Leckie×Leckie
Scotland's leading educational publishers

National 4 & 5
HISTORY
COURSE NOTES

N4 & 5 HISTORY
COURSE NOTES

Maxine Hughes • Chris Hume
Holly Robertson

001/26032018

10 9 8 7 6 5 4 3 2 1

ISBN 9780008282134

Published by
Leckie & Leckie Ltd
An imprint of HarperCollinsPublishers
Westerhill Road, Bishopbriggs, Glasgow, G64 2QT
T: 0844 576 8126   F: 0844 576 8131
leckieandleckie@harpercollins.co.uk   www.leckieandleckie.co.uk

Special thanks to
Sonia Dawkins (project management); Roda Morrison (project management/ copy edit); Louise Robb (proofread); Ink Tank (cover design); Jouve (layout)

Printed in United Kingdom.

A CIP Catalogue record for this book is available from the British Library.

Acknowledgements

Scottish: Migration and Empire, 1830–1939
Impact Spread: © Print Collector/Getty Images; Fig 1: © Crown copyright 2012; Fig 2: Print Collector/Getty Images; Fig 3: Public Domain; Fig 4: SSPL via Getty Images; Fig 6: Public Domain; Fig 7: © Getty Images; Fig 10: © Getty Images, Fig 11: © Getty Images; Fig 12 © Boston Globe via Getty Images; Fig 14: © Crown copyright 2012; Fig 15: © Crown copyright 2012; Fig 16: Reproduced with the permission of the Scottish Jewish Archives Centre; Fig 17: © Roger Viollet/Getty Images; Fig 18: © Print Collector/ Getty Images; Fig 20: © Getty Images; Fig 21: © Crown copyright 2012; Fig 23: Public Domain; Fig 24: Public Domain; Fig 28: Public Domain; Fig 29: Public Domain; Fig 30 © AFP/Getty Images; Fig 31: © Getty Images

The Era of the Great War, 1900–1928
Impact Spread: © Print Collector/Getty Images; Fig1: © Print Collector/Getty Images; Fig 2: © Imperial War Museums (Q 48958); Fig 3: Public Domain; Fig 4: © Imperial War Museums (Q 45786); Fig 5: © Imperial War Museums (Q 8443); Fig 6: © Imperial War Museums (Q 4649); Fig 7: Public Domain; Fig 10: © Imperial War Museums (Q 4649); Fig 11 Public Domain; Fig 12: Public Domain; Fig 13: Public Domain; Fig 14: © Time & Life Pictures/ Getty Images; Fig 15 © Imperial War Museums (Q 1580); Fig 16: © Imperial War Museums (CO 2533); Fig 17: licensed under a Creative Commons Attribution Share-Alike 3.0 License; Fig 18: Public Domain; Fig 19: Public Domain; Fig 20: Public Domain; Fig 21: © Imperial War Museums (Q 54605); Fig 22: © Popperfoto/Getty Images; Fig 23: Public Domain; Fig 24: reproduced with the permission of Glasgow City Council, Glasgow Museums; Fig 25: © Getty Images; Fig 26: © Getty Images

British: The Atlantic Slave Trade, 1770–1807
Impact Spread: © Getty Images; Fig 1: Creative Commons CC0 1.0 Universal Public Domain Dedication. Source British Library; Fig 2: This fileislicensed under the Creative Commons Attribution-Share Alike 3.0 Unported licence; Fig 3: Public Domain; Fig 5: Creative Commons Attribution Share-alike license 2.0 ; Fig 6: Creative Commons Attribution Share-alike license 2.0; Fig 7: Creative Commons Attribution-Share Alike 3.0 Unported licence; Fig 8: British Library/Robana via Getty Images; Fig 10: © Getty Images; Fig 11: © Getty Images; Fig 12: Public Domain; Fig 13: © British Library/Robana via Getty Images; Fig 14: Public Domain; Fig 15 : © Time & Life Pictures/Getty Images; Fig 16: This fileismade vailable under the Creative Commons CC0 1.0 Universal Public Domain Dedication; Fig 17: Creative Commons CC0 1.0 Universal Public Domain Dedication/source British Library; Fig 18: Creative Commons Attribution-Share Alike 3.0 Unported/Author Urban Walnut; Fig 19: © Getty Images; Fig 20: © De Agostini/Getty Images; Figure

21: Creative Commons CC0 1.0 Universal Public Domain Dedication; Fig 22: Public Domain; Fig 23: Public Domain; Fig 24: Public Domain; Fig 25: Creative Commons Attribution-Share Alike 3.0 Unported. Attribute to Tropenmuseum of the Royal Tropical Institute (KIT); Fig 26: Public Domain; Fig 27: © Getty Images; Fig 28: Public Domain; Fig 29: Public Domain; Fig 30: Public Domain; Fig31: Public Domain

British: Changing Britain, 1760–1914
Impact Spread: © SSPL via Getty Images; Fig 1: © Getty Images; Fig 2: © Time & Life Pictures/Getty Images; Fig 3: © Getty Images; Fig 4: © UIG via Getty Images; Fig 5: Public Domain; Fig 6: © Print Collector/Getty Images; Fig 7: US public domain tag; Fig 8: © Popperfoto/Getty Images; Fig 9: Public Domain; Fig 10: Public Domain; Fig 12: © UIG via Getty Images; Fig 13: © UIG via Getty Images; Fig 14: © Print Collector/Getty Images; Fig 15: © SSPL via Getty Images; Fig 16: © Getty Images; Fig 18 © SSPL via Getty Images; Fig 19: © SSPL via Getty Images; Fig 20: © UIG via Getty Images; Fig 21: SSPL via Getty Images; Fig 22: Public Domain; Fig 23: British Library/Robana via Getty Images; Fig 25: © Getty Images; Fig 26: Public Domain; Fig 27: Public Domain

European and World: Red flag: Lenin and the Russian Revolution, 1894–1921
Impact Spread: © Getty Images; Fig 1: © UIG via Getty Images; Fig 2: UIG via Getty Images; Fig 3: Public Domain; Fig 4: Public Domain; Fig 5: Public Domain; Fig 6: Public Domain; Fig 7: © Getty Images; Fig 8: © UIG via Getty Images; Fig 9: © Heritage Images/Getty Images; Fig 10: © UIG via Getty Images; Fig 11: © Heritage Images/Getty Images; Fig 12: Public Domain; Fig 13: Public Domain; Fig 14: Public Domain; Fig 15: Public Domain; Fig 16: Public Domain; Fig 17: © Getty Images; Fig 18: © Heritage Images/Getty Images; Fig 19: Public Domain; Fig 20: © Print Collector/Getty Images; Fig 21: © AFP/Getty Images; Fig 22: © AFP/Getty Images; Fig 23: © Getty Images; Fig 24: Public Domain; Fig 25: © Heritage Images/Getty Images; Fig 26: Creative Commons Attribution-Share Alike 3.0 Unported/ Author Hoodinski ; Fig 28: © Image Asset Management Ltd./Alamy; Fig 29: Public Domain

European and World: Hitler and Nazi Germany, 1919–1939
Impact Spread: © Mondadori via Getty Images; Fig 1: Public Domain; Fig 2: © Getty Images; Fig 3: Bundesarchiv, Bild 102-00015/CC-BY-SA; Fig 4: © Popperfoto/Getty Images; Fig 5: Public Domain; Fig 6: Public Domain; Fig 7: © UIG via Getty Images; Fig 8: © Print Collector/Getty Images; Fig 9: © Getty Images; Fig 10: Public Domain; Fig 11: © Getty Images; Fig 12: Bundesarchiv, Bild 183-1989-0630-504/CC-BY-SA; Fig 13: © Getty Images; Fig 14: Bundesarchiv, Bild 183-C06886/CC-BY-SA; Fig 15: © Getty Images; Fig 17: The LIFE Picture Collection; Fig 18: © Time & Life Pictures/Getty Images; Fig 19: © SSPL via Getty Images; Fig 20: © Getty Images; Fig 21: Bundesarchiv, Bild 183-S72707/CC-BY-SA; Fig 22: © Getty Images; Fig 23: © Getty Images; Fig 24: © Popperfoto/Getty Images; Fig 25: © Getty Images; Fig 26: © Getty Images; Fig 27: © Getty Images; Fig 28: © Getty Images

European and World: Free at Last? Civil Rights in the USA, 1918–1968
Impact Spread: © Getty Images; Fig 1: Public Domain; Fig 2: © Getty Images; Fig 3 : ©Print Collector/Getty Images; Fig 4: © Getty Images; Fig 5: © Getty Images; Fig 6: Public Domain; Fig 7: Public Domain; Fig 8: © Getty Images; Fig 9: © Getty Images; Fig 10: © Getty Images; Fig 11: Public Domain; Fig 12: © Time & Life Pictures/Getty Images; Fig 13: © Getty Images; Fig 14: © © Everett Collection Historical / Alamy; Fig 15: Public Domain; Fig 16: Public Domain; Fig 17: © Time & Life Pictures/ Getty Images; Fig 18: © The LIFE Picture Collection; Fig 19: © Getty Images; Fig 20: © Getty Images; Fig 21: © Time & Life Pictures/Getty Images; Fig 22: © Time & Life Pictures/Getty Images; Fig 23: © Time & Life Pictures/ Getty Images; Fig 24: © NY Daily News via Getty Images; Fig 25: Public Domain; Fig 26: © Black Star / Alamy; Fig 27: © Getty Images; Fig 28: © Getty Images; Fig 29: © Everett Collection Historical / Alamy; Fig 30: © AFP/Getty Images; Fig 31: © Getty Images; Fig 32: Public Domain; Fig 33: Public Domain; Fig 34: Public Domain; Fig 35: © Getty Images; Fig 36: © Popperfoto/Getty Images; Fig 37: © Getty Images

All other images © Shutterstock.com

Introduction

About this book

This book is designed to lead you through your National 4 or National 5 History course. The book has been organised to map the course specifications and is packed with examples, explanations, activities and features to deepen your understanding of the topics and help you prepare for the assessment.

At the beginning of each topic you will find a list of the level 4 experiences and outcomes that this topic covers, meaning that you can start it in S3 as part of your broad general education. The themes, ideas and skills in this topic build upon what you have already learned as part of your broad general education in S1–S3.

Throughout the topics you will see that there are activities and exam style questions for you to complete, usually with some of the section outcomes (1.1, 1.2, etc.) indicated below them. Completing these pieces of work successfully means you will be compiling evidence that you are meeting the standard for National 4 or 5, depending on which you are studying.

In History there is a choice of topics for each section. This book covers the following topics:

Section 1: Scottish: Migration and Empire, 1830–1939; The Era of the Great War, 1900–1928

Section 2: British: The Atlantic Slave Trade, 1770–1807; Changing Britain, 1760–1914

Section 3: European and World: The Red Flag: Lenin and the Russian Revolution, 1894–1921; Hitler and Nazi Germany, 1919–1939; Free at Last? Civil Rights in the USA, 1918–1968

Features

Learning intentions

This is a list of what you will learn as you work your way through the chapter.

HINT

Hints give you advice and tips to support your learning.

> **Hint**
>
> The Great War of 1914–18 is also known as the First World War or World War One.

MAKE THE LINK

Make the Link helps you to connect what you are learning to other sections within the course and to other subjects you might be studying. History is about what has happened in the past and you will find that what you learn has links to lots of other subjects, such as Modern Studies, Geography, English, RMPS and many more.

> **Make the Link**
>
> If you study Modern Studies you will learn in detail about what makes a democracy.

KEY WORD

Key words or phrases which will help you understand the topic more are highlighted and explained.

> 📖 **Key Word**
>
> • **Philanthropist**
> Someone who seeks to help others, usually by donating money to charities or worthwhile causes.

ACTIVITY

Activities will get you thinking about what you have learned and help you to practise and develop the skills you will need for your assessment. There are different kinds of activities, including individual research work, paired discussion and group work.

> **GO! Activity 16**
>
> Imagine it is 1900 and you have left Scotland for India. Write a diary entry describing all the things you have seen that Scots had a hand in developing.
> **(Unit outcomes: National 4/5: Outcome 2.1)**

Exam style questions

Exam style questions are included throughout each topic to test your knowledge and understanding of what you have learned. Many of these questions will also help you to develop and practise the skills you will need for your final exam.

Learning checklist

Each topic closes with a summary of learning statements showing what you should be able to do when you complete the topic. You can use the checklist to check that you have a good understanding of the areas covered in the topic; you can make a note of how confident you feel using the traffic lights so that you know which areas you might need to revisit.

Assessment

At National 5 you will sit a final exam which will cover all three sections. Each section will feature a mixture of source-handling skills and knowledge and understanding questions. The exam is worth 80 marks and will last 2 hours and 20 minutes.

As well as this, National 5 candidates will complete an Assignment worth 20 marks. The assignment is a piece of work in which you decide on the issue and question yourself, conduct research on it, and then write it up in class in an hour. You can take an A4 resource sheet in to help you when you write it up, meaning you don't have to remember all your research. This piece of work will be sent off to SQA to be assessed.

Studying this topic will provide you with a good understanding of the causes and results of the movement of population into and away from Scotland in the years between 1830 and 1939. As well as this, by focusing on the experiences of those who arrived in Scotland in this period, and of those Scots who left to start new lives abroad, you will gain an understanding and appreciation of the impact emigrants can make in their new countries or communities.

You will develop your skills and be able to:

❖ evaluate the usefulness of a source
❖ compare two sources by saying what they agree or disagree about
❖ put a source into context by saying how fully it describes an issue.

This topic is split into four sections:

❖ Immigration to Scotland, 1830s–1939
❖ The experience of immigrants in Scotland, 1880s–1939
❖ Scottish emigration, 1830s–1939
❖ The experience of Scots abroad, 1830s–1939

Level 4 experiences and outcomes relevant to this topic:

I can evaluate conflicting sources of evidence to sustain a line of argument. **SOC 4-01a**

By studying groups in past societies who experienced inequality, I can explain the reasons for the inequality and evaluate how groups or individuals addressed it. **SOC 4-04a**

I can present supported conclusions about the social, political and economic impacts of a technological change in the past. **SOC 4-05a**

I have investigated a meeting of cultures in the past and can analyse the impact on the societies involved. **SOC 4-05c**

Having critically analysed a significant historical event, I can assess the relative importance of factors contributing to the event. **SOC 4-06a**

I can assess the impact for those involved in a specific instance of the expansion of power and influence in the past. **SOC 4-06d**

Section 1: Scottish: Migration and Empire, 1830–1939

Background

Make the Link

In Geography you will learn about both urban and rural economies.

By the 1830s the industrial revolution was well under way in Scotland, leading to a real change in where people lived and worked. There was a clear move from the more agricultural Lowlands and Highlands of Scotland towards the larger urban and industrialised cities in and around the central belt. As we will learn, there were various reasons for this. As this movement occurred, cities like Glasgow struggled to keep up with the large number of people settling there. These cities also attracted many people from other nations, most notably from Ireland, who were looking to start new lives in places where there were jobs.

By 1922 the British Empire ruled over around 458 000 000 people, one quarter of the world's population at that time. As part of the British Empire, Scotland was beginning to make the most of new markets in which to sell its goods. From Canada to India to Australia, the British Empire allowed Scottish companies to engage in trade with nations thousands of miles away. This undoubtedly helped the Scottish economy to grow and made many Scots very rich indeed. Furthermore, the Empire allowed Scots to travel freely to places where new opportunities, and challenges, awaited them. The impact that many Scots made on their new home countries can clearly be seen when we examine the history of these countries in this period.

Overall, the migration of Scots in this period was significant in the development of the British Empire and, indeed, the other countries they settled in. By the same token, those immigrants who arrived in Scotland also left their mark, helping to shape the nation that we live in today.

Figure 1: *A poster advertising emigration to the colonies.*

Key words/concepts for this topic:

- Emigrant: someone who has left his or her country of birth or residence to settle elsewhere.
- Emigration: the process of leaving the country of birth or residence to settle elsewhere.
- Immigrant: someone who has arrived to live in a new country.
- Immigration: the process of arriving in a new country to live there.
- Push factors: reasons why people would want to leave the country that they live in.
- Pull factors: reasons why people are attracted to live in new countries.
- Economic: anything that relates to the economy or the making/exchange of money.
- Industry/industrial: anything that relates to the production of goods and materials on a large scale, generally in factories.
- The industrial revolution: this was a period from the late 1700s into the 1800s when new inventions and techniques massively changed and improved the way farming and manufacturing occurred. It began in Britain and soon spread to other countries, such as Germany and the USA.
- Assimilate: to become part of a new country or society, usually by adopting certain aspects or ways of a new culture.

All these different concepts and words will feature throughout the topic. The following activity will help you produce a visual aid that you can refer back to throughout the topic.

GO! Activity 1

Create a poster/illustrated mind map/presentation that explains all key concepts/words and then present the finished product to your group.

Rules: You cannot use more than 30 words in your piece of work so will also have to use pictures to help explain the key concepts and words.

1 Immigration to Scotland, 1830s–1939

During the nineteenth century many people from many different nations settled in Scotland. These people often made the decision to leave their home countries because they were unhappy with their lives there. We call these **push** factors, because it is almost like they were being pushed out of their countries by their experiences there. Others were attracted to Scotland because of the opportunities they saw there. We call these **pull** factors because these immigrants were almost being pulled towards Scotland.

Irish immigration

Push factors

Figure 2: *For many, living conditions in Ireland were terrible*

In 1830 Ireland was a poor nation where living conditions for most were generally terrible and literacy levels low. These low literacy levels meant that most Irish could only do unskilled jobs, such as labouring or farm work. These jobs paid low wages and so poverty was widespread. Those who farmed their own land only produced enough to survive. All this was made significantly worse by the fact that Ireland's population doubled between 1791 and 1841, meaning there was less land to go around. Many landlords, keen to make a profit

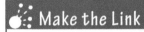
Make the Link

If you study Modern Studies or Geography you will learn about the causes and effects of poverty in a society.

from their land, believed they could make more money by combining their tenants' lands and using new farming technology and techniques instead of workers. As a result, landlords put the rent up on their land, sometimes to force their tenants off. Those who couldn't pay were thrown off their land and came to rely on growing one crop, the potato, on any scrap of land they could. This situation in itself was certainly terrible for many Irish, but worse was to come in the autumn of 1845 when the potato blight hit Ireland. (1)

By 1800 90% of the Irish population was dependent on the potato for their main calorific intake and for selling. In September 1845 a fungus began to infect potatoes all across Ireland. Crops were ruined and people starved. Journalists at the time reported seeing families reduced to eating grass from the fields and seaweed from the beaches. The famine that followed devastated Ireland, with some historians believing around 2 000 000 people may have starved to death. It is thought that another 2 000 000 left for new lives abroad. Also, at this time Ireland was industrially backward, so there was a real lack of jobs in the cities. (2)

Pull factors

Scotland was undoubtedly attractive to many Irish, often for economic reasons. Employers in the shipyards and factories were always looking for workers to do unskilled jobs. For the immigrant Irish, wages in Scotland, even for these unskilled jobs, were better than in Ireland – often six times as high. For those Irish families who came to Scotland there were jobs for them all, whether it was down a coal pit or in the jute factories of Dundee. What is more, housing in Scotland was much better than in Ireland and many employers would often provide accommodation with a job. For those Irish who were skilled, Scotland offered higher wages than in Ireland. (3)

📖 Key Words

- **Tenant**
  Someone who rents land or a home from a landlord.

- **Famine**
  When people starve and often die due to not having any food.

Figure 3: *A drawing of a poor Irish family in the 1840s. How can you tell that they are poor?*

🔬 Make the Link

In Health and Food Technology you may have learned about the importance of having a balanced and varied diet. What effect do you think having a diet restricted mainly to potatoes would have on someone's health?

🔍 Hint

Countries that had not gone through the industrial revolution were not as wealthy and full of job opportunities as those that had.

Figure 4: *Irish immigrants were attracted to jobs in the jute mills of Dundee.*

Figure 5: *Steamers were cheap and quick, two important factors for those Irish who were poor and needed a job as soon as possible.*

Ease of transport was also a crucial factor in attracting Irish to Scotland. Steam boats, with low fares, travelled between the two countries regularly meaning even the poorest Irish could afford the trip to Scotland. Also, many Irish had visited Scotland previously for work on the railways or at harvest time, and it was therefore familiar to them. Some even had family and friends who had stayed across in Scotland, meaning that it would be easier for them to organise jobs and housing in advance. (4)

GO! Activity 2

1. Divide a piece of paper into two columns: Push and Pull. This is where you will take notes throughout the following task.

2. Get into groups of four and number yourselves 1–4. You will see that each of the preceding paragraphs has a number in brackets at the end of it. You will become an expert on the paragraph that matches your number by reading it very carefully and creating a **quick, rough teaching aid** (a poster) on it. You will then explain it clearly and in detail to others in your group while they take notes on what you say.

3. Your teaching aid is going to be a poster explaining your topic. The poster should have no more than fifteen words on it, so you should use pictures too.

   Your teacher will decide on an appropriate amount of time for the whole activity.

4. As you listen to each person in the group explaining their paragraph using their teaching aid, note down the push and/ or pull factors they mention.

   (Unit outcomes: National 4/5: Outcome 2.2)

Exam style question

Source A is from *The Cork Examiner*, an Irish newspaper, and was written in 1846.

> Disease and famine have fastened onto the young, the old, the strong and feeble, the mother and the infant; whole families lie together on the damp floor. Without food or fuel, bed or bedding, whole families are shut up in hovels, dropping into the arms of death one by one.

5. Evaluate the usefulness of **Source A** as evidence of why so many Irish settled in Scotland in the nineteenth century.   **SH 5**

   (You may want to comment on who wrote it, when they wrote it, why they wrote it, what they say or what has been missed out.)

   (Unit outcomes: National 4: Outcome 1.1; National 5: Outcomes 1.1 and 2.1)

Italian, Lithuanian and Jewish immigration

Push factors

Italians began arriving in Scotland in larger numbers after 1880. Many were looking to escape extreme poverty, low wages, poor living conditions and the droughts that often caused food shortages in Italy. All these factors convinced many Italians to seek a better life abroad.

Between 1880 and 1914 a large number of Jews arrived in Scotland. Many were escaping religious persecution in Russia. Pogroms became more common and increasingly violent. In addition to these pogroms, many Jews were leaving because of economic persecution. In Russia Jews were often discriminated against when applying for jobs or starting businesses, making it hard for them to earn a living.

📖 Key Words

- **Pogrom**

A violent massacre or persecution of an ethnic or religious group, particularly one aimed at Jews.

- **Persecution**

The mistreatment of people or individuals by another individual or group.

Make the Link

In 'Lenin and the Russian Revolution, 1894–1921', you learn in more detail about how minorities were treated by the Tsar (the Russian Emperor).

Figure 6: *A political cartoon from 1904 asking the Russian Tsar to stop his oppression toward the Jews. What else can you learn from the cartoon?*

Source B is from the website www.historytoday.com and was written by Murdoch Rodgers.

> For the vast majority of Lithuanians America was the ultimate destination and Scotland was regarded, at least in the early part of this period, as only a temporary stop on that longer journey. There were sound financial reasons for having such a break… [such as the] ample opportunities to earn money by working in the expanding coal and iron and steel industries in Lanarkshire and Ayrshire.

Source C was written by a modern historian.

> There were many different reasons why Lithuanians left their home on the shores of the Baltic: some were escaping conscription into the Russian army; some were simply economic migrants, desperate to escape the crushing poverty at home and prepared to go anywhere in search of a better life. Others saw America in their sights and bought tickets for Scotland only because it was cheaper than going to the USA directly.

Hint

Remember to quote from the sources when you compare them so that you are backing up each point you make.

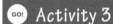 **Activity 3**

Exam style question

Compare the views of **Sources B** and **C** on the reasons why Lithuanians were attracted to Scotland in the nineteenth century. (Compare the sources overall and in detail.) **SH 4**

(Unit outcomes: National 4/5: Outcome 1.3)

Pull factors

Figure 7: *Many Italians saw Scotland as the stopping off point on their way to the USA. Do you know what the statue in the picture is and where it is?*

Hint

The USA was very attractive to immigrants because, like Scotland, it offered employment opportunities.

 **Make the Link**

Immigration is a major political issue in Britain today and you may have encountered it in Modern Studies. Some of the reasons immigrants come to Britain today are the same as they were 150 years ago: can you think of any?

Many Italians were initially attracted to Scotland because it was cheaper to stop off in Scotland on the way to America than go there directly! They saw Scotland, essentially, as a stopping off point but a significant number ended up staying. Also, like the Irish, many were attracted to Scotland by the promise of higher wages, better living conditions and a more stable, reliable jobs market.

Lithuanians and Jews were both attracted to Scotland for similar reasons to begin with, notably the fact that it was often cheaper to travel to America via Scotland than go there direct. For those Lithuanians who had planned to settle in Scotland from the beginning, the booming iron, coal and steel industries offered opportunities to earn money; for those Jews with similar intentions, the freedom from economic and religious persecution that had blighted their lives in Eastern Europe made Scotland an attractive destination.

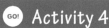

Activity 4

Using the information on the previous two pages, write an article for a History website explaining why Italians, Lithuanians and Jews came to Scotland in the nineteenth century. You must show/describe at least three push or pull reasons for each group and use at least one quote from the sources.

(Unit outcomes: National 4/5: Outcome 2.2)

The impact of the Empire on Scotland

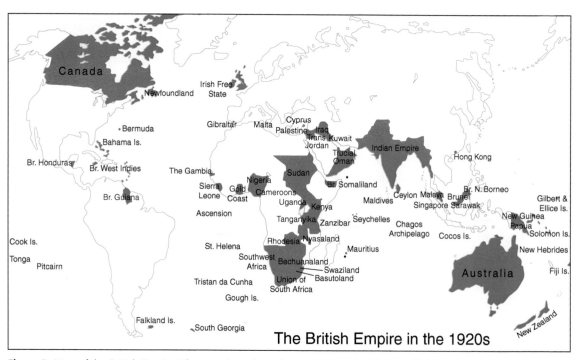

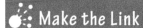

Figure 8: *Map of the British Empire. The areas in red are those countries that Britain ruled over.*

The British Empire made a massive impact upon Scotland. In terms of Scotland's economy, the Empire meant that Scottish industries had large markets where they could sell their goods and products. For example, as the historian Tom Devine notes, 38% of all Scottish coal went abroad to countries in the Empire in the 1910s. Also, the Scottish based North British Locomotive Company sent almost all its engines to the British Empire in the years before the First World War. What is more, the Empire supplied raw materials such as sugar and tobacco that Scottish companies could sell on to other countries for a profit. The growth of the Scottish economy also meant more jobs for ordinary Scots.

However, the picture is not wholly positive. By the 1930s, Scotland's economy had become too reliant on trade within the Empire and had lost its competitive edge. Other countries in the Empire had, by this

Make the Link

If you study Business Management or Economics you will learn more about domestic and international trade.

13

time, developed industries which rivalled and often bettered Scotland's in terms of price and quality. For example, the once booming jute industry in Dundee had been overtaken by the jute industry in India which could provide the same product much cheaper. In the 1920s, the Glasgow cotton industry was also finished off by competition from India, where, again, prices were lower. India had also begun to produce its own locomotives by 1895, challenging companies in Britain for international contracts and exports. As well as this, by relying on selling products to the Empire, Scotland had become complacent and had not modernised machinery or techniques. By 1939 the Scottish economy was struggling and there was rising unemployment.

Scotland's important role in producing goods and products that helped run the Empire meant that people from other countries were attracted to the 'workshop of the world' safe in the knowledge that jobs would be available. The many immigrants that settled in Scotland from countries within the Empire, such as India, have helped give Scotland its distinct, diverse culture. Also, the Empire allowed those Scots who wanted to leave Scotland the opportunity to travel to new countries where English was spoken and the prospect of a better life was very real. On the other hand, the fact that so many ambitious, educated Scots left for opportunity and fortune within the Empire was perhaps the Empire's gain and Scotland's loss.

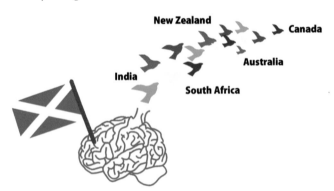

Figure 9: *Some historians believe a 'brain drain' in Scotland in the nineteenth and twentieth centuries saw the brightest and best people leave Scotland for new lives in the Empire and elsewhere.*

GO! Activity 5

Using the information above, bullet point all the ways that the Empire impacted upon Scotland. Beside the bullet points, in brackets, note whether the impact can be considered a pro or a con for Scotland and why. For example:

- The Empire encouraged immigration from countries such as India (pro, because it has helped Scotland develop a diverse culture).

Once you have done this, write a paragraph explaining whether you think the Empire made a positive contribution to Scotland or not.

(Unit outcomes: National 4/5: Outcome 2.1)

2 The experience of immigrants in Scotland, 1880s–1939

In this section you will learn about:

- The experiences of four different immigrant groups in Scotland: Irish, Italians, Lithuanians, Jews.
- The difficulties these groups faced.
- The extent to which each group managed to assimilate.

The experience of Irish immigrants in Scotland

In the nineteenth century Irish immigrants tended to settle in west and central Scotland, mainly in Glasgow and the surrounding towns. Many Irish also made it over to Dundee and, to a lesser extent, Edinburgh. The Irish settled in these places because there were lots of jobs available.

When Irish immigrants first arrived they faced a significant amount of resentment from native Scots. Many Scots felt that the arrival of the Irish meant there were fewer jobs and less decent housing to go round and that this kept wages low and rents high. Many Scots landlords even refused to rent their properties to Irish families. This, combined with high rents, forced many Irish to settle in the poorest areas of the cities: the slums.

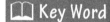

> ### 📖 Key Word
>
> - **Slum**
>
> A crowded and heavily populated area where housing and conditions are below the normal standard.

Figures 10 & 11: *These are photos of the slums in Glasgow. Conditions remained terrible in these areas well into the twentieth century when these photos were taken. Irish immigrants generally settled in these areas as the rent was low.*

Conditions in the slums were terrible for Irish people. Buildings were badly made, often unsafe to live in, and they lacked ventilation or

access to natural sunlight. These tenement buildings also had no water supply making it difficult to keep homes clean. With no toilets or sewers either, people simply threw their waste out into the back courts or into gutters in the street.

In this overcrowded, damp and dirty atmosphere, disease and illness spread quickly. Outbreaks of cholera, typhus and tuberculosis (TB) became a regular occurrence. Soon Scots began to associate the Irish with these diseases, blaming them for the filth they lived in, even though many Scots lived in similar conditions.

Irish immigrants were generally uneducated and unskilled and faced discrimination in the jobs market, usually because they were Catholic. They took on unskilled jobs in factories, textiles, mines and railway construction for low pay and often difficult conditions. Some Scots disliked that the Irish were willing to work for so little because they felt it meant fewer jobs for them.

Figure 12: *Some Scots employers refused to employ Irish immigrants.*

In terms of assimilation, religion was a big factor. The vast majority of Irish immigrants were Catholic, whereas Scotland was a Protestant country. This led to anti-Catholic feeling in areas where the Irish Catholic population was high. Because of this, the Irish tended to keep themselves to themselves, and thriving communities developed as a result.

To begin with, Irish priests worked hard to provide some stability for the immigrants. Churches were built, Catholic schools established and priests worked hard to help immigrants find jobs and housing. However, as Irish Catholic communities began to grow, so did the suspicions of the native Protestant Scots.

Some Scots were suspicious of the fact that Irish immigrants lived in their own communities and rarely strayed from them. Some Protestant Scots believed that the growing number of Irish immigrants was threatening the identity and culture of Scotland. The result of such suspicion and mistrust was the establishing of the Orange Lodge organisation in Scotland. The Orange Lodge was a Protestant society that focused on maintaining and celebrating the history of Protestants. Members would sometimes go on marches and violence often flared up between Catholic and Protestants on such occasions.

Perhaps the most obvious evidence today of Irish immigration to Scotland is the existence of three football clubs: Glasgow Celtic, Hibernian and Dundee United. All three clubs can trace their roots to the descendants of Irish Catholics, and all were formed to represent the Irish communities that existed in Glasgow, Edinburgh and Dundee. Even today, the main rivalries in these cities exist between clubs that represent two different religions: Catholicism and Protestantism.

When considering the Irish experience in Scotland we must recognise that Protestant Irish also arrived in Scotland, generally from the 1880s onwards. These immigrants mixed well with native Scots due to their shared religion and faced much less difficulty in gaining jobs in skilled industries than their Catholic counterparts.

By the 1930s Irish Catholics were on the road to being accepted as part of Scottish society and assimilated well. Over the years Scots and Irish had intermarried and worked side by side in a variety of industries, political parties and trade unions. Both groups also had much in common, such as their love of football. That being said, by 1939 there still remained a sectarian divide in some areas in Scotland and the historian Tom Devine suggests that Irish assimilation in Scotland was not complete until the 1960s.

Figure 13: *The badge of Glasgow Celtic. The club was established after the Irish began arriving in Scotland in larger numbers.*

📖 Key Word

- **Trade union**
  An organisation that represents workers' rights.

GO! Activity 6

1. You will complete this activity by working in threes so number yourselves 1, 2 or 3. All members of the group will read the information in this section and take notes on their issues.

   1s: Note down as much information as you can on three issues:
   Where immigrants settled   Employment   Housing and disease
   2s: Note down as much information as you can on two issues:
   Scottish attitudes towards the Irish   Assimilation
   3s: Note down as much information as you can on three issues:
   Religion   Sport   Protestant Irish
   Your teacher will give you an appropriate amount of time to take notes on your issues. Once this time is up, you will take it in turns to teach one another about your topics. When one person is speaking, the other two will be taking notes.

   (Unit outcomes: National 4/5: Outcome 2.1)

Exam style question

2. Describe the experience of Irish immigrants in Scotland. **KU 4**
   (Unit outcomes: National 4/5: Outcome 2.1)

🔍 Hint

When writing an answer about Irish immigrants' experiences in Scotland remember to write about the different experiences Catholic and Protestant Irish had, and why this was.

The experience of Italian immigrants in Scotland

Source D is from Tom Devine, *The Scottish Nation 1700–2000*.

> The Italian community did not attract much hostility from native Scots because most Italians worked in family run businesses, kept close ties with their homeland and hoped to return there one day. Marriages were often kept within the Italian family network and consequently there was limited assimilation or integration with native Scots.

Source E is adapted from www.educationscotland.gov.uk.

> Initially working as 'hokey pokey' men selling ice cream from barrows, Italian immigrants moved into working-class areas, combining ice cream making with selling fish and chips. In addition to catering, Italians found themselves in hairdressing, establishing the College of Italian Hairdressers in Glasgow in 1928.

Source F is a photo taken in Glasgow around 1900.

Figure 14 and Source F: *Italian ice cream shop in Glasgow around 1900.*

Source G was written by Joe Pieri, in his *Memoirs of a Scots-Italian*.

> The counter (in our café) between myself and our customers acted as a barrier. We were aliens, foreigners, the Tallies who worked all day to serve them fish and chips and ice-cream, and we were tolerated as such.

Source H was written by a modern historian.

> Italians experienced some hostility from native Scots. Italian cafes began opening on Sundays, in the process angering Church leaders. The fact that Italians were Catholics also soured relations with many Protestant Scots.

Source I is adapted from *New Arrivals* by Tony Jaconelli in *Our Glasgow Story*.

> School was a nightmare for me. A few times I found myself surrounded by classmates chanting at me because I was a foreigner. Within a couple of years I lost all trace of my mother tongue and developed a strong, guttural Glasgow accent. In no time at all I was a complete Glaswegian.

GO! Activity 7

1. Make up a table like this, leaving enough space to write a sentence or two in each box.

Source	Employment/ jobs	Problems they faced	Evidence of assimilation
D			
E			
F			
G			
H			
I			

Review each source and fill in the table as you go. Each source will tell you something about the jobs Italians did, the problems they faced or whether they assimilated. Leave a box blank if you can't find any information that fits.

Exam style question

2. Evaluate the usefulness of **Source I** as evidence of the Italian immigrant experience in Scotland.   **SH 5**

   (You may want to comment on who wrote it, when they wrote it, why they wrote it, what they say or what has been missed out.)

   (Unit outcomes: National 4: Outcome 1.1; National 5: Outcomes 1.1 and 2.1)

The experience of Lithuanian immigrants in Scotland

Lithuanian immigrants tended to settle in the industrial towns in the west of Scotland, hoping to find jobs in coal mines and factories. The largest Lithuanian community to develop in Scotland in this period was in the town of Coatbridge where there was a large coal mine. At its peak, the Lithuanian population of Coatbridge was around 6000.

At first Lithuanians were not fully welcomed by Scots and there was often open hostility towards them. This was the case even though many Lithuanians had changed their surnames to local sounding names in an attempt to integrate into their new communities more easily. Scots were concerned that Lithuanians would work for less than them and, on a social level, many considered the immigrants dirty and often drunk. These accusations could have been levelled at the Scottish miners at the time, but the Lithuanians were easy targets because they were immigrants and because they were Catholic.

Over time, however, the situation improved as Lithuanian miners began to strike alongside their Scottish counterparts for better pay and conditions. This won them respect, as did the fact that they had a strong sense of community, often being found organising social events like trips to the seaside and sports days. Their children attended local schools, and many Lithuanians moved out of the mines and factories to establish local businesses. These Lithuanians even established two local newspapers and insurance societies!

Figure 15: *Lithuanian miners in Lanarkshire, around 1900.*

By 1914, Lithuanians had assimilated well into their communities. However, with the start of the Great War many men left to fight for Russia. After the war these men did not return to Scotland and the remaining Lithuanians began to drift back to their home country. By the mid-1920s there remained little evidence of a Lithuanian community having existed in Scotland. This is perhaps partly because those who did stay had assimilated so well by then.

> ### Make the Link
>
> You should be able to see from other parts of this topic that Catholic immigrants often experienced discrimination because of their religion. Remember to discuss this in any answer you write.

The experience of Jewish immigrants in Scotland

Jewish immigrants settled mainly in Glasgow but in Edinburgh there was also a sizeable Jewish community by 1939. Both cities offered economic opportunities.

Jewish families tended to settle in the same areas, thereby creating Jewish communities in areas like the Gorbals where accommodation was cheap. By the 1930s Jewish newspapers had been established and synagogues built. Jews tended to interact mainly with other Jews but this was no different to other immigrant groups. Because the Jewish community was never large, local Scots communities didn't perceive Jews as a threat as they often did with the Irish. This certainly helped relations between the two groups. That being said, it would be untrue to say that Jews did not face anti-Semitism and prejudice in Scotland.

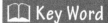

📖 **Key Word**

- **Anti-Semitism**
Prejudice, hatred or discrimination against Jews for reasons connected to their Jewish religion.

Figure 16: *A Jewish linen merchant in Main Street in the Gorbals, 1907. Note the writing in English and Yiddish.*

Jewish immigrants tended to work as hawkers and peddlers, selling goods door to door, although they also set up businesses as tailors, bakers, watchmakers and jewellers. It was not long before Scottish resentment of Jewish presence in industry came to the fore, with many accusing Jews of undercutting wages and running 'sweated trades'. 'Sweated trades' describes those jobs and industries where employees worked for long hours for low pay, often with very few rights in the workplace. Despite the fact that there was little evidence to connect Jews with the sweated trades, trade unions and newspapers began to focus on it and in many people's minds it became fact. The same can be said for the myth that Jews were connected with cholera outbreaks, which was clearly untrue and based on little else than thinly disguised anti-Semitism. These stereotypes and prejudices inevitably led to instances of anti-Semitism, sometimes violent.

Overall, despite the challenges Jews faced it is fair to say that they had assimilated fairly well into Scottish society by the 1930s. Although they tended to stay in their own communities Jews had generally integrated well with Scots, both in the workplace, in schools, and in general society too.

🔅 **Make the Link**

If you study 'Hitler and Nazi Germany, 1919–1939', you will learn about how the Nazis used negative stereotypes to encourage anti-Semitism.

🔅 **Make the Link**

It is a key part of the Curriculum for Excellence to become a responsible citizen and to respect the different cultures and people that make up Scotland. Can you think of any lessons we can learn from this topic about the importance of treating immigrants fairly and not believing stereotypes?

> **GO! Activity 8**
>
> Working alone or in pairs, create an A5 booklet or presentation on Lithuanian and Jewish immigration with pages/slides on:
>
> - where both groups settled
> - problems they experienced and negative stereotypes that developed
> - employment
> - whether they assimilated into Scottish society.
>
> **(Unit outcomes: National 4/5: Outcome 2.1)**

> **Make the Link**
>
> You may learn more about immigration in Modern Studies.

Figure 17: *In the 1930s, some Italians came into conflict with Scots because of their support for the Italian fascist dictator, Benito Mussolini.*

> **Hint**
>
> Remember that at National 5 each point you make in an answer should be clear and detailed, ideally with an example to back up your point.

The political impact of immigrants on Scotland

Immigrants made a considerable impact on the politics of Scotland in this period. Irish Catholics initially voted for the Liberal Party because the Liberals supported Irish independence but soon became unhappy with the way the Liberals dealt with the issue. By the 1920s Irish Catholics were voting mainly for the Labour Party, playing an important role in its rise in Scotland.

Italians did not engage significantly with politics in Scotland. In the 1920s and 1930s some Italians associated themselves with Mussolini's Fascist Party, leading to some clashes with Scots when the Second World War broke out.

Lithuanians and Jews played an important role in the trade union movement that fought for better conditions in the workplace. Also, many joined the Independent Labour Party which fought for changes in the political system that would help the working class.

> **GO! Activity 9**
>
> 1. Create a small mind map with a minimum of five points, summarising the political impact of immigrants on Scotland.
>   **(Unit outcomes: National 4/5: Outcome 2.1)**
>
> **Exam style questions**
>
> 2. Explain why many Italians, Jews and Lithuanians arrived in Scotland in the nineteenth and early twentieth century. **KU 6**
>   **(Unit outcomes: National 4/5: Outcome 2.1)**
> 3. To what extent had immigrant groups assimilated in Scotland by 1939? **KU 9**
>   **(Unit outcomes: National 5: Outcome 2.3)**

3 Scottish emigration, 1830s–1939

In this section you will learn about:

- The push and pull factors that led Scots to emigrate.
- The countries Scots immigrated to.
- The different areas in Scotland that saw high emigration.

Between 1830 and 1939 it is thought that around 2 500 000 Scots emigrated overseas. Historians investigating this movement have pinpointed key push and pull factors that largely explain the high level of Scottish emigration in this period.

Push factors for emigration

Scots living in the Highlands experienced great changes in the nineteenth century. The population had grown quickly and there was a lack of quality land to farm. The result was that each bit of land that a family had to survive on got smaller and smaller, leading to food shortages and poverty. Landowners were often not paid rents for their lands and so they sought different ways to make a profit. This led to the now infamous Highland Clearances.

The Highland Clearances occurred throughout the nineteenth century when landowners made the decision to evict their tenants in favour of using their land for more profitable enterprises, such as sheep farming. Scots whose families had been farming the same land for generations were effectively cleared off their land and from their homes, often with little or no money to go elsewhere.

Many Highland communities relied heavily on potatoes to survive. In 1846 the potato blight wiped out the potato crop on the west coast of Scotland, meaning thousands of Highlanders were left starving. The landowners often tried their best to help their tenants, with some even going bankrupt in the process, but they could not afford to support them indefinitely. The potato blight forced many landowners, if they hadn't done so already, to change the way they made money from their lands and was another factor explaining the Highland Clearances.

 Hint

When trying to remember what the Highland Clearances were all about, think: sheep, potato blight, profit, landowners.

Make the Link

Over the years Scottish emigration, and the Highland Clearances specifically, has inspired many painters, writers and musicians to create important pieces of work. Next time you're in Art, Music or English, try using what you've learned as inspiration for your own piece of work.

🔍 Hint

Blackhouses got their name because the fires that were lit in them gave off soot and smoke that had nowhere to escape to due to the lack of a proper chimney or windows. So the houses were often very dark, or black, inside.

The living conditions in the Highlands were poor in the nineteenth century. Many Scots in the west Highlands lived in blackhouses, which lacked a proper ceiling or paved floor, and often didn't even have a window or chimney. Animals often lived in blackhouses alongside humans, meaning the houses were often dirty and smelly.

Figure 18: *Scots in the north and west Highlands would often live in simple blackhouses like the one above. Conditions inside were very basic.*

Many Highlanders who left their homes decided to try their luck in the growing towns and cities in the south. However, upon arrival in these alien places, they sometimes found it difficult to settle in and adjust to their new lives. Many Higlanders only spoke Gaelic and not English, and these language difficulties, combined with problems adapting their existing skills to factories and industrial work, forced some Highlanders to try their luck abroad instead.

Figure 19: *A sketch showing victims of the Highland Clearances leaving on board a ship.*

In the Lowlands the population had grown considerably, and new machines like steam powered threshers and reapers had begun to replace farm workers. With a lack of jobs available many Scots in these areas were forced to look elsewhere for employment and opportunities.

It was not just in rural areas that Scots experienced these 'push' factors. In the ever-growing cities of Glasgow, Edinburgh and Dundee workers experienced terrible living and working conditions and wages were low. This was despite the fact that Scotland was, by the 1830s, an industrial powerhouse where many Scottish businessmen were becoming very rich indeed.

🔍 **Hint**

The industrial revolution may have meant more jobs in the cities, but in rural areas it often meant fewer jobs on farms as machines replaced workers.

Pull factors for emigration

Cheap land abroad attracted many Scots to places such as Canada, the United States, Australia and New Zealand. Those emigrating from rural areas in the Highlands and Lowlands of Scotland would have had the necessary skills to develop and tend land and so would have been 'pulled' to these new countries in the hope of a better, more stable and prosperous life. Some countries were even known to offer free land to emigrants, something that would have attracted many Scots abroad.

Figure 20: *Many Scots were attracted abroad by the prospect of employment.*

Those Scots who left cities like Glasgow or Edinburgh were often attracted by the better wages on offer in countries like the United States or Canada. These Scots would also often have skills that were highly desirable and so they could command higher wages than they would get in Scotland, just for doing the same job.

Figure 21: *Some Scots were attracted to Australia by the promise of gold.*

Scots were often given help to emigrate by landowners, charities and government organisations. Landowners sometimes offered to pay the fares of those people whom they had moved off their land, and this of course would have encouraged these Scots to go abroad.

Charities were often set up to help Scots move abroad, especially after the potato blight and the famine that followed. In fact the Highlands and Islands Emigration Society helped landlords to resettle over 16 000 Scots abroad. The British government also set up schemes to provide grants of land in places like Canada and Australia, as well as to provide loans for the cost of getting there by ship. In 1922 the Empire Settlement Act was passed which meant emigrants were now entitled to help with the cost of moving abroad, such was the government's desire to relieve unemployment in Britain.

Governments in the British colonies employed agents to attract Scots to their countries. These agents would travel throughout Scotland, telling stories of the many opportunities that could be found abroad and often enticing potential emigrants with the offer of free passage.

Perhaps the biggest 'pull' factor for many Scots was the letters home that they received from family and friends who had already settled in colonies abroad. These letters would often talk of the great opportunities to be had abroad and must have convinced their recipients to go and join them. The next two sources are perfect examples:

Source K is from a letter written by James Thomson in 1844, who was living in Montreal, Canada.

> 📖 **Key Word**
>
> • **British colonies**
> Countries that the British Empire controlled.

> Servants here dress almost as fine as their mistresses. In summer white dresses, black veils and silk parasols are quite common among them. In that way they are just like everyone here by being better dressed than people at home. I have seen fewer ragged people here than in Aberdeen. The country people are dressed in thick, grey home-made clothes. They all wear the same as if they were a regiment of soldiers. I plan to stay here all winter and go up the country early in spring. Until then I would not want to give anyone advice about coming to America although what I have seen confirms my opinion that any steady person who is willing to work would do better than at home.

Figure 22: *A poster advertising emigration to Canada.*

Source L is a letter written from Mr Donald of Melbourne, published in the Aberdeen Journal on 12 May 1852.

> I think I will like this country well. Servants here earn wages of £26 to £30 with a free house and fuel, and it is expected wages will be higher soon. Scottish servants are preferred to all other nationalities. I will not advise you to leave everything and come here if you have a permanent job, but any man or woman can do far better here than at home and with half the care and trouble too! I hope many more Aberdeenshire folk will come out – they will do well.

GO! Activity 10

Exam style questions

1. Evaluate the usefulness of **Source K** as evidence of the reasons Scots were attracted abroad between 1830 and 1939.   **SH 5**

   (You may want to comment on who wrote it, when they wrote it, why they wrote it, what they say or what has been missed out.)

   (Unit outcomes: National 4: Outcome 1.1; National 5: Outcomes 1.1 and 2.1)

2. Compare the views of **Sources K** and **L** as evidence of what Scots thought of their new countries. (Compare the sources overall and in detail.)   **SH 4**

   (Unit outcomes: National 4/5: Outcome 1.3)

🔍 **Hint**

Improved transport was another consequence of the industrial revolution.

Many of the ships and railways that moved Scots around the world had actually been built in Scotland, often by Scots and immigrants.

Improved transport also played a key role in attracting Scots abroad. From the 1880s steamships could cross the Atlantic much quicker and by 1914 it took only one week to travel from Scotland to North America. This encouraged many Scots to go across to Canada or the USA, earn some money, and then return to share it with their families. The improvement of railway travel also meant travel to ports was easier than ever before.

The importance of religion in Scottish emigration must also be recognised. Scottish Christians were often attracted to countries in Africa and Asia to spread the word of God. Their ultimate aim was to convert the natives to Christianity and many were very successful. Perhaps the best known of Scotland's missionaries was David Livingstone who became famous as an explorer of Africa. Livingstone and others set up schools, hospitals and churches wherever they could and inspired other Scots to follow in their footsteps.

📖 **Key Word**

- **Missionary**
Someone who has been sent on a religious mission, often to promote Christianity in a foreign country.

Make the Link

You may learn more about missionaries in RMPS or Modern Studies.

Activity 11

1. Your teacher will give you an appropriate amount of time for this activity.

   Take an A3 piece of paper and divide it up as shown below.

Push factors	Pull factors
Where Scots went:	
Areas Scots left:	

   Using all the information in this section, including the sources, you are going to fill in the boxes, ensuring you show at least five pull factors and five push factors. However, you can only use a maximum of fifty words, so you'll have to use pictures and diagrams to get your points across. Once you have finished, you will be expected to present your poster to your group who will assess if you have been successful.
   (Unit outcomes: National 4/5: Outcome 2.2)

Exam style questions

Source M is from David Ross, *Scotland: History of a Nation* (2007).

> As early as 1814, the clearances began in Sutherland when Strathnaver was turned over to sheep rearing. The inhabitants were forcibly transferred to coastal locations where they were expected to make a living by fishing. The potato famine of the 1840s added to the miseries of the people. In the 1850s, emigration societies, including the quaintly named Scottish Patriotic Society, were formed, and emigration became an industry.

2. How fully does **Source M** explain the reasons for Scottish migration in the nineteenth century? (Use **Source M** and recall.) **SH 6**

   (Unit outcomes: National 4: Outcome 1.2; National 5: Outcomes 1.2 and 2.2)

3. Explain why so many Scots settled in Canada between 1830 and 1939. **KU 6**

   (Unit outcomes: National 4/5: Outcome 2.2)

4 The experience of Scots abroad, 1830s–1939

In this section you will learn about:

- The countries Scottish emigrants made an impact in.
- The role of Scots in five different countries, focusing on: industry, economy, education and politics.
- The impact of individual Scots in their new countries.

Scots in Canada

In Canada today it is thought that around one in ten people have Scottish ancestry. It is perhaps no surprise that so many Scots settled in Canada, since it was part of the British Empire and its people spoke English, like most Scots. Also, by 1910, the journey from the west of Scotland by steamship only took a week. Between 1830 and 1939 Scots made a significant impact on Canada's economy, industry, politics and education, helping to shape the country as it stands today.

Figure 23: *The flag of Nova Scotia in Canada shows the Scottish impact there. Nova Scotia means 'New Scotland' in Latin.*

By 1878 it was thought that one third of Canada's richest and most influential businessmen were of Scots origin. Scottish immigrants to Canada were therefore very important in developing the Canadian economy and industry. Many Scots took up the offer of free or cheap land and established thriving farms throughout Canada. Others became involved in the fur trade, and within a few years had come to dominate it. It was this fur trade, as well as timber, that had formed the basis of the Hudson Bay Company, a massive trading company in Canada in which Scots played a vital role. Scots also came to dominate the paper industry in Canada and made a huge impact on the railway industry in Canada, by creating and then building the Canadian-Pacific Railway.

The Scot Lord Mount Stephen created the Canadian-Pacific Railway, which stretched right across Canada, benefiting all aspects of the economy and industry. It was a feat of engineering and exploration, covering 3700 miles, and the chief engineer, Sandford Fleming, was also a Scot. Fleming also came up with the idea of dividing the world into different time zones, with all countries working on one standard time. Since 1883 the world has been running on standard time, meaning whenever you go abroad and put the time forward or back, it is because of Sandford Fleming.

Figure 24: *Sandford Fleming in the tall hat watches as the last spike is driven into the Canadian-Pacific Railway.*

Hint

When looking at how Scots impacted on a country focus on industry, politics and education. That way you'll have plenty to write about when doing activities.

The Scottish influence on education in Canada can easily be seen by the fact that Scots founded six universities in Canada. As one author wrote in 1896 'There is not a college or University in Canada, where at least one "son of the heather" is not to be found in some high capacity.' In politics, too, Scots were crucial in Canada's development. The first two Canadian Prime Ministers, Sir John McDonald and Alexander McKenzie, were both born in Scotland. It was these men that guided Canada to independence and then prosperity.

GO! Activity 12

Create a comic strip or poster that summarises the four previous paragraphs using mainly pictures. You can only use 30 words in your piece of work.

(Unit outcomes: National 4/5: Outcome 2.1)

Scots in the United States

Although the United States was not a part of the British Empire many Scots continued to settle there, mainly because of the shared language and the many economic opportunities that it offered. These economic opportunities lay in the many factories and industries that had made the USA so wealthy by 1939, and the skills that Scots brought with them made them very welcome indeed.

Figure 25: *A United States postal stamp issued in 1960 in honour of Andrew Carnegie.*

Some Scots made a bigger impact than others, and perhaps none more so than Andrew Carnegie. Carnegie was born in Dunfermline in 1835 and just before his thirteenth birthday, in 1848, he and his family moved to America. The Carnegie family settled in Pittsburgh and Andrew and his father gained jobs in the textile mills there. Andrew Carnegie excelled in every job he did, making the most of the many industries that were growing rapidly in the USA at this time. By 1889, he was the head of the largest steel firm in the world, the Carnegie Steel Corporation. By this point he had become known as one of America's 'builders', as his business had helped to build and shape America's economy. Carnegie's rags to riches tale is certainly worthy of a Hollywood film, although for many it was what he did with his wealth that makes his story so memorable.

Make the Link

If you take Modern Studies you may look at the USA in Unit 3.

In Business Education you might learn about successful entrepreneurs. Can you think of any modern day individuals who are similar to Andrew Carnegie?

By the turn of the century in 1900, Carnegie was one of the wealthiest people in the world. In 1901 he made the dramatic decision to sell his company for around $480 000 000 and, using the profits, began helping others. He donated millions of dollars to the New York Public Library and it is thought that all his donations over the years helped open 2800 new libraries. In terms of an impact on education and learning, this is hard to beat. He also set up funds and awards for teachers and supported peace projects. While Carnegie had been an astute and clever businessmen, by the end of his life in 1919 he was also known as one of the great philanthropists of the modern age, having given away $350 000 000.

Key Word

- **Philanthropist**

Someone who seeks to help others, usually by donating money to charities or worthwhile causes.

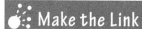

Another impressive Scottish immigrant to the USA was John Muir. Muir loved nature and explored vast areas of North America. It was his exploration and writings that convinced the United States government to establish the now world famous Yosemite National Park.

Activity 13

Using the preceding information and, ideally, the internet, create a Facebook page for either Andrew Carnegie or John Muir. You could do this on a computer or a piece of A3/4 paper. It must show all his achievements and the impact other Scots like him had on the USA.

Make the Link

The John Muir Award is an environmental award that encourages people of all backgrounds to connect, enjoy and care for wild places. You may be able to do this in your school.

Figure 26: *A commemorative coin issued by the United States mint, showing John Muir.*

Scots in Australia

Between 1788 and 1900 over 200 000 Scots immigrated to Australia. Some of these Scots were convicts, forcibly removed from Scotland and sent to Australia to serve their sentence. Some of these convicts, upon release, decided to remain in Australia, often establishing businesses and contributing to the economic development of Australia. Generally speaking, however, most Scots chose to settle in Australia, and many made a significant impact on their new country's development.

Scots were heavily involved in mining, whether it was for coal, copper, silver or gold. Scots could also be found running successful farms, often rearing sheep. In fact, a Scot named John MacArthur set up the first Australian sheep ranch, and Scots became important figures in the export of wool from Australia. The growing sugar industry of the 1880s also saw the involvement of Scots, as did shipping and trade generally, and Robert McCracken from Ayrshire was the founder of Australia's brewing industry.

Politically, Scots also played an important role. For example, Andrew Fisher from Ayrshire became Australian Prime Minister three times and is considered by many to be one of Australia's most successful politicians. He also established the Commonwealth Bank, one of Australia's leading banks. Just as impressive was Catherine Helen Spence from the Borders town of Melrose, who immigrated to Australia in 1839. She became Australia's first female political candidate and first woman journalist. She also campaigned for women to have the vote and has been called 'Australia's greatest woman'. She is fondly remembered in Australia and even appears on the Australian $5 bank note.

Figure 27 and Source N: *The Australian $5 note honours Scots-born Catherine Helen Spence.*

Figure 28: 'First Scottish Colony for New Zealand' – 1839 poster advertising emigration from Scotland to New Zealand.

 Hint

Throughout this topic sheep farming has been mentioned. Sheep farming helped to push Highlanders off their land, yet Scots abroad often started sheep farms!

GO! Activity 14

1. Imagine it is 1900. Create an advert designed to attract Scots to Australia. Show what other Scots have done in Australia and the impact they have made.

   (Unit outcomes: National 4/5: Outcome 2.2)

Exam style question

2. Evaluate the usefulness of **Source N** for investigating the impact of Scots abroad between 1830 and 1930. **SH 5**

   (Unit outcomes: National 4: Outcome 1.1; National 5: Outcomes 1.1 and 2.1)

Scots in New Zealand

Those Scots who made the long journey to New Zealand made a significant impact there. In 1848 Scots created the town of Dunedin (the Scottish Gaelic name for Edinburgh), which is now one of the largest in New Zealand. Dunedin lies in the Otago province in the South Island of New Zealand and it was Scots who dominated this region. Even today towns, houses and streets in Otago look Scottish and the nickname of the Dunedin rugby team is 'The Highlanders'!

In New Zealand, Scots were successful in many different industries, helping the New Zealand economy to grow. Men like Donald Reid from Perthshire established sheep farms from which they made money exporting wool. Scots could also be found mining gold after it was discovered in the mid-nineteenth century. The paper-making business in New Zealand was founded by Scots and Henry Nichol, who came from Greenock, even built a shipyard in Auckland in 1843. It soon became very successful, launching 180 ships into the Pacific.

In education and politics Scots made an impact. The Scottish education system that was established in 1872 provided the basis for the one that New Zealand adopted in 1877. Also, Scots helped to create the first girls' school in New Zealand and had a hand in shaping the curriculum of New Zealand's first university in Otago. In terms of politics, at least four New Zealand Prime Ministers were Scots.

Activity 15

Exam style question

Source O is from James Adam, *Twenty-Five Years of an Emigrant's Life in the South of New Zealand* (1876).

> The Scot has certainly made his mark on this land, not only in commerce but also in the field of education, setting up schools throughout the area. Several of the Scots' descendants have also become doctors. It must be stated, however, that not all of the emigrants have made their presence a wholly welcome one in this land. Thankfully, this type of immigrant is far from common-place.

Evaluate the usefulness of **Source O** as evidence of the impact Scots made in their new countries. **SH 5**
(Use **Source O** and recall.)

(Unit outcomes: National 4/5: Outcome 2.2)

Scots in India

The East India Company ran India until 1857. It was dominated by Scots, with many making their fortunes there through trade. Following the British takeover of India, the first three Governors-General of India were Scottish. This clearly shows the important role Scots played in India's development in the nineteenth and early twentieth century, yet the story does not end there.

James Dalhousie was a Scottish aristocrat who served as Governor-General of India between 1848 and 1856. During his time in charge, Dalhousie oversaw the creation of an extensive railway network throughout India which helped to modernise and unite the country. He also encouraged the building of schools and roads, all with a view to improving India. However, Dalhousie remains a controversial figure because he believed that India needed to be 'civilised', to be made more like Britain. Some historians argue that he didn't respect the cultures and practices of Indians and was more concerned with making them behave like the British.

Many Scots travelled to India as missionaries and helped to establish schools throughout the country. They spread the word of God, hoping to convert Indians, yet by focusing on the importance of education, they helped many poor, illiterate Indians to read and write.

 **Make the Link**

If you take Modern Studies you may look at India in Unit 3.

Figure 29: *Sir Thomas Lipton.*

From 1830 onwards, Scots became involved in exporting jute, tea, timber, coal, sugar and indigo as well as cotton. By 1880 India had overtaken China as leaders of tea distribution and, perhaps unsurprisingly, Scots were at the heart of this too. One of the most notable figures here was Thomas Lipton, who was born in Glasgow in 1850. Lipton made a fortune by establishing tea plantations in India and it is thought that by the turn of the century he controlled around 10% of the world tea trade. Even today the Lipton tea brand is going strong.

> ### GO! Activity 16
>
> Imagine it is 1900 and you have left Scotland for India. Write a diary entry describing all the things you have seen that Scots had a hand in developing.
>
> **(Unit outcomes: National 4/5: Outcome 2.1)**

Scots' relations with native societies

While Scots certainly had a positive impact on the countries they settled in, the story is not quite that simple. In the USA some Scots were involved in the slave trade, becoming slave owners, trading in slaves and opposing an end to slavery. Elsewhere, Scots immigrants often came into conflict with Aborigines in Australia, Maoris in New Zealand and Native Americans in Canada and the USA. This was usually because Scots had settled, and planned to farm, on land that was not theirs. The terrible irony here is that some Scots who had been thrown off their land in the Highlands then travelled abroad and did the same to others. There is plenty of evidence to prove that Scots used brutal force when claiming land in Australia, New Zealand and Canada. There are, however, also examples of Scots cooperating and developing good relations with the local populations in these countries.

Figure 30: *Scots immigrants were involved in the ill treatment of Australian Aborigines.*

Make the Link

If you are studying 'The Atlantic Slave Trade, 1770–1807', you will learn about how some Scots were involved in the slave trade and how they benefited from it.

Figure 31: *Some Scottish immigrants in the USA were involved in the slave trade.*

Source P was written by a modern historian.

> Scots often forced native people off their land and killed them if they resisted. Scots tried to impose their religion and culture on North American Indians, playing a role in their destruction. Scots settlers often brought diseases to their new countries which native people had no resistance to, leaving many dead.

GO! Activity 17

Exam style questions

1. How fully does **Source P** describe relations between Scots immigrant and native societies? (Use **Source P** and recall.) **SH 6**

   (Unit outcomes: National 4/5: Outcome 2.2)

2. To what extent did Scots make a positive impact on the countries they settled in? **KU 9**

   (Unit outcomes: National 5: Outcome 2.3)

Hint

Remember that questions for 8 marks require several paragraphs, a balanced answer, and a clear conclusion that answers the question.

Summary

In this topic you have learned:

- why immigrants came to Scotland
- the impact of the British Empire on Scotland
- what life was like for immigrants in Scotland
- how well immigrants assimilated in Scotland
- where Scots emigrated
- why Scots emigrated
- the impact Scots emigrants had on the countries they settled in, both positive and negative.

You should have developed your skills and be able to:

- evaluate the usefulness of a source
- compare two sources by saying what they agree or disagree about
- put a source into context by saying how fully it describes an issue.

Learning Checklist

Now that you have finished **Migration and Empire, 1830–1939**, complete a self-evaluation of your knowledge and skill to assess what you have understood. Use traffic lights to help you make up a revision plan to help you improve in the areas you identified as red or amber.

- Explain the reasons for Irish immigration to Scotland. ◯ ◯ ◯

- Explain the reasons for Italian immigration to Scotland. ◯ ◯ ◯

- Explain the reasons for Lithuanian immigration to Scotland. ◯ ◯ ◯

- Explain the reasons for Jewish immigration to Scotland. ◯ ◯ ◯

- Evaluate the impact the Empire had on Scotland. ◯ ◯ ◯

- Describe the experience of Irish immigrants in Scotland. ◯ ◯ ◯

- Describe the experience of Italian immigrants in Scotland. ◯ ◯ ◯

- Describe the experience of Lithuanian immigrants in Scotland. ◯ ◯ ◯

- Describe the experience of Jewish immigrants in Scotland. ◯ ◯ ◯

- Evaluate how well immigrants assimilated into Scotland. ◯ ◯ ◯

- Explain the reasons for Scottish emigration.

- List five countries that Scots immigrated to.

- Describe the impact of at least one Scottish immigrant in their new country.

- Evaluate the impact of Scots in Canada.

- Evaluate the impact of Scots in the USA.

- Evaluate the impact of Scots in Australia.

- Evaluate the impact of Scots in New Zealand.

- Evaluate the impact of Scots in India.

- Evaluate the overall impact of Scottish immigrants abroad.

Studying this topic will provide you with a good understanding of the ways in which the Great War affected the lives of those serving on the Western Front and those at home in Scotland. It will allow you to understand the impact new technology had on soldiers and what life was like for them in the trenches. Also, by focusing on all aspects of life in Scotland during and after the war, you will gain an understanding of the ways in which the war affected Scotland and its people in the short and long term.

You will develop your skills and be able to:

❖ evaluate the usefulness of a source

❖ compare two sources by saying what they agree or disagree about

❖ put a source into context by saying how fully it describes an issue.

This topic is split into four sections:

❖ Scots on the Western Front

❖ The domestic impact of war—society and culture

❖ The domestic impact of war—economy and industry

❖ The domestic impact of war—politics

Level 4 experiences and outcomes relevant to this topic:

I have developed a sense of my heritage and identity as a British, European or global citizen and can present arguments about the importance of respecting the heritage and identity of others. **SOC 4-02a**

I can evaluate conflicting sources of evidence to sustain a line of argument. **SOC 4-01a**

I can make reasoned judgements about how the exercise of power affects the rights and responsibilities of citizens by comparing a more democratic and a less democratic society. **SOC 4-04c**

I can present supported conclusions about the social, political and economic impacts of a technological change in the past. **SOC 4-05a**

I can evaluate the changes which have taken place in an industry in Scotland's past and can debate their impact. **SOC 4-05b**

Having critically analysed a significant historical event, I can assess the relative importance of factors contributing to the event. **SOC 4-06a**

I can express an informed view about the changing nature of conflict over time, appreciate its impact and empathise with the experiences of those involved. **SOC 4-06b**

I can assess the impact for those involved in a specific instance of the expansion of power and influence in the past. **SOC 4-06d**

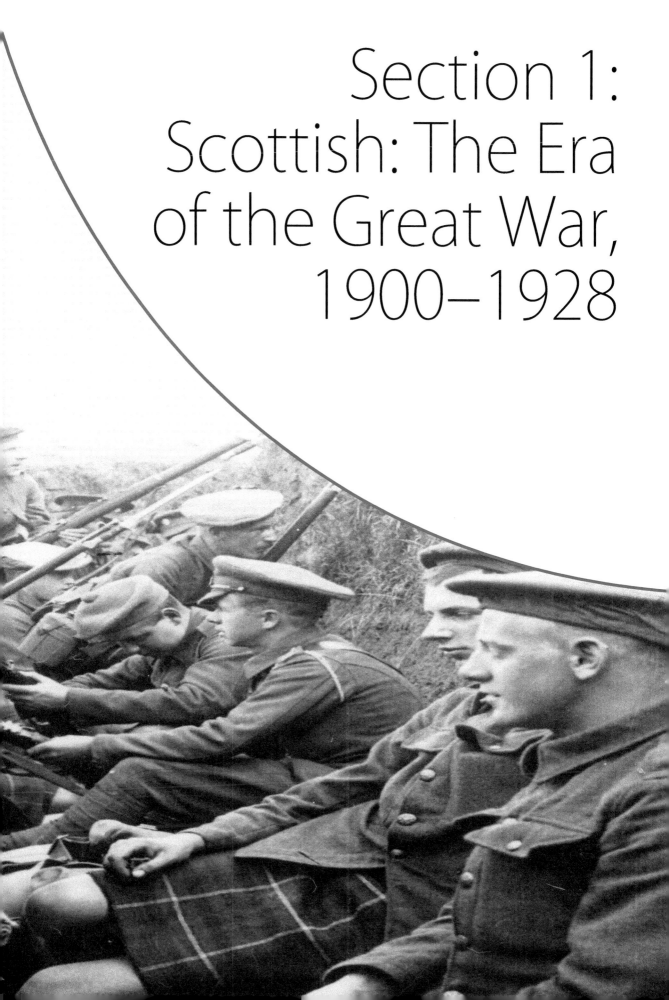

Section 1: Scottish: The Era of the Great War, 1900–1928

Background

In 1900 Scotland appeared to be economically strong, a country making the most of its important role within the British Empire and boasting industries that were well known and respected throughout the world. By 1928, however, Scotland's economy was struggling, unemployment was rising, and its role within the Empire was being called into question. The years in between, therefore, saw Scotland go through major changes and the Great War, the major world event of the era, was right at the heart of this.

By the start of the twentieth century, Scotland, as part of the United Kingdom and the British Empire, had helped make Britain the most powerful country in the world. Scotland's shipbuilding, coal, iron and steel industries helped make and power the ships, machinery and weaponry that maintained Britain's position in the world. Because of this Scotland's economy relied heavily on the Empire for trade and the jobs that went with it. In addition, Scots soldiers played an important role in the British Empire, helping to ensure new colonies were well run and disturbances dealt with quickly. In short, Scotland's ties with the British Empire were strong, and it is no surprise that, when it went to war in 1914, Scotland and its people were among the first to lend their support to the cause.

Figure 1: *Scots played an important role in the Empire. When war broke out in 1914, many were keen to sign up and fight to protect it. These soldiers were from the Argyll and Sutherland Regiment.*

The Great War was a terrible conflict for all countries involved and Scotland was no different. Scottish troops experienced the full horror and impact of modern warfare, from machine guns and gas attacks, to airplanes and tanks. Casualty rates were devastatingly high at 26%, leaving a permanent mark on the towns and cities of Scotland. On the home front Scots adjusted to 'total war', which meant that the economy

Hint

The Great War of 1914–18 is also known as the First World War or World War One.

and society generally was geared towards fighting a successful campaign. In this time of increased government control over people's everyday lives, from what they ate to where they worked, many Scots became more politically aware and active.

Following the armistice in November 1918, many expected Scotland to simply slot back into its pre-1914 role as a major cog in the machine that was the British Empire. However, the economic situation after the war was very different and Scotland's industries struggled. With so many Scots having failed to return from the war, and many of those who remained at home having seen their lives change massively, Scotland in 1928 was very different to Scotland in 1900. The era of the Great War, therefore, saw Scotland and its people experience significant changes. It is these changes, and the event that caused many of them, that you will learn about in this topic.

GO! Activity 1

Read the background information. Create a poster/illustrated mind map/presentation entitled: **Scotland 1900–1928: Background.**

Rules: Your piece of work cannot feature more than thirty words so you will also need to use pictures to get all the points across. You will be expected to present your piece of work to someone else once it is finished, so make sure it makes total sense.

1 Scots on the Western Front

In this section you will learn about:

- Why so many Scots volunteered for the armed forces in 1914.
- The defensive trench system on the Western Front.
- The new technology and tactics that were used in the war.
- What life was like in the trenches.

Recruitment: why so many Scots volunteered for the armed forces in 1914

When the war broke out in August 1914, many believed it would be over by Christmas. Some Scots rushed to sign up because they were afraid of missing out on the action and adventure of war. The war offered these men a break from the daily grind of work and many were genuinely excited by the prospect of travelling abroad, often for the first time. For those Scots who lived in small towns, it was often the case that if one or two signed up, many others would follow. This sense of comradeship, of friendship and mutual support, meant that many communities saw a large proportion of their men leave in August 1914.

Figure 2: *Soldiers of the Black Watch leaving for France in August 1914*

There was a strong military tradition in Scotland, where the army was seen as a good career choice and soldiering a noble thing to do. This led many men to join up, often following in the footsteps of fathers, brothers or uncles. Other Scots were motivated by the prospect of a decent wage and employment. For those already employed, pressure was sometimes put on them to join up by their employers. For many, the stories of German atrocities in Belgium were enough to convince them to sign up, simply because it was 'the right thing to do'. For others, peer pressure from friends and family was enough to convince them to enlist. Perhaps the biggest motivating factor for many Scots was simply patriotism: they felt it was their duty to fight for king and country. This was something that the British government focused on in its wartime propaganda.

Propaganda

Right from the beginning of the war the British government created posters that were designed to recruit as many men as possible. This wartime propaganda often focused on the factors outlined above, such as patriotism and peer pressure. A recurring theme in wartime propaganda is the idea that it was a man's duty to sign up, not only to his country and Empire, but also his family.

Daddy, what did YOU do in the Great War?

YOUR KING & COUNTRY NEED YOU

A WEE 'SCRAP O' PAPER' IS BRITAIN'S BOND.

TO MAINTAIN THE HONOUR AND GLORY OF THE BRITISH EMPIRE

YOUR COUNTRY'S CALL

Isn't this worth fighting for?
ENLIST NOW

LINE UP, BOYS!

ENLIST TO-DAY.

📖 Key Words

- **Patriotism**

Strongly supporting and loving your country.

- **Propaganda**

Spreading information that is designed to promote a cause.

🔍 Hint

During the Great War all governments engaged in propaganda in an attempt to convince people to do what politicians thought was best for the country.

🔍 Hint

In the National 5 exam you could well encounter a poster or picture source and be asked to evaluate its usefulness. Be prepared to analyse picture sources in detail, as well as written sources.

Source A: *'Your King and Country Need You', a government recruitment poster from 1915.*

⚛ Make the Link

If you study 'Hitler and Nazi Germany, 1919–1939', you will learn how the Nazis used propaganda effectively to spread their ideas.

Figure 3a–d: *These are all recruitment posters from the Great War. What do you think each poster is trying to make Scots feel in an attempt to boost army recruitment?*

> **GO!** **Activity 2**
>
> 1. Imagine it is August 1914 and you have just signed up along with some of your closest friends. Write a diary entry explaining why you signed up and why four of your friends signed up. Also, describe some of the posters that you have seen around your town and the effect they had on you.
>
>   **(Unit outcomes: National 4/5: Outcome 2.2)**
>
> **Exam style question**
>
> 2. Evaluate the usefulness of **Source A** for investigating why so many Scots volunteered for the armed forces at the beginning of the war. **SH 5**
>
>   (You may want to comment on who wrote it, when they wrote it, why they wrote it, what they say or what has been missed out.)
>
>   **(Unit outcomes: National 4: Outcome 1.1; National 5: Outcomes 1.1 and 2.1)**

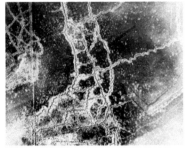

Figure 4: *By 1915, opposing lines of trenches stretched across Europe, covering vast distances. This aerial photograph shows the opposing lines with no man's land in the middle. Why do you think it was called 'no man's land'?*

The defensive trench system on the Western Front

When the war began in August 1914, it was a war of movement. In the first weeks of the war the German army made good ground, advancing through Belgium and into France. However, when the Germans were stopped by artillery and machine gun fire, they began to dig trenches so as to maintain their position. In return, the French and British dug in and so trench warfare began.

As you can see from Figures 5–8 trenches were built for defence and to keep troops safe.

Figure 5: *The first trenches were basic, often resembling long ditches dug in the ground.*

Figure 6: *As the war progressed, trenches became larger, deeper and sturdier.*

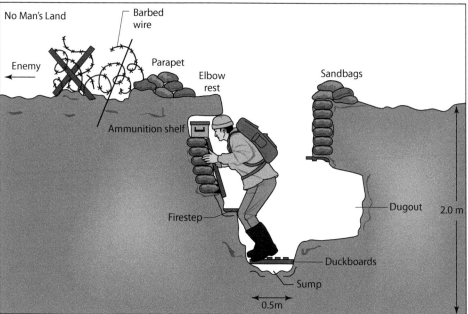

Figures 7 and 8: *Trenches were constructed to provide protection from bullets, artillery shells and water that collected at the bottom. Can you see which parts of the trench protected troops?*

In addition to the way that trenches were constructed, the system of trenches on the Western Front also made them difficult to attack. As Figure 9 shows, there were several lines of trenches, all manned by troops and well protected, meaning attacking troops faced many problems.

A typical attack would see troops go 'over the top' into no man's land in an attempt to reach the enemy trench. However, this was very difficult, as Figure 9 shows. Trench warfare saw huge losses of life simply because it was so difficult to attack trenches. All along the Western Front there were very few breakthroughs and a stalemate developed where neither side was able to take much land and hold it. For the next four years this deadlock remained, as army leaders struggled to devise tactics that would lead to a breakthrough.

> **Hint**
>
> In some sources Scots soldiers mention going 'ower the bags'. This means the same as going over the top, as the 'bags' that they referred to were the sandbags that protected the trenches.

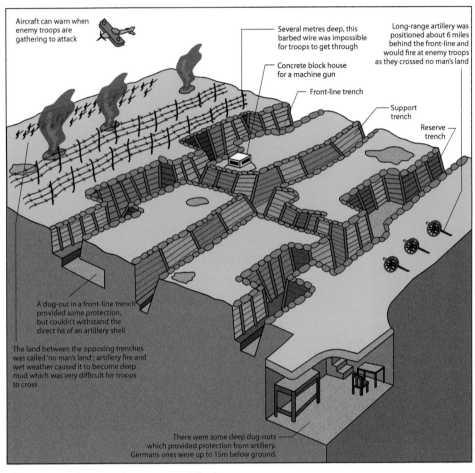

Aircraft can warn when enemy troops are gathering to attack

Several metres deep, this barbed wire was impossible for troops to get through

Long-range artillery was positioned about 6 miles behind the front-line and would fire at enemy troops as they crossed no man's land

Concrete block house for a machine gun

Front-line trench

Support trench

Reserve trench

A dug-out in a front-line trench provided some protection, but couldn't withstand the direct hit of an artillery shell

The land between the opposing trenches was called 'no man's land'; artillery fire and wet weather caused it to become deep mud which was very difficult for troops to cross

There were some deep dug-outs which provided protection from artillery. Germans ones were up to 15m below ground.

Figure 9: *Attacking trenches was very difficult, as you can see.*

> ### GO! Activity 3
>
> Create a poster/presentation that clearly explains:
>
> - why the trench system developed
> - how trenches were laid out
> - what made defending trenches easier than attacking them
> - why there was a stalemate on the Western Front.
>
> Use words, pictures and diagrams in your piece of work.
>
> **(Unit outcomes: National 4/5: Outcome 2.2)**

New technology and tactics

Artillery

Figure 10: *Artillery was known as the 'King of the Battlefield' because it was such a devastating weapon.*

Artillery refers to large guns that fired explosive shells across large distances in an effort to destroy enemy troops, guns and trenches. During the Great War artillery was the cause of more than half of all casualties. By 1918 the British had begun to use accurate artillery barrages, along with tanks, to make gains on the Western Front.

Machine guns

Machine guns were used to terrible effect in the Great War. They could fire hundreds of bullets a minute, and were crucial in defending trenches from attack. However, because they were so heavy and often required up to six men to operate them and stop them overheating, they could not be easily moved around the battlefield. This meant that they were essentially a defensive weapon. Machine guns certainly contributed to the stalemate on the Western Front.

Gas

The Germans first used poison gas in 1915 and the French and British soon followed. Chlorine, phosgene and mustard gas were the most commonly used. Chlorine and phosgene choked those who inhaled it, burning their throats and internal organs, and often killed soldiers. Mustard gas caused horrific burns when it was exposed to skin, which was particularly worrying for Scottish soldiers who wore kilts. It could also cause blindness and, in severe cases, death. By the end of the war, troops on both sides were using well-made gas masks to protect themselves but the fear of getting caught in an attack still remained. That being said, chlorine gas, for example, was actually a rather unreliable weapon as it relied on the wind blowing the right way to be successful. Overall, gas attacks were horrendous and understandably feared, but they didn't claim anywhere near as many lives as machine guns and artillery.

Figure 11: *The machine gun was known as the 'Queen of the Battlefield' as it was second only to artillery in the damage it could do to the enemy.*

Make the Link

In Modern Studies you may learn about the banning of poison gas as a weapon.

Make the Link

In English you may study poetry from the Great War; the famous poem 'Dulce Et Decorum Est' by Wilfred Owen describes someone injured by a gas attack.

Make the Link

Improved wartime technology was the result of the industrial revolution which Scotland had gone through in the nineteenth century. If in History you study the topic 'Changing Britain, 1760–1914' you will learn about this in more depth.

Figure 12: *Poison gas was one of the most feared weapons due to the terrible effects it had if it touched skin or was inhaled.*

Tanks

Figure 13: *By 1918 tanks were beginning to make a real impact on the battlefield.*

The British first used tanks in 1916 but they were not effective. They got stuck in mud, broke down and were slow. However, the British continued to improve them and by late 1917 they were making more of an impact in battles. They became more reliable, had stronger armour, were a little quicker, and could go through barbed wire. By 1918 British generals were using tanks and artillery together to provide troops with more cover in the field. These new tactics meant that the British were able to advance quicker than ever before. The decision by the Germans not to focus on building as many tanks as the British was one they must have regretted by 1918.

Aircraft

Figure 14: *Later in the war, planes were fitted with machine guns and were even used to drop bombs on the enemy.*

When war broke out planes were used mainly to spot the enemy position and report back to headquarters. However, four years later planes looked very different. They were stronger and faster and could now carry machine guns and drop bombs. Some German bombers even flew over London to drop bombs on factories.

Zeppelins were huge oval shaped airships that Germany used in the early part of the war for bombing raids. They carried machine guns and bombs. However, in late 1916 they were abandoned because they were easy to shoot out of the sky and planes were now capable of dropping bombs.

🔵 **GO!** Activity 4

1. Imagine it is August 1918 and you have been in the army four years now. You want to let new recruits know about all the new technology on the Western Front. Your challenge is to create a five page booklet entitled 'A soldier's guide to World War I weapons'. You must:

   - Describe each weapon, perhaps using drawings to help.
   - Explain, where possible, how the weapon had improved by 1918.
   - Explain the impact each weapon had on the tactics in WWI.

   (Unit outcomes: National 4/5: Outcomes 2.1 and 2.2)

2. **Internet based activity: important battles of the Great War**

   Go online and, with guidance from your teacher as to what sites to visit, research what happened to Scottish troops in the following battles:

   - Battle of Loos 1915
   - Battle of the Somme 1916
   - Battle of Arras 1917

   You should produce a presentation describing all three battles.

   (Unit outcomes: National 4/5: Outcome 2.1)

🔍 Hint

You may well face questions in your National 5 exam on some of these battles so it is worthwhile doing your research on them.

Life in the trenches

Life in the trenches was very difficult for soldiers. However, it must first be remembered that troops did not spend their whole time on the front line. They would rotate between three lines: the front line, the support line and the reserve line, and then spend a short period in rest, before beginning the cycle again. In busier times they would be expected to spend longer on the front line.

The typical daily routine would begin with the 'morning hate'. This was when soldiers would be woken up at dawn to stand to attention in their trenches to make sure the enemy didn't attack. Each side would bombard the other with artillery to disrupt the beginning of the day for soldiers. Understandably, soldiers hated starting the day like this, as the nickname suggests! Breakfast would follow, then the cleaning of rifles, and the rest of the day would see soldiers joining work parties in the trenches, perhaps fixing duckboards or re-filling sandbags. Evenings might be spent writing letters home, keeping up with diaries or playing cards with friends. It certainly wasn't always action-packed!

Soldiers received ration packs with food in them, but did not have the luxury of hot meals for much of the war. There was not a great deal of variety in the food they were given, although some soldiers would receive parcels from home or from the Red Cross. Despite this, soldiers came to hate the food they were given as it was often tasteless or too salty. Bully beef and plum and apple pudding, two staple foods that were given to troops throughout the war, have been described in some Scottish soldier's diaries as being more feared and hated than the enemy!

Figure 16: *Soldiers would often spend their spare time writing letters home or catching up on sleep.*

Make the Link

If you study Health and Food Technology you will learn about a balanced diet. Do you think that the ration packs would provide the soldiers with all the nutrients they needed?

Figure 15: *Black Watch soldiers receiving their ration packs in France in 1918.*

Source B is from the diary of Sergeant S. Saunders, 6th Battalion Gordon Highlanders, who fought in the Great War (taken from *Scottish Voices from the Great War* by Derek Young).

> It is HELL – that's the only way of putting it. Everyone is coated with mud from head to toe – I've never seen men in such a mess. Food is none too plentiful and water is scarce … Rum was issued this morning before breakfast – it upset some of the men being taken on an empty stomach … The trenches are not deep enough and as one walks along one has to stoop down … all of course in thick mud.

Lice were a major irritant to Scottish troops, although picking them out of the pleats of their kilts would sometimes provide some brief entertainment. The itching and discomfort, however, was terrible. Rats were one of the worst aspects of trench life. Rats would sometimes feed on the corpses in no man's land and became confident enough in time to try their luck with sleeping soldiers, nibbling on their ears or fingers! These rats would often grow much bigger than normal because they had such a ready supply of troops, with some soldiers claiming that they grew as large as cats and that they would eat a wounded man if he couldn't defend himself.

A constant source of fear in the trenches was trench foot. Trenches were often water logged and standing in this cold, dirty water for hours on end, without then being able to properly clean your feet or keep them dry, would result in feet going numb and turning blue or red. This was trench foot. If untreated, feet could develop infections and gangrene, resulting in amputation.

Hint

Edinburgh born Douglas Haig was made Commander in Chief of the British and Allied forces in December 1915. Some historians believe his tactics helped the Allies win, but others blame him for the high number of casualties British forces suffered.

GO! Activity 5

1. Imagine that you are serving in the trenches. Write a letter home to a loved one describing what your life is like. You should include at least five good, detailed points about life in the trenches. You could also include sketches and drawings beside the text to make it more interesting to read.

   (Unit outcomes: National 4/5: Outcome 2.1)

Exam style questions

2. Evaluate the usefulness of **Source B** as evidence of life in the trenches   **SH 5**

   (You may want to comment on who wrote it, when they wrote it, why they wrote it, what they say or what has been missed out.)

   (Unit outcomes: National 4: Outcome 1.1; National 5: Outcomes 1.1 and 2.1)

3. Describe the experience of Scots on the Western Front.   **KU 4**

   (Unit outcomes: National 4/5: Outcome 2.1)

2 The domestic impact of war— society and culture

In this section you will learn about:

- The effects of DORA: rationing, conscription and conscientious objectors.
- Propaganda and censorship.
- The changing role of women.
- Casualties, death and memorials.

The effects of DORA: rationing, conscription and conscientious objectors

DORA

On 8 August 1914 the British government introduced the Defence of the Realm Act (DORA). DORA was designed to give the government new powers and more control of various aspects of life in Britain during the war. The idea was that the government would use these new powers to ensure that Britain won the war. Some parts of DORA were welcomed by the British people because they recognised the need to win the war. However, some aspects of DORA were unpopular.

DORA introduced new laws and controls into British life. Under DORA the government took over the running of various industries such as coal mining, shipbuilding and railways. This meant that the government could direct all the resources and energy necessary towards winning the war. DORA also put in place laws that may sound strange now, but were designed to ensure that British workers were as productive as possible:

- British Summer Time was introduced to give more daylight for extra work.
- Opening hours in pubs were cut.
- Beer was watered down.
- Customers in pubs were not allowed to buy a round of drinks.

DORA also passed new laws to prevent sensitive information being heard or seen:

- No one was allowed to talk about naval or military matters in public places.
- No one was allowed to buy binoculars.
- No one was allowed to use invisible ink when writing abroad.
- The government could censor newspapers.

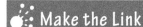

Make the Link

In Modern Studies you will learn more about civil liberties and times when they have been restricted.

📖 Key Word

- **Censorship**

When information is controlled and limited. In Britain during the war, the government censored newspapers as they didn't want sensitive information being available to the enemy.

🔍 Hint

David Lloyd George became Prime Minister in December 1916. Some historians see his strong leadership of Britain during the war as being crucial to the eventual Allied success, but during the war many Scots resented some of his policies, such as those concerning DORA.

⁂ Make the Link

In Health and Food Technology you may have learned about the importance of a balanced diet. Why do you think cutting down on some of the foods mentioned gave people in wartime Britain a more balanced, healthy diet?

Food shortages and rationing

One of the main ways that DORA impacted on ordinary people's lives was through the introduction of rationing in 1918. Since the beginning of the war the British government had encouraged citizens to save food and not waste it. When German U-boats began to attack British ships bringing food into the country, Britain began to run out of everyday basics. In April 1916 Britain had only six weeks' worth of wheat left. The price of food went up meaning the rich could afford it but poorer people couldn't. As a result, cases of malnutrition were seen in some communities. Any areas that could be used to grow vegetables and keep animals were converted to do so. However, there was still not enough food for everyone. To make matters worse, food had to be sent off to the soldiers on the Western Front. By early 1918 it was clear that the government had to act and rationing was introduced as part of DORA.

Source C describes the introduction of rationing in January 1918.

> By April 1918, every person had a ration card (including the king and queen). This allowed each person:
>
> - 15 oz (425g) of meat per week
> - 5 oz (142g) of bacon per week
> - 4 oz (113g) of butter or margarine per week.
>
> Sugar was also rationed, and the government controlled the availability of many other goods. As with most other areas of government control, most people accepted it even though they did not like the idea. Rationing solved the problems of rising prices and food queues. Even more surprising, the health of the majority of people actually improved as a result of rationing! The poor got a share of better food than they could have afforded before. The well off ate less of the food that was bad for them.

Conscription and conscientious objectors

In January 1916 the government extended the powers of DORA by passing the Military Services Act. This introduced conscription for single males, aged 18–40. This was put in place because Britain was running out of volunteers for the army. Conscription was later extended to include all males aged 18–50. Some men objected to conscription arguing that it went against their religious views or their consciences. These men came to be known as conscientious objectors.

Conscientious objectors were often treated very harshly by the authorities and sometimes by the general public. The authorities decided whether someone was allowed to refuse conscription based on their conscience or religious beliefs and could grant them an exemption, meaning they didn't have to sign up. However, exemptions for conscientious objectors were quite rare and most were told they would have to go to the Western Front to help in some way or face prison. Those who agreed to go to the front line worked in non-combat roles

📖 Key Word

- **Conscription**

When males of a certain age are told by the government that they must join the army.

⁂ Make the Link

If you study RMPS you will look at conscience and beliefs in more detail.

such as stretcher-bearers, and were known as non-combatants. Soldiers sometimes gave non-combatants a hard time. Those who absolutely refused to go to war were known as absolutists, and were sent to jail. Absolutists faced a difficult time in jail, where conditions were not good and fellow prisoners gave them a very hard time, calling them cowards and much worse. Many members of the general public viewed conscientious objectors as cowards who were not doing their duty.

Figure 17 and Source D: *Postcard, 1916. Postcards such as this ridiculed men who refused to be forced into the armed forces.*

GO! Activity 6

1. Imagine it is April 1916 and you are a journalist working for a major Scottish newspaper. You have been asked to write a front page article explaining the effects of DORA on ordinary people. You should include information on all aspects of DORA, including rationing, conscription and conscientious objectors.

    (Unit outcomes: National 4/5: Outcomes 2.1 and 2.2)

Exam style questions

2. How fully does **Source C** describe the effects of food shortages during the war?   **SH 6**

    (Use the source and recall.)

    (Unit outcomes: National 4: Outcome 1.2; National 5: Outcomes 1.2 and 2.2)

3. Evaluate the usefulness of **Source D** for investigating attitudes to conscientious objectors during the Great War.   **SH 5**

    (You may want to comment on who wrote it, when they wrote it, why they wrote it, what they say or what has been missed out.)

    (Unit outcomes: National 4: Outcome 1.1; National 5: Outcomes 1.1 and 2.1)

4. Describe the impact that DORA made on people's lives in Scotland.   **KU 4**

    (Unit outcomes: National 4/5: Outcome 2.1)

5. Explain why rationing was introduced.   **KU 6**

    (Unit outcomes: National 4/5: Outcome 2.2)

Propaganda and censorship

During the war the British government used propaganda and censorship in an attempt to convince people to think a certain way and to do what the government believed was best. Newspapers and soldiers' letters were censored to ensure only the stories the government approved of were heard. Films were produced to show British soldiers as heroic and strong, and Germans as cowardly brutes. The government even encouraged newspapers to make up and spread lies about German atrocities in Belgium. Newspaper headlines such as 'Belgium child's hands cut off by German' were not uncommon. Posters were designed to boost morale and keep everyone working for the war effort.

Make the Link

In English or Media you may study the use of propaganda or persuasive language.

Figure 18: *Posters like this one encouraged people to put the war effort first.*

Key Word

- **Munitions**

  Military weapons or equipment.

GO! Activity 7

Create your own piece of wartime propaganda. You could write a newspaper article with a headline, create a poster or postcard or even design a film poster. Think about what your piece of work is aiming to do to help Britain. Share it with others and see if they can guess the message you're trying to get across.

(Unit outcomes: National 4: Outcome 2.1)

The changing role of women

During the Great War the number of women in work increased greatly as women stepped into the jobs that men had vacated when they went off to fight. From the beginning of the war women took on jobs as tram and bus conductors, as well as typists and secretaries in offices. Others worked as mechanics and in industries like shipbuilding and mining. Some joined the Women's Land Army and worked in agriculture, helping to produce enough food for Britain to survive on. By 1918 women had joined the Women's Auxiliary Army Corps (WAAC) and the Women's Royal Air Force (WRAF) working in clerical and support jobs. Some became nurses and joined the Voluntary Aid Detachment (VAD). However, perhaps the most famous role women took on was in munitions factories.

Source E was written by a modern historian.

Munitions work was hard and dangerous due to working with TNT explosives. Those women who worked in munitions factories came to be known as 'canaries' because the TNT turned their skin yellow. By 1917 over 30 000 women were working in munitions factories in Scotland, up from 4000 before the war. The biggest munitions factory in Scotland was in Gretna Green where women worked long hours mixing the explosive cordite. It resembled porridge when being mixed so came to be known as 'devil's porridge' since it was so dangerous and toxic.

Some men were worried when women began working, as they believed women would drive down wages and threaten the status of their jobs. In short, men were worried women would 'dilute' the work force. The government came to a 'dilution' agreement with trade unions (which represented male workers) whereby women could not be fully trained up in skilled jobs. This kept male workers happy as it meant their skills and their jobs were safe, but it does show that in the workplace women were nowhere near equal with men.

The Great War saw a great change in women's role in society but when the war ended women generally returned to their previous roles as housekeepers, wives and mothers. Despite this, the Great War had shown both men and women that women could do 'male' jobs. In 1918 some women were given the vote for the first time. Some historians believe this was due to their contribution to the war effort.

Make the Link

In Business Management you will learn about how trade unions operate today.

Hint

You will look at the reasons why women got the vote in more detail later in this topic.

GO! Activity 8

1. Create a poster or presentation which describes the changing role of women during the war. You can use a maximum of thirty words.

   (Unit outcomes: National 4/5: Outcome 2.1)

Exam style questions

2. How fully does **Source E** describe the work done by women during the war.   **SH 6**

   (Use the source and recall.)

   (Unit outcomes: National 4: Outcome 1.2; National 5: Outcomes 1.2 and 2.2)

3. Evaluate the usefulness of **Source F** as evidence of the changing role of women in Scotland during the war.   **SH 5**

   (Unit outcomes: National 4: Outcome 1.1; National 5: Outcomes 1.1 and 2.1)

4. To what extent did the Great War change the role of women in Scotland?   **KU 9**

   (Unit outcomes: National 5: Outcome 2.3)

Figure 19 and Source F: *A female tram driver and conductor on board their tram, in Scotland.*

Casualties, death and memorials

In the years following the war, memorials were erected in London and elsewhere to remember the fallen. A National War Memorial was created at Edinburgh Castle and, throughout Scotland, towns and villages created their own memorials. It was important to Scots that they had their own memorials to reflect the sacrifices made by Scottish troops in the First World War.

Source G was written by a modern historian.

> When the war ended in November 1918 there was a real sense of loss in Scotland. There wasn't a town or village in the country that had not lost some of its men in the war. In fact over one quarter of all adult males who enlisted in Scotland were killed, a figure significantly higher than the 11·8% for the whole of Britain and Ireland. This desire for separate Scottish memorials was informed by these high casualty figures of Scots battalions and by the fact that Scots were often the first troops sent over the top to lead the line.

Source H is from *The Scottish Nation 1700–2000* by Tom Devine, a Scottish historian.

> The terrible carnage on the Western Front and the endless list of casualties soon changed the collective mood to one of national grief. The human losses were enormous and unprecedented. Of the 557 000 Scots who enlisted in all services 26·4% lost their lives. This compares with an average death rate of 11·8% for the rest of the British army between 1914 and 1918 .... The main reason for the higher than average casualties among the Scottish soldiers was that they were regarded as excellent, aggressive shock troops who could be depended upon to lead the line in the first hours of battle.

🔵GO! Activity 9

1. Create an A5 postcard which summarises the information above in no more than fifteen key words and statistics. On the front of the postcard draw your own design for a First World War memorial.

Exam style question

2. Compare the views of **Sources G** and **H** on the reasons why Scots wanted their own war memorials. **SH 4**

   (Compare the sources overall and in detail.)

   (Unit outcomes: National 4/5: Outcome 1.3)

Hint

Remember to quote from the sources when you compare them so that you are backing up each point you make.

3 The domestic impact of war— economy and industry

In this section you will learn about:

- War work and reserved occupations.
- Scottish industry before, during and after the war.
- The rise of new industries in the 1920s.

War work and reserved occupations

It was important to the government that the country did not grind to a halt when men went off to war. One solution, as we have seen, was that women took on many of the roles that men had previously held. However, there were industries that required experienced and skilled men to remain, such as shipbuilding, mining and agriculture. The government recognised this, so when they introduced conscription in 1916 they also introduced 'reserved occupations'.

A reserved occupation was any job that the government felt was so important that anyone who worked in it did not have to join the armed forces. Exemption certificates were granted to these men. At certain points in the war men working in munitions factories, down coal mines and in shipyards were considered to be doing reserved occupations. These men therefore avoided conscription. However, the government did not publish a definite set of 'reserved occupations' in 1916 in case people thought it was an easy way to get out of conscription. Instead, they kept the situation vague, informing industries if and when those who worked in them were considered important enough to be counted among the reserved occupations. If someone in a particular district or area had a skill which was necessary for that area to function, then they could also be put on the reserved occupations list for that area.

> 📖 **Key Word**
>
> - **Industry**
> The mass manufacture and production of goods, usually in factories.

> **GO! Activity 10**
>
> Create a comic strip/presentation that explains what reserved occupations were and the different types of war work that existed in Scotland during the war.
>
> **(Unit outcomes: National 4/5: Outcome 2.2)**

🔍 Hint

When an industry 'booms' it means it does very well very quickly. During the war many industries in Scotland boomed.

Figure 20: *William Beardmore's shipbuilding firm in Glasgow did very well during the war.*

✺ Make the Link

In Business Management you will study supply and demand.

✺ Make the Link

If you study 'Changing Britain, 1760–1914', you will learn about why the coal mining industry was so important to Britain before 1900.

📖 Key Words

- **Strike**

When unhappy workers stop working in an attempt to force their employers to provide them with better working conditions or pay.

- **Agriculture**

The science or occupation of farming.

Economy and industry

The Great War had a major impact on the economy and industry of Scotland. While some industries experienced a 'boom' during the war, others suffered, and after the war Scotland's economy went into decline.

Shipbuilding

Before the war an estimated 14% of adult males in Scotland relied on shipbuilding in some way for their wages. The naval race between Britain and Germany had seen orders for warships flood into the Clyde shipyards in Glasgow. Before this, however, the industry had been struggling and some shipyards had been on the verge of closure.

During the war, shipyards such as Beardmore's in Glasgow rolled out hundreds of warships and the industry boomed. Between 1914 and 1918, 481 warships were built on the Clyde. In fact some shipbuilding firms, keen to make the most of the wartime boom, began producing airships and aircraft. The Scottish economy was boosted by the shipbuilding industry's success.

When the war ended orders for warships obviously dried up. Countries throughout the world had less money than before and Scotland's shipbuilding industry went into decline. For example, between 1921 and 1923 the number of ships built on the Clyde was cut by more than a third. By 1930, yards were beginning to close. The shipbuilding industry had, quite simply, relied too heavily on orders from the Empire.

Coal mining

In 1900, Scotland was producing a lot of coal but the industry looked stronger than it actually was. There was growing competition from foreign coal producers and new fuel sources such as gas and oil were threatening coal's status as the main energy source for factories and machinery.

During the war the government took control of coal mines. This meant that demand remained high because the government was buying coal from the pits. This in turn led to higher wages for miners. The coal mining industry boomed because coal was vital to the factories that produced the weapons of war.

After the war the government no longer needed to control the mines and the demand for coal decreased. The problems that had existed before the war returned and Scottish mines began to struggle. In the 1920s Scottish miners went on strike several times to try to avoid redundancies and wage cuts but they had little success.

Agriculture

Agriculture in Britain was doing quite well before the war but Britain still relied mostly on imports for its food. Scotland employed, at its peak, 107 000 workers in farming and agriculture, demonstrating the importance of the industry to the Scottish economy.

The war initially hit farming hard. Many horses were taken to serve on the Western Front, and many farm workers signed up to fight. The pre-war high of 107 000 workers had fallen to 89 000 by the end of the war. However, many farmers did very well during the war, and some farm workers saw their wages double. Farms that reared sheep for wool made a lot of money as the government needed wool for soldiers' blankets and uniforms. By 1918 sheep prices were 60% higher than in 1914.

Make the Link

If you study Geography you will look at the economics of farming in detail.

Figure 21: *Members of the Women's Land Army shearing sheep on a farm during the First World War.*

Following the war, agriculture in Scotland declined as the number of workers fell and machines began to replace workers and animals. Wool was no longer in demand as it had been during the war, and the government was no longer prepared the help control the prices. This meant that the 1920s were hard for many farms.

Jute

Jute is a textile that, before the war, was produced mainly in Dundee. Raw jute was imported from India and made into various products, such as bags and sacks for packaging foodstuffs. Dundee was home to the largest jute factory in the world and, by 1914, most people in the city relied on jute for their employment. It is no surprise that Dundee was nicknamed 'Juteopolis'! However, from 1900 onwards the jute industry in Dundee was beginning to face fierce competition from Calcutta, India, and was not as strong as it had once been.

The outbreak of war in August 1914 provided a huge boost to the jute industry in Dundee. The armies of the Triple Entente required millions of sandbags to reinforce their trenches and orders flooded into Dundee. In one month during the war, Dundee produced 6 000 000 sandbags. Profits for jute firms in Dundee rocketed.

Hint

In the Great War the Triple Entente was the name of the alliance between Great Britain, France and Russia.

When the war ended there was less demand for jute, as sandbags were no longer needed. Also, the jute industry in Calcutta was able to produce jute cheaper than in Dundee and easily overtook it as the world leader in jute production. The jute industry in Dundee went into terminal decline as orders dried up, meaning unemployment was a growing problem in Dundee in the 1920s and 1930s.

Fishing

Before the First World War, the fishing industry was very important to the Scottish economy, employing over 32 500 men. Scotland exported large amounts of herring to Eastern Europe, particularly Germany and Russia. Fishermen, on the whole, earned a decent wage.

The war greatly affected the fishing industry. The North Sea almost totally closed to fishing due to the threat of German naval attacks. Scottish ships were now mostly restricted to the west coast. Also, many fishing boats were taken over by the British navy to be used as patrol boats and minesweepers. The war meant that the herring trade with Germany and Russia was also lost.

When the war ended the fishing industry struggled to get back on its feet. The herring trade to the east was lost, fuel costs had risen, and the boats the navy returned to fishermen were often damaged and compensation was slow in coming. By the 1930s the fishing industry was slowly recovering but it didn't return to its successful pre-war days.

Summary

Overall, it is clear that the war saw a temporary boom in most Scottish industries but this was followed by a severe and long economic decline in the 1920s. The war had disguised the existing problems in Scotland's economy and industries before 1914, such as a failure to modernise equipment and techniques, and an over-reliance on the Empire for trade.

GO! Activity 11

1. On an A3 piece of paper, create a table like the one below. Use the information in this section to fill it in as fully as you can.

Industry	Before the war	During the war	After the war
Shipbuilding			
Coal			
Agriculture			
Jute			
Fishing			

(Unit outcomes: National 4/5: Outcome 2.1)

Exam style question

2. To what extent did the Great War have a positive impact on Scotland's economy? KU 9

(Unit outcomes: National 5: Outcome 2.3)

The rise of new industries in the 1920s

As the old industries that Scotland had relied on before the war struggled to survive, with some disappearing altogether, so some Scots looked to new industries to make money. Despite the problems and high unemployment of the 1920s, there were some areas of progress in the Scottish economy. Some businesses tried to develop the internal combustion engine although car manufacturing did not take off in Scotland. Other Scots tried to start businesses in electrics, but made little progress. In the new industry of man-made fibres for clothing, some Scots made a little headway but, again, they were ultimately unsuccessful. These new industries didn't take off for various reasons.

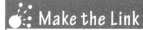

Make the Link

In Science you may learn more about the development of the internal combustion engine.

- The skills that Scottish workers had developed in old industries could not be used in the new ones and there wasn't the money to train workers in the skills necessary to build, for example, cars.

- There was no money for the new machinery necessary to produce these new products or for the investment which was badly needed to allow scientific research and development in the new industries.

- The government did not offer effective support to these new industries.

In short, Scotland didn't have the skilled workers, money or government support to really allow these new industries to develop and grow.

Source I is from *The Scottish Nation, 1700–2000*, by Tom Devine, a Scottish historian.

> The inter-war period was not all doom and gloom for Scottish industry. For those who were in a job, standards of living rose for much of the period. As a result the relatively small part of the manufacturing economy geared to domestic consumers did well. Carpets, linoleum, hosiery and knitwear were especially successful although they were relatively modest employers of labour. But the giants of the nineteenth century economy were either in the doldrums in most years or were in acute crisis.

⊙ Activity 12

1. Imagine you are looking for a job in Scotland in the 1920s. Write a diary entry describing your search for a job in the new industries. Explain why they are struggling to take off and grow in Scotland.

   (Unit outcomes: National 4/5: Outcome 2.2)

Exam style question

2. Evaluate the usefulness of **Source I** for investigating the rise of new industries in Scotland in the 1920s. **SH 5**

   (You may want to comment on who wrote it, when they wrote it, why they wrote it, what they say or what has been missed out.)

   (Unit outcomes: National 4: Outcome 1.1; National 5: Outcomes 1.1 and 2.1)

4 The domestic impact of war—politics

In this section you will learn about:

- The campaigns for women's suffrage.
- The rent strikes.
- The extension of the franchise.
- The effect of DORA on Scottish politics.
- Red Clydeside.
- The housing issue: 'Homes fit for heroes'.

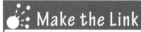

Make the Link

If you study Modern Studies you will learn about how a population can participate in democracy.

Between 1900 and 1928 Scotland underwent many political changes. As the government became more involved in people's lives than ever before, many Scots began to take a more active role in politics, simply by standing up for what they believed in.

The campaigns for women's suffrage

Figure 22: *Women suffragettes from Dundee, Scotland, demonstrate in London.*

Key Word

- **Suffrage**

Having the vote.

Make the Link

In the British topic 'Changing Britain, 1760–1914' you learn about the growth of democracy up until 1867. Many advances were made in this period, but they only advanced men's voting rights.

In 1900 women in Britain did not have the vote. Since the 1860s women had begun to organise groups that called for all women to have the right to vote, and the first national organisation formed in 1897. It was called the National Union of Women's Suffrage Societies (NUWSS). This group was soon given the nickname the suffragists, because they were campaigning for the vote.

The suffragists used peaceful, legal tactics to try to win support. They wrote letters to MPs, sent petitions to Parliament, distributed leaflets, organised meetings and held rallies and marches. However, by 1900

the suffragists had made little progress and so in 1903 another, more militant, group formed, called the Women's Social and Political Union (WSPU). The first Scottish branch of the WSPU was formed in 1906. Journalists soon nicknamed the WSPU 'the suffragettes'.

The suffragettes did not believe that peaceful methods of campaigning were working and decided to use more militant tactics.

Source J is from the website 'SCAN Education: Women's Suffrage in Scotland'.

> Scottish Suffragettes poured acid into pillar boxes, chained themselves to railings, smashed windows and slashed portraits of the King. They also set fire to important buildings such as Leuchars Railway Station, Ayr Racecourse and the Whitekirk in East Lothian.

Source K was written by a modern historian.

> Some Suffragettes would chain themselves to railings, smash windows and pour acid on golf greens at men only clubs. Others cut telegraph poles and were even involved in arson. In Glasgow, the Suffragette Emily Green was arrested for smashing windows in Sauchiehall Street, whilst Janet Arthur was arrested for trying to blow up the Robert Burns Cottage in Alloway.

📖 Key Word

• **Militant**
To be forceful, aggressive or even violent in achieving your aims.

🔍 Hint

Emmeline Pankhurst founded the WSPU (the suffragettes). Emmeline and her daughters, Sylvia, Adela and Christabel, were all central to and active in the suffragettes.

🔵 GO! Activity 13

1. Create two simple comic strips showing and describing the different methods used by suffragists and suffragettes. Use a full A4 page to draw up a comic strip like the one below.

Suffragists	Picture	Picture	Picture	Picture
Real name: NUWSS	Explanation	Explanation	Explanation	Explanation
Suffragettes	Picture	Picture	Picture	Picture
Real name: WSPU	Explanation	Explanation	Explanation	Explanation

(Unit outcomes: National 4/5: Outcome 2.1)

Exam style questions

2. Compare the views of **Sources J** and **K** on the methods used by the suffragettes to gain the vote. **SH 4**

   (Compare the sources overall and in detail.)

   (Unit outcomes: National 4/5: Outcome 1.3)

3. Describe the tactics employed by women in their fight for the vote. **KU 4**

   (Unit outcomes: National 4/5: Outcome 2.1)

Figure 23: This is a suffragette poster about the 'Cat and Mouse Act'. What do you think its aim is?

The Cat and Mouse Act 1913

When suffragettes were sent to prison they often protested by refusing to eat and went on hunger strike. The government could not allow suffragettes to become seriously ill or die in prison so they chose to force feed them. The process was often brutal and extremely painful and distressing for the women. When the public found out that women were being brutally force fed in prison the government had to stop doing it. However, the Liberal government decided to get round the problem of the continuing hunger strikes by temporarily releasing those involved until they were fit and healthy, at which point they would be re-arrested and put back in jail. This came to be known as the 'Cat and Mouse Act', as cats often toy with mice they've caught by letting them go and catching them again.

The government's treatment of those on hunger strike provided the suffragettes with good publicity for their cause and some men even sympathised with them. However, the majority of men and women viewed the suffragettes as a menace, as did the newspapers and politicians of the time. Most believed a woman's place was in the home and that they shouldn't have the vote. Some historians have argued that, before the war, the suffragettes' tactics actually harmed women's fight for the vote. Others disagree, noting how the issue of women's suffrage was now being discussed by everyone around Britain, and that this was down to the suffragettes.

Rent strikes

During the war, the suffragettes suspended their militant actions and got behind the war effort. Despite the more peaceful role that suffragettes adopted during the war, there were instances where women were prepared to fight for what they believed in. The most famous of these was the rent strikes in Glasgow in 1915.

As Glasgow's industry boomed during the war, workers flooded into the city for work. However, there was not enough housing to go around and demand soared. Landlords took this opportunity to raise rents knowing that people would be forced to pay but, unfortunately for them, the women of Govan and Partick had different ideas.

Led by Mary Barbour and Helen Crawford these Glaswegian women made it clear that they would not stand for the rent increases. They continued to send landlords the old rent amount and, when the landlords' representatives rejected it and came to collect the new, higher figure, these women would pelt them with flour and whatever else they could lay their hands on! Significantly, these rent strikes were backed by major trade unions in Glasgow, many of whom represented workers in the vital munitions factories and shipyards. When a strike

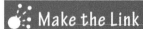

Make the Link

In Business Management and Modern Studies you will learn more about how pressure groups work to influence the government today.

of over 10 000 workers, women and Independent Labour Party members took place in November 1915, the government was so shocked and worried that it passed the 'Rent Restrictions Act'. This act froze rent at pre-war levels not only in Scotland but throughout Britain. The women of Glasgow, backed up by men, had forced the government to act and had shown that direct action could make a difference.

Figure 24 and Source L: *This is an image of a rent strike in Glasgow in 1915.*

> ### 🔵 GO! Activity 15
>
> 1. Create a comic strip/video/presentation which explains what the rent strikes were and why they succeeded.
>
>   **(Unit outcomes: National 4/5: Outcome 2.2)**
>
> **Exam style question**
>
> 2. Evaluate the usefulness of **Source L** for investigating the rent strikes.   **SH 5**
>
>   **(Unit outcomes: National 4: Outcome 1.1; National 5: Outcomes 1.1 and 2.1)**

The extension of the franchise

As we have seen earlier, women played a significant role in the war by taking on many of the roles vacated by men who were fighting. Women proved themselves in these jobs and impressed men with their work ethic and professionalism. In Scotland the activism of women in the rent strikes showed that they were politically aware and that they could succeed in making positive changes to society. When the war ended in 1918 the Liberal government passed the Representation of the People Act, giving the vote to all women over thirty. Although many of the women who had put their lives on the line by working in munitions factories were under thirty and therefore denied the vote, it was a significant step forward for the women's suffrage movement. This Act of Parliament also gave the vote to an additional 13 000 000 men meaning that more people than ever before had the vote. Ten years later, in 1928, all men and women over the age of twenty one were given the vote. For the first time in British and Scottish history, men and women were able to vote on an equal footing.

Activity 16

1. Draw three columns with these headings:

   The war   Women's suffrage movement   Other factors

   Discuss the issue in pairs and fill in these columns with reasons why each factor may have led to the government passing the 1918 Act.

   (Unit outcomes: National 4/5: Outcome 2.2; National 5: Outcome 2.3)

Exam style question

2. To what extent was the Great War responsible for women gaining the vote?   KU 9

   (Unit outcomes: National 5: Outcome 2.3)

The effect of DORA on Scottish politics

The Defence of the Realm Act (DORA) changed people's lives in significant ways. In Scotland this made some people become more politically active during the war as they sought to challenge the control that the government had over their lives.

Under DORA the government had introduced conscription in 1916. Some Scots refused to serve in any way and were jailed. Others, like the socialist school teacher John Maclean, not only refused to serve but made speeches attacking the government and DORA. Maclean was imprisoned during the war for undermining the war effort with his speeches, breaking a law which had been passed under DORA. His imprisonment angered many of his supporters who said it went against the basic right of freedom of speech. What is more, DORA actually gave the government the power to imprison someone without a trial. Many Scots were worried that the rights they had fought for over many years were now being pushed aside. Some said the British government was turning into a dictatorship and turned for answers to political groups who opposed the government.

Under the 1915 Munitions of War Act, the government made it compulsory for all workers in important industries to obtain a leaving certificate from their employers before they could change jobs. This was to allow for the maximum output of munitions, including warships, so as to keep the war effort on track. Workers felt it unfair that they could no longer freely leave their jobs if they wanted to. What is more, the Act made it illegal for workers in these industries to strike, meaning they had very few ways to express their displeasure in the workplace. These two factors led many Scots working in the factories and shipyards of Glasgow to join trade unions and the left wing Independent Labour Party.

📖 Key Word

- **Socialist**

Someone who believes that the government should run the country and its factories in the interests of the workers.

🔴 Make the Link

In 'Hitler and Nazi Germany, 1919–1939' you will learn about what a real dictatorship was like.

🔍 Hint

In politics, if a group, political party or person is 'left wing', then they believe in socialism or communism.

Activity 17

1. Explain in a comic strip, small poster or an illustrated mind map:

   • why some Scots resented DORA (four examples)

   • what this resentment led many Scots to do.

   (Unit outcomes: National 4/5: Outcome 2.2)

Exam style question

2. Explain why DORA was unpopular among many Scots.   **KU 6**

   (Unit outcomes: National 4/5: Outcome 2.2)

Red Clydeside

The Clydeside area of Glasgow was vital to the war effort. Warships were built here, as were weapons and equipment used on the Western Front. The government was becoming increasingly concerned by the power of the trade unions and the influence of the Independent Labour Party, both of whom were calling for better conditions and pay for workers. They were worried production might grind to a halt. From the workers' point of view, the government's attempts to cut wages, extend working hours and bring in women to do skilled jobs concerned them. Also, the issue of leaving certificates and strikes being made illegal created much resentment.

Activity 18

Answer these questions in paragraphs or by creating a quick poster or comic strip.

1. Explain why the government was so worried about the industries on the Clyde during the war.

   (Unit outcomes: National 4: Outcome 2.2)

2. Explain why workers were not happy with the government.

   (Unit outcomes: National 4: Outcome 2.2)

Hint

The Communist Party was a left wing political party that wanted to overthrow the government in a workers'-led revolution.

During the war there were several disputes over wages and working hours on Clydeside and many workers joined left wing political parties. These left wing parties had long adopted the colour red for their flags, banners and posters, and some people even nicknamed groups like the communists 'Reds'. As the workers on Clydeside became more and more left wing in their thinking, so the term 'Red Clydeside' was born. For some, Red Clydeside not only posed a threat to the production of war materials, but also to the British government generally.

Make the Link

If you study 'Lenin and the Russian Revolution, 1894–1921', you will learn in detail about who the communists were and what they believed in.

> **GO!** Activity 19
>
> Explain in a picture, diagram or couple of sentences why the industrial area around the Clyde came to be known as 'Red Clydeside'.
>
> **(Unit outcomes: National 4/5: Outcome 2.2)**

By the end of the war the membership of the Independent Labour Party had tripled in Scotland and, with the extension of the franchise in 1918, more working class Scots could vote than ever before. What is more, there had been a communist revolution in Russia where the Russian Emperor (the Tsar) had been murdered and the communists had taken power. The British government was worried that the same might happen in Britain. With the huge fall in demand for ships and munitions after the war, workers on the Clyde feared for their jobs.

In 1919 workers went on a 40 hour strike hoping to improve working conditions and pay. The protest of 100 000 people quickly escalated to a riot, with the red flag of the communists being raised in George Square. The police responded with baton charges, but many in the British government believed this was the beginning of a revolution so they sent in 12 000 troops, machine guns and tanks to crush the protest. This became known as 'the Battle of George Square'. Once order had been restored, the strikers' demands were dismissed, and many of the leaders were arrested.

In reality there was no real threat of a communist revolution in Glasgow in 1919. What it did show was how the working classes in Glasgow now viewed left wing parties as their true representatives, not the Liberal government.

Figure 25 and Source M: *Police officers return from a baton charge during the 1919 disturbances on Clydeside.*

> **GO!** Activity 20
>
> 1. A major Hollywood producer wants to make a film about Red Clydeside. You have been hired to make up a storyboard to explain what happened there during and after the war. You should have a sentence or two explaining each picture on your storyboard. If you finish, you can decide on a title for your film and create an A5 size film poster to advertise it.
>
>   **(Unit outcomes: National 4/5: Outcome 2.2)**
>
> **Exam style question**
>
> 2. Evaluate the usefulness of **Source M** for investigating Red Clydeside.   **SH 5**
>
>   **(Unit outcomes: National 4: Outcome 1.1; National 5: Outcomes 1.1 and 2.1)**

Homes fit for heroes

Before the war housing was a major political issue in Scotland. Many Scots lived in terrible conditions, often in one or two roomed tenement flats. Following the war, the government promised that soldiers would not have to return to the awful living conditions they had left. They promised 'Homes fit for heroes'. The 1919 Housing Act gave local councils money to build more houses, with the government promising that 500 000 would be built in three years. However, not enough money was provided so local councils could not build as many houses as they wanted and they still had to charge rent that many returning soldiers could not afford. Scots began to lose faith in the Liberal government and moved their support to the Labour Party who seemed to care more about working class people. In the end, Scottish housing did not improve significantly in this period and the 'Homes fit for heroes' never really happened.

> **Make the Link**
>
> In Geography you will learn about housing in both developed and developing countries. How do you think the housing in Scotland at this time would compare to housing in a developing country today?

> **GO! Activity 21**
>
> Explain what 'Homes fit for heroes' was and why its failure led to a rise in support for the Labour Party.
>
> **(Unit outcomes: National 4/5: Outcome 2.2)**

Figure 26: *A 1922 General Election poster for the Labour Party. Note how Labour have focused on areas that many voters felt the Liberal government had not succeeded in improving after the war.*

The decline of the Liberals

The Liberal government may have led Britain to victory in the First World War but after it their power declined rapidly. One reason was that the members of the Liberal Party wanted to go in different directions and the party eventually split. In the 1918 election there were essentially two Liberal Parties that people could vote for and it became very clear that the Liberals were in crisis. As a result they lost support from many people who had previously voted for them. Also, in 1918 more people than ever before could vote, including all working class men and some women. Many of these working class voters cast their votes for the Labour Party. Others, put off by the split in the Liberal Party, turned towards the Conservatives. By 1928, the Liberals were the third party in Britain, trailing behind Labour and the Conservatives in votes and support.

Scottish politics after the war: a summary

Overall, in the years following the war the Labour Party saw its membership grow rapidly. Its support of the rent strikes and the workers on the Clyde made them popular, as did their promises to deal with growing unemployment in Britain. Also, the Liberal government's introduction of the unpopular DORA, its dealings with Red Clydeside and its failed housing policy meant they lost support in elections. This, coupled with their decline in the early 1920s, meant that by 1928 Scotland was generally voting Labour or Conservative, and the Liberals were no longer a political force.

 Activity 22

Exam style question

To what extent did the Great War have an impact on politics in Scotland? **KU 9**

(Unit outcomes: National 5: Outcome 2.3)

Summary

In this topic you have learned:

- why Scots signed up for the armed forces
- trench system, life and technology on the Western Front
- the impact of the war on people's lives in Scotland
- the changing role of women in the war
- the impact the war had on the Scottish economy and its industry
- the impact the war had on Scottish politics.

You should have developed your skills and be able to:

- evaluate the usefulness of a source
- compare two sources by saying what they agree or disagree about
- put a source into context by saying how fully it describes an issue.

Learning Checklist

Now that you have finished **The Era of the Great War, 1900–1928**, complete a self-evaluation of your knowledge and skill to assess what you have understood. Use traffic lights to help you make up a revision plan to help you improve in the areas you identified as red or amber.

- Explain the reasons why Scots signed up for the armed forces.

- Describe how trenches were set up on the Western Front.

- Describe the new technology used on the Western Front.

- Describe life for Scots soldiers in the trenches.

- Describe how DORA impacted upon people's lives.

- Explain why rationing was brought in.

- Evaluate the impact women had on the war effort.

- Provide examples of British wartime propaganda.

- Explain why Scottish war memorials were erected following the armistice.

- Describe how the Scottish economy was doing before, during and after the war, making reference to Scotland's main industries.

- Evaluate the overall impact of the war on Scotland's economy.

- Provide examples of war work and reserved occupations.

- Describe some of the new industries that emerged in the 1920s.

- Describe women's campaign for the vote.

- Explain what the rent strikes were.

- Evaluate why some women got the vote in 1918.

- Explain why DORA was unpopular among some Scots.

- Explain how DORA affected Scottish politics.

- Explain what Red Clydeside was.

- Describe what happened on Red Clydeside in 1919.

- Explain what 'Homes fit for heroes' meant.

- Evaluate the overall impact of the Great War on Scottish politics.

This topic looks at the Atlantic slave trade and Britain's involvement from 1770–1807. It will provide you with an understanding of the complex relationship between the rise of British industry and its reliance on slave labour in the British colonies. It will look at how slaves were acquired in West Africa and the work they did on the plantations. Finally, you will look at the work of the abolitionists to stop the slave trade in the British Empire in 1807.

You will develop your skills and be able to:

❖ evaluate the usefulness of a source

❖ put a source into context by saying how fully it describes an issue.

This topic is split into four sections:

❖ The triangular trade

❖ Britain and the Caribbean

❖ The captive's experience and slave resistance

❖ The abolitionist campaigns

Level 4 experiences and outcomes relevant to this topic:

I can evaluate conflicting sources of evidence to sustain a line of argument. **SOC 4-01a**

I have developed a sense of my heritage and identity as a British, European or global citizen and can present arguments about the importance of respecting the heritage and identity of others. **SOC 4-02a**

By studying groups in past societies who experienced inequality, I can explain the reasons for the inequality and evaluate how groups or individuals addressed it. **SOC 4-04a**

I can make reasoned judgements about how the exercise of power affects the rights and responsibilities of citizens by comparing a more democratic and a less democratic society. **SOC 4-04c**

I can present supported conclusions about the social, political and economic impacts of a technological change in the past. **SOC 4-05a**

I have investigated a meeting of cultures in the past and can analyse the impact on the societies involved. **SOC 4-05c**

I can assess the impact for those involved in a specific instance of the expansion of power and influence in the past. **SOC 4-06d**

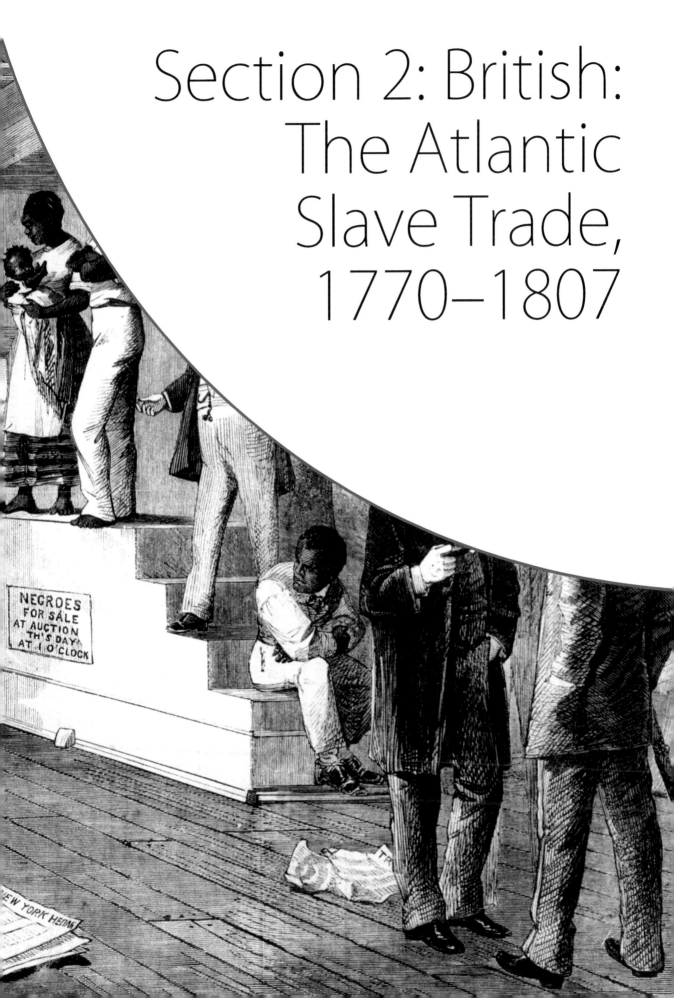

Section 2: British: The Atlantic Slave Trade, 1770–1807

Background

Slavery has existed for thousands of years. The ancient Egyptians, Greeks and Romans used slaves, and slavery was accepted as part of their culture. However, the Atlantic slave trade grew because of the need to have access to unpaid labour on a large scale to allow the procurement of raw goods in the New World and maximum profits to be made. The raw goods were to be used to make the mass-produced items of the industrial revolution.

Key Words

- **Procurement**

The acquisition of goods.

- **Raw goods**

Things like sugar or cotton in their most basic forms. They could be transformed into different products like clothing and sold for a profit.

Figure 1: *Slaves cutting sugar cane.*

Africa was known as the 'dark continent' by Europeans and the African people were relatively unknown and mysterious. They seemed backward in terms of their education and religion – indeed, very few if any were Christian. Ideas of white superiority and a lack of understanding about African tribes and culture may have led to European slave traders easily justifying the enslavement of black people and forcing them to work on the plantations. It is estimated that between 9 000 000 and 12 000 000 black people were taken from Africa by Europeans during the slave trade. The conditions the slaves were kept in on the journey to the New World and their treatment on the plantations led a group of people known as the 'abolitionists' to fight for the end of the slave trade. Their campaigns, conducted nationally and in Parliament, finally led to the end of the slave trade in 1807 with the Abolition of the Slave Trade Act. It would take a further twenty six years until slavery itself was abolished in the British Empire in 1833.

In many places around the word slavery still exists today. In Niger, slavery was only outlawed in 2003 and it is estimated that close to 1 000 000 people are still enslaved. In Pakistan and other South Asian nations the problem of bonded servitude means many people are working in appalling conditions to pay off debts. In many cases it is disputed if these debts even exist.

Hint

In 2004, twenty three Chinese people drowned in Morecambe Bay. They were effectively working under slave labour conditions, working for less than $2 per day. The case highlighted that slavery and forced labour still exist and was even taking place in the United Kingdom.

Activity 1

Write down the questions: What is slavery? What is a slave?

Take 10 minutes and come up with as many suggestions/ examples as you can.

Discuss your ideas with your group/class.

1 The triangular trade

In this section you will learn about:

- The organisation and nature of the slave trade.
- The effect of the slave trade on British Ports.
- The effect of the slave trade on African societies and West Indian plantations.
- Slave factories on the African coast.
- The economics and conditions of the 'Middle Passage'.

The organisation and nature of the slave trade: the triangular trade

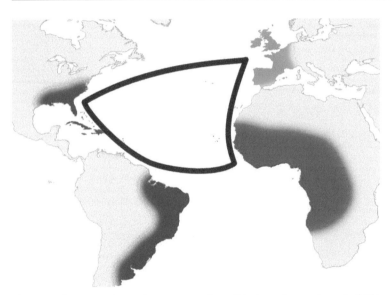

Figure 2: *The triangular trade route went from Britain to the west coast of Africa, to the West Indies and then back to Britain again. The journey was completed repeatedly.*

By the eighteenth century a well-established trade route had grown up between Europe, Africa and the Americas. The trading of slaves was only one part of a three-part route known as the triangular trade.

Goods created in Britain through new methods of industrialisation were transported from ports on the west coast like Bristol and Liverpool to West Africa where they were traded for slaves. Desirable goods included pots and pans, clothing, alcohol and guns. Ships would leave Britain between July and September and would take four to six weeks to reach the coast of Africa.

Slave merchants would spend between 200 and 300 days on the west coast of Africa trading for slaves. Most slaves were obtained from areas along the Guinea west coast of Africa although nearly 50% of slaves came from the area around the Bight of Benin, named the 'slave coast'.

Once the slave ships had a full cargo of slaves, the ship would set sail on the Middle Passage. This journey took between thirty and fifty days. When the slaves reached the Caribbean they would be sold at auction and put to work on plantations. Most of the plantations in the Caribbean produced sugar cane. The slave merchants would spend about fifty days in the Caribbean. The sugar was loaded on to the slave ships which returned to Britain. The last part of the journey took about fifty days.

Once the ships returned to Britain the sugar was sold on for a profit. Other raw goods like cotton were used in the new factories of the industrial revolution to create the goods that were so valuable for trading. The process would then begin again.

The triangular trade route could take up to a year and a half to complete in full.

> ## 🔵 Activity 2
>
> Using a large piece of poster paper, create a detailed diagram of the triangular trade. Make sure you include the following:
>
> - Britain; West Africa; Caribbean
> - details of how long each leg of the journey took
> - details of the goods carried on each leg of the journey.
>
> **(Unit outcomes: National 4/5: Outcome 1.1)**

The effect of the slave trade on British ports

The slave trade benefited some British ports. Between 1630 and 1807 Britain's merchants made around £12 000 000 profit from the 2 500 000 Africans who were bought and sold. Cities such as Liverpool and Bristol grew rich because of these profits and because of the employment opportunities that came with the new-found wealth.

Geographically, Liverpool and Bristol were well-placed for the slave trade – easy access to the Atlantic meant they were in prime position for taking part in the Atlantic slave trade. Businesses and employment grew as a direct result. For example, shipbuilding and repair was big business in Liverpool. Other enterprises included the trading of slave-produced goods like sugar, cotton and tobacco and, in turn, the industrial production of desirable goods like clothing. Exportable goods like pottery were also produced – these could then be used to trade for slaves in Africa. The slave trade was so profitable that banks were set up to deal directly with the money made from slavery – Barclays Bank is one example. Further, insurance companies made huge profits from insuring businesses linked to the slave trade. It was rare for a bank to turn down a loan to anyone if the business involved slavery; such was the guarantee of profit from the trade.

📖 Key Word

- **Enterprise**

Business or company or a project; normally associated with making money.

Make the Link

In Business Management you learn about sources of finance in the present day.

Initially, London had also been involved in the slave trade but, by 1792, 131 ships set sail from Liverpool compared to London's 22, proving its success. Liverpool's slave trade legacy is still apparent today. Street names such as Penny Lane, Bold Street and Rodney Street are named after slave traders. The carvings on the town hall depict the route taken by the slave traders.

Figure 3: *The legacy of the slave trade can be seen on some of Liverpool's landmarks – the town hall depicts some of the images seen by the slave traders on their journey on the triangular trade route.*

Individuals could amass large personal wealth if they were involved in the slave trade. Thomas Leyland was one such individual. After a lottery win of around £20 000 he invested the money in the slave trade. On one trip he made £12 000 profit. He invested his money in the banking industry and became a significant figure in local politics. He was mayor of Liverpool three times.

Figure 4: *Thomas Leyland, slave trader and three times mayor of Liverpool.*

Figure 5: *Auchencruive House in Ayrshire, built with the wealth accrued from investment in the slave trade.*

Glasgow and Ayrshire also had a role in the slave trade. Glasgow grew to be an industrial town because of the raw goods like cotton and tobacco transported there from across the Atlantic. One merchant, Richard Oswald, made a lot of money from the slave trade and his accumulated wealth was shown when he returned to Scotland and built Auchincruive house. His wife, Mary Ramsay, was the daughter of a rich plantation owner in Jamaica.

The legacy of Glasgow's involvement in the slave trade can still be seen today, Street names such as Buchanan Street are named after slave merchants and Jamaica Street after a colony.

Hint

Robert Burns wrote a poem on the death of Mary Ramsay. He was very critical of the way she had made her money and her attitude towards it.

Burns had actually considered taking a job on a plantation as a bookmaker but decided against it and instead became a critic of the slave trade.

Figure 6: *Buchanan Street in Glasgow was named after a British slave colony.*

Activity 3

1. Using the preceding information, describe in detail the effect of the slave trade on Britain. Use at least three examples from the information in your answer.

Exam style question

2. Explain the reasons why Britain was able to profit so well from the slave trade. Think about Britain's position geographically, the payment of slaves and the use of raw goods. **KU 6**

(Unit outcomes: National 4/5: Outcome 2.2)

The effect of the slave trade on West African societies

Most of the slaves taken from Africa came from the west coast. It was renamed the slave coast because of the high procurement of slaves from that area. Many slaves were kidnapped by Europeans but African chiefs became involved in the trading of slaves, exchanging people for the desirable goods produced in Britain. Of these goods, alcohol and guns were the most popular – more sophisticated weapons gave African chiefs a distinct advantage over opposing tribes in conflicts.

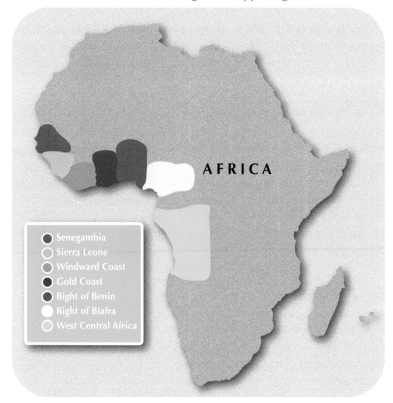

Figure 7: *This map shows some of the primary areas slaves were taken from during the time of the slave trade.*

Source A: John Newton (former slave trader and later abolitionist) wrote of the effect of taking slaves in Africa.

> I verily believe that the far greater part of wars, in Africa, would cease, if the Europeans would cease to tempt them, by offering goods for sale. I believe the captives reserved for sale are fewer than the slain.

States such as Angola under Queen Nzinga Nbande put up a very strong fight against slavery. However, many African tribal chiefs worked with the Europeans to provide slaves to be used on the plantations in exchange for goods.

Many historians believe that the African population was greatly affected by the slave trade in that their tribal culture was influenced by European thoughts and practices as well as European religion (Christianity). Historians sometimes point to the idea that African societies were often left underdeveloped because much of the population was taken from Africa.

The Ashanti

It has been argued that the Ashanti tribe were able to grow and prosper as a result of wars with European slave traders. It is likely the Ashanti were formed out of a number of smaller tribes who collaborated against the European invaders initially but grew to trade slaves with them in the latter half of the eighteenth century, making them partners in the Atlantic slave trade. Their tribe grew especially powerful because trading with Europeans brought them new-found wealth and firearms. Eventually, the Ashanti were able to use the weapons against their trading partners. The British tried to colonise the Ashanti because they were positioned on the Gold Coast, where, as the name suggests, gold was in abundance. The Ashanti fought the British off for a considerable time until in 1902 the Gold Coast was colonised into the British Empire.

The effect of the slave trade on West Indian plantations

The population of black slaves outnumbered the number of white plantation owners and workers in the West Indies. Plantations were populated with slaves from Africa but the number of slaves also grew as slaves reproduced in the colonies. Most of the plantations in the West Indies grew sugar. The climate was ideal for growing sugar cane and the African workers were perceived as being ideal for the climate – they were used to hot and tropical conditions whereas European workers were not.

Slave factories on the west coast of Africa

Many conflicts between African tribes were over the issue of trading slaves. Slave ships would sail along the west coast filling their ships until they had enough cargo to cross the Atlantic. Other European slave traders would set up slave fortresses or 'factories'. Slaves would be captured and held until they could be sold to European slave traders. It was not uncommon for African tribal chiefs to be involved in the running of the slave factories and filling them with supplies of slaves.

Trading slaves was not always a simple process. Slave traders would not be permitted to move inland to trade for slaves; trading always took place on the coast. It could take a long time to select the perfect cargo of slaves. Merchants could afford to be picky – their cargo had to make it through the Middle Passage and be sold for a profit when they reached the West Indies. It was in their interest to be selective and only trade for the best cargo. Any slaves not chosen would either be enslaved by the African chief who had captured them or killed.

> ### 🔍 Hint
>
> Around 12% of the population of the United States is made up of African Americans, almost all direct descendants of slaves. The population of black people in the Caribbean is much higher, often over 90%.

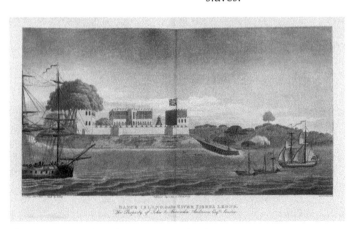

Figure 8: *British slave fort on Bance Island.*

In **Source B** William Bosman, a Dutch slave trader, describes what happened to slaves when they were brought to a slave factory:

> When slaves are brought from the inland countries, they are put in prison together. When we buy them, they are all brought out together and thoroughly examined by our surgeons. Those which are approved as good are set on one side; in the meantime a burning iron, with the name of the company, lies in the fire. Our slaves are branded on the chest after we have agreed a price with the owners of the slaves.

SLAVERS REVENGING THEIR LOSSES.

📖 Key Word

- **Coffle**
The term applied to a group of slaves fastened at the neck, hands and sometimes feet.

Figure 9: *A painting of a coffle. Captured slaves would be fastened together by the hands and neck and marched to the coast for trading.*

Figure 10: *A drawing of a barracoon. These were basic wooden cages that slaves would be kept in until traded and put aboard a ship on the Middle Passage.*

🔵 Activity 4

Imagine you are a slave trader who has approached a slave factory on the west coast of Africa. Write a letter home describing trading on the coast for slaves. Include details of the following:

- Description of the slave fort.
- Description of the goods traded for slaves.
- Where you think the African chief gets his slaves.
- How long you think it will take to get the number of slaves you need and the reason you are not in a rush.

(Unit outcomes: National 4/5: Outcome 1.1)

The economics and conditions on the Middle Passage

Make the Link

You may learn more about the spread of disease in Science, Health and Food Technology and Geography.

Key Words

- **Typhoid**

Infection passed to humans through infected urine or faeces. Causes stomach pains and diarrhoea and can lead to internal bleeding and death.

- **Bloody flux**

Also known as dysentery – caused severe sickness and diarrhoea and eventual death from dehydration.

The conditions on the Middle Passage were horrendous. The slaves would be shackled together between six and fourteen weeks, sailing from Africa to the Caribbean before being sold to plantation owners in the New World. Slaves would be carried on the boat in either 'Tight Pack' or 'Loose Pack' formation. Tight pack required the slaves to be set on their sides. This way more could be carried on board – between 200–250 slaves. Loose pack meant the slaves would be placed on their backs, carrying about 170–200 slaves. Since the slaves were shackled together for the journey, they ate, slept and went to the toilet in their shackled positions. Occasionally there would be a toilet 'pot' at one end of the ship. The temperatures below deck were stiflingly hot. Slaves would be fed rice mixed with palm oil and pepper and water was rationed. Slaves would get sea sick and, due to the unhygienic conditions below deck, disease was rife. Typhoid and the bloody flux killed many slaves but dehydration was the biggest cause of slave and sailor deaths before they reached the Caribbean. Sometimes slaves were brought up on deck to be exercised and sometimes the crew would rape the women aboard the slave ship. Slaves that died on the passage would be thrown overboard. Many slaves attempted suicide as the experience was so awful and they did not know what their future held, if the journey was ever going to come to an end.

Source C is from *The Interesting Narrative of the Life of Olaudah Equiano* (1789). Olaudah Equiano was a slave who bought his right to freedom. He was well educated and wrote about his experiences of being a slave in the book. It charts how he was captured and used as a slave in Africa before being taken to the West Indies and his life beyond being a slave.

Figure 11: *Drawing of slaves aboard the slave ship* Wildfire. *They were forced to sit on deck for the whole journey.*

The closeness of the place, and the heat of the climate, added to the number in the ship, which was so crowded that each had scarcely room to turn himself, almost suffocated us. This produced copious perspirations, so that the air soon became unfit for respiration, from a variety of loathsome smells, and brought on a sickness among the slaves, of which many died, thus falling victims to the improvident avarice, as I may call it, of their purchasers. This wretched situation was again aggravated by the galling of the chains, now become insupportable; and the filth of the necessary tubs, into which the children often fell, and were almost suffocated.

GO! Activity 5

1. With a partner, use the internet to research the conditions on the Middle Passage. You must find five pieces of **primary source** evidence which show the conditions on the passage. Make sure you give the **details** of the source – who wrote/produced it and the date. Then explain the evidence from the source. You can quote if it is a written source but then explain the content in your own words. If it is a picture source, make sure you describe what the source shows. Complete the following table:

Source	Evidence from the source showing conditions on the Middle Passage
1 Write the **origin** of the source **here** (who wrote it and the date)	Quote from the source or describe its detail which shows the conditions on the Middle Passage **here**.
2	
3	
4	
5	

(Unit outcomes: National 4/5: Outcome 1.2)

Exam style questions

2. Describe, in detail, the conditions on the Middle Passage. 　　　　　　　　　KU 4

(Unit outcomes: National 4/5: Outcome 2.1)

3. Using the image of the slave ship *Wildfire* and **Source C:**

   How fully do the sources explain the conditions on the Middle Passage? 　　　SH 6

   (Use **Source C** and recall.)

2 Britain and the Caribbean

In this section you will learn about:

- The importance of tropical crops such as sugar.
- The influence of the British in the Caribbean.
- The impact of the Caribbean trade on the British economy.
- The negative impact of the slave trade on the development of the Caribbean islands.

The importance of tropical crops such as sugar

Figure 12: *A seventeenth century coffee house.*

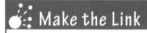
Make the Link

In Health and Food Technology you will learn about the nutritional make up of sugar.

The key tropical crop grown in the West Indies was sugar. Sugar was a valuable commodity; it had become fashionable to consume sugar in Britain. People used it to sweeten food and it was popular in the new coffee and tea houses of the time. Rum, which is made from sugar, could be made in the West Indies and sold in Britain. People consumed sugar and rum in vast quantities so demand was very high. Since sugar was farmed on the plantations of the West Indies and the workers were not paid, large profits could be made selling the sugar when it was back in Britain. The climate of the Caribbean was ideal for growing sugar cane and since the working conditions were hot and humid it seemed that slave workers from Africa were right for the job.

The profits made by the slave traders were on a scale hitherto unknown by any merchants in Britain. The new machinery of the industrial revolution could make desirable products quickly and relatively cheaply. In turn, these products could be sold on for profit or indeed used to trade for slaves on the west coast of Africa. It is estimated that Britain made £3 800 000 in profit (around £450 000 000 in today's money) from its West Indian plantations and around £1 300 000 from trading in 1770 alone. During the course of the slave trade from 1750–1807 it is likely that Britain accumulated £60 000 000 from the sale of human beings, about £8 billion in today's money.

In **Source D**, historian Clive Ponting assesses the importance of sugar in Britain in the eighteenth century (from *World History: A New Perspective*).

> [Sugar was] the most valuable commodity in European trade — it made up a fifth of all European imports and in the last decades of the century four-fifths of the sugar came from the British and French colonies in the West Indies.

Hint

Rum, a product made from the sugar on the plantations was not only sold in Britain, it was traded in Africa for slaves. The triangular trade was generated and perpetuated by slavery.

📖 Key Words

- **Generated**
Produced and created.

- **Perpetuated**
Kept going.

🔵 Activity 6

Exam style questions

1. Evaluate the usefulness of **Source D** in assessing the importance of sugar in the Atlantic slave trade.   **SH 5**

   (You may want to comment on who wrote it, when they wrote it, why they wrote it, what they say or what has been missed out.)

2. 'Britain's wealth was created through investment in the slave trade.'

   Give the evidence to support this statement. Find three pieces of evidence and explain your points clearly.

The influence of the British in the Caribbean and the impact of the Caribbean trade on the British economy

The influence of the British in the Caribbean has left a legacy lasting 400 years. When the British arrived they set up plantations, most of which grew sugar. As they used slave labour, the profits accrued had a massive impact on the British economy. Some historians would argue that the rapid growth of the British economy is almost entirely down to investment in the slave trade.

The key towns which grew quickly because of the slave trade were Liverpool and Bristol. They had the geographical advantage of being situated on the west coast of Britain, which gave them direct access to the Atlantic. This meant that raw goods from the West Indies could be imported to these towns straight from the Atlantic and used in the new industrial factories. The end products could be shipped out of the same ports and transported elsewhere – to continental Europe for further trading or back to Africa to trade for slaves. Britain was able to trade with its colonies and beyond, for example India became a valuable trading post in its own right. However, Britain did face competition from its European neighbours such as Spain and Portugal.

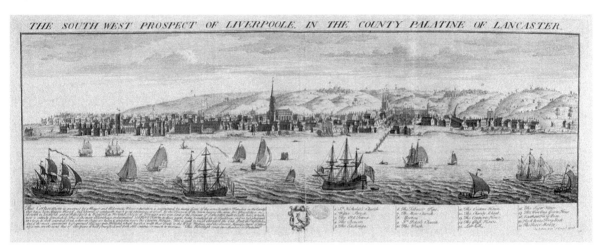

Figure 13: *Liverpool in the eighteenth century.*

The profits made from slavery were invested in the industrial revolution in Britain. Canals, agricultural improvement, roads and mills were seen as sound and profitable investments. It cost between £10 000 and £15 000 to build a mill and invest in the materials and labour to run it. However, so attractive were the profits made by merchants involved in the slave trade that this was done on a large scale. Of course, the shipbuilding industry flourished and the need for harbours and related workers – carpenters, sail-makers, blacksmiths and sailors – generated employment opportunities. By 1807, 87% of British growth came from exports.

Glasgow and Ayrshire also grew because of the slave trade. Glasgow grew to be Scotland's largest city, employing thousands in the industrial revolution. The investors of the slave trade and industrial revolution grew rich. The population of Scotland and the rest of Britain grew rapidly. During this time Liverpool became the most valuable port in Britain, eclipsing London.

In **Source E** Rosemary Rees describes the effect of the slave trade on Liverpool (from *Britain and the Slave Trade*).

> In 1700 Liverpool was a small fishing port of 5000 people. One hundred years later over 78 000 people lived and worked in Liverpool. Prosperity depended on the slave trade. Liverpool's wealth came from trading in slaves and slave-produced cotton. Liverpool's slave merchants rose to positions of power and influence in the town. At least twenty six of Liverpool's mayors between 1700 and 1820 were slave merchants. Thousands of people found work because of the slave trade. More and more ships were needed. These had to be built and equipped. Carpenters, rope-makers, dockers and sailors were all needed. Many found jobs in banking and insurance. Gradually the prosperity of the whole town and those who lived there began to depend more and more on the slave trade.

In **Source F** F.G. Kay describes some of the social changes that also took place because of the growth of the slave trade (from *The Shameful Trade*).

> The slave trade created a new class of wealthy colonial families. The industrialists of the Midlands and Lancashire, the London bankers, the directors of the shipping firms in Glasgow and Liverpool enjoyed, quietly, the profits from the slave trade. But the retired and absentee plantation owners soon became envied and admired with their grand houses newly built in spacious parks, and their lavish parties in towns like Bath.

GO! Activity 7

Exam style questions

1. To what extent did the slave trade lead to economic and social changes in Britain?   **KU 9**
   (Unit outcomes: National 5: Outcome 2.3)
2. How fully do **Sources E** and **F** describe the effect of the slave trade on British towns?   **SH 6**
   (Use **Sources E** and **F** and recall.)

The negative impact of the slave trade on the development of the Caribbean islands

Many historians think that the Caribbean has been impacted negatively because of their involvement in the slave trade. The plantations were very specific in what they farmed and most only grew one type of crop. Many slaves did not have opportunities to gain other skills so found themselves tied to plantation work even after slavery had ended. Slaves also found it difficult to adjust to freedom and many continued working on the plantations after the abolition of slavery.

3 The captive's experience and slave resistance

In this section you will learn about:

- Slave auctions.
- Living and working conditions on the plantations.
- Discipline and fear of revolt.
- Resistance on the plantations.
- Other forms of slave labour on the Caribbean islands.

Slave auctions

Key Word

- **Auction**

When goods are sold to the highest bidder. Slaves were regarded as being goods for sale.

When slaves arrived in the West Indies they were sold at auction. They would be prepared beforehand – rubbed with oil to make their skin gleam, grey hair covered up and any injuries sustained on the Middle Passage covered up. Young adult males fetched the best prices. Families would often be separated during the sale – brothers and sisters, mothers and fathers could be bought by different plantation owners. There were also 'scramble' auctions when the slaves were kept in a large cage and the price was agreed between the slave traders and plantation owners. When a signal was sounded the buyers rushed into the cage to try to grab the slaves they wanted.

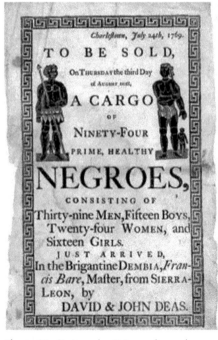

Figure 14: *Poster advertising a slave sale.*

Figure 15: *A slave auction. Slaves were typically sold to the highest bidder.*

Activity 8

Create your own slave auction poster. It must contain details of the cargo of slaves to be sold, the time and the price expected for the cargo.

Life on the plantations

A plantation is a farm that only grows one kind of crop. The majority of plantations in the British owned Caribbean were sugar plantations. Slaves were forced to work from sun up to sun down, from as young as the age of three or four. Slaves were often split into 'gangs' to

Figure 16: *Painting by W Clark in 1823 showing slaves working in the fields on a sugar plantation in Jamaica.*

Figure 17: *Painting by W Clark showing slaves working in a boiling house in Antigua.*

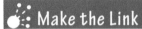
complete the work required. The First Gang of fieldworkers tended to be the strongest slaves. They were expected to prepare the ground for the sugar cane, maintain the land, harvest the sugar cane and load it on to carts to take to the boiler house. The work was gruelling. Even the youngest slaves were made to pick up debris and hunt for animal fodder. Slaves on the sugar plantations were also required to work in the boiling houses, hot and dangerous work where they would extract the raw juice from the sugar cane and put it through a process of being boiled at different temperatures until it resembled something similar to the sugar crystals we use today.

Figure 18: *Rose Hall, an impressive plantation house in Montego Bay, Jamaica.*

Slaves were also required to work in the 'big house'. Sometimes, this was a popular job as it meant working closely with the masters and afforded some slaves certain privileges. However, for many, it meant they were treated more cruelly than if they had been field hands. Maids would have to get up at 4 a.m. to make sure the fires were lit and the kitchen put into action. A long day of cooking and cleaning followed and they would have to work late into the evening because the people of the big house would have to be served dinner and then be cleaned up after.

The accommodation for slaves was vastly different to that of the plantation owners. Slaves stayed in wooden huts, sometimes resembling the huts they inhabited in Africa. Life was basic and they had no home comforts – the most they owned would be a few farmyard animals and vegetable patches to grow some food. Rations from the plantation owners were small and would consist of maize, yams and mackerel.

Figure 19: *A typical slave cabin.*

In **Source G** Josiah Henson describes his living conditions (*The Life of Josiah Henson*, published in 1849).

> We lodged in log huts, and on the bare ground. Wooden floors were an unknown luxury. In a single room were huddled, like cattle, ten or a dozen persons, men, women, and children. All ideas of refinement and decency were, of course, out of the question. We had neither bedsteads, nor furniture of any description. Our beds were collections of straw and old rags, thrown down in the corners and boxed in with boards; a single blanket the only covering.

Depending on the plantation owner, the slaves would be allowed to have some free time in the evening. They told stories, often about life in Africa. They sang songs and were sometimes allowed instruments. However, plantation owners were suspicious of the slaves who wanted to play drums – they thought they might be sending signals to slaves on other nearby plantations with plans to escape. The plantation owners were also suspicious of the African traditions and religions practised by slaves. Many plantation owners tried to convert their slaves to Christianity and even allowed them to be baptised and attend church on Sundays. Slaves would sing songs in the evening and during the day to motivate them while working in the fields. These songs became known as negro spirituals.

Humanitarian and religious concerns about slavery

The life of slaves on the plantations came under criticism from humanitarian societies such as the Quakers who insisted this was an awful way to treat other human beings. They argued that if slaves were to be converted to Christianity then they should not be enslaved people – Christianity promoted equality.

 Make the Link

You may learn about the songs sung by slaves if you study Music.

Make the Link

You will learn about the beliefs of Christians if you study RMPS.

Discipline and fear of revolt

The fear of slave revolt was never far from the mind of plantation owners. They knew deep down they were outnumbered by slaves and that an organised rebellion could result in them being killed. They opted to control the slaves with a fear of punishment. Different acts of resistance by the slaves carried different punishments. The most common form of punishment was whipping. However, iron muzzles, thumb screws and the cutting off of limbs were also used. Running away could be punishable by death. Plantation owners would threaten the slaves with separation from their families – probably the most effective form of punishment.

In **Source H** Olaudah Equiano recalls some of the punishments given out to slaves, just for minor acts of resistance (from *The Interesting Narrative of the Life of Olaudah Equiano*, 1789).

> It was very common in several of the islands, particularly in St Kitts, for the slaves to be branded with the initial letter of the master's name and a load of heavy iron hooks hung about their necks. Indeed on the most trifling occasions they were loaded with chains, and often instruments of torture were added. The iron muzzle, thumbscrews, etc. were sometimes applied for the slightest faults. I have seen a Negro beaten till some of his bones were broken for even letting a pot boil over.

📖 Key Word

• **Overseer**

An overseer would watch over the slaves to check they were doing their job properly.

Plantation owners did not always give out the punishments themselves. The overseers (normally white men or promoted slaves) would likely give them out but it was common for other slaves to punish their fellow workers.

Figure 20: *A drawing of a slave carrying out a punishment on a fellow slave.*

The harsh punishments given out by the plantation owners had the opposite effect of keeping the slaves under control – it built on the resentment already felt by slaves and contributed to acts of resistance and rebellion.

Activity 9

Essay board activity

'The life of a slave was a comfortable and happy one.'

To what extent do you agree with the above statement?

- Take an A3 piece of paper and write the question at the top.
- Create an 'introduction box' and write two to three sentences addressing the question and outline some of the key factors which will feature on your essay board.
- You will now add four sections to your essay board:
  1. work
  2. resistance
  3. punishments
  4. traditions and religion.
- For each section, give details about the heading and explain whether life for slaves on the plantations was comfortable and happy. Include one piece of evidence from a primary source in each section to exemplify the points you are making. You can use the information from the sources in this section or carry out further research.
- Now add a 'conclusion box' – summarise your key arguments and answer the question.

  (Unit outcomes: National 5: Outcome 2.3)

Slave resistance

Slaves did resist, sometimes by running away but sometimes by committing smaller acts of sabotage –crops were ruined, tools were broken and instructions were misunderstood. However, any acts of resistance on a large scale were often crushed quickly as the slaves were disorganised and lacked the more sophisticated weapons of the whites.

Saint Domingue (now known as Haiti) was controlled by the French and had the largest enslaved population in the Caribbean. It had a booming sugar industry that had created the world's richest colony, with 500 000 enslaved Africans. It produced more than 30% of the world's sugar and more than half its coffee. Slaves had to live in windowless huts and were overworked and often underfed. Some owners put tin masks on the slaves to keep them from chewing sugar cane in the fields. Slaves were whipped regularly and salt, pepper and even hot ashes were poured onto bleeding wounds. A rebellion began in 1791, when slaves attacked plantation buildings with hooks, machetes and torches. They set fire to everything connected with their work on the sugar plantations. The rebellion sent shock waves throughout Europe, as European men and women were killed in their hundreds.

Nevertheless, rather than encouraging the better treatment of slaves on other plantations it reinforced the belief of plantation owners that it was better to treat the slaves as harshly as possible to stop the possibility of a rebellion.

Figure 21: *Toussaint L'Ouverture, leader of the slave revolt on Haiti.*

Other forms of slavery on the Caribbean islands

It was not only slaves that were treated harshly on the Caribbean islands; some white men were often treated no better than the slaves. Many white workers on the plantations were 'indebted servants' – men who worked for nothing to pay off a debt. They were treated only marginally better than slaves but they did tend to have the better positions on the plantations, such as overseers. Those in indebted servitude also had a limited number of years which they had to work to pay off their debts, and they were then free.

GO! Activity 10

1. Imagine you are a plantation owner on one of the Caribbean islands and you have heard of the rebellion on Haiti. Write a letter home to a family member and include the following details:
   - details of the rebellion on Haiti
   - your personal fears
   - what you feel should be done to avoid rebellion among your slaves.

   (Unit outcomes: National 4/5: Outcome 1.1)

Exam style questions

2. Explain the reasons why slaves found it difficult to rebel on the plantations. **KU 6**
3. Explain the reasons why people in Britain began to have concerns about the treatment of slaves on the plantations. **KU 6**

   (Unit outcomes: National 4/5: Outcome 2.2)

4 The abolitionist campaigns

In this section you will learn about:

- The origins of the abolitionist movement.
- The arguments of the abolitionists: Christian, humanitarian, economic.
- The decision to concentrate on the slave trade.
- The methods of the abolitionists, including meetings and publicity.
- The influence of slaves and former slaves, e.g. Olaudah Equiano.
- The key abolitionists.
- Arguments for the slave trade.
- The debate over reasons for the eventual success of the abolition campaign.

The abolitionist movement: origins and arguments

During the course of the eighteenth century, most people did not question the slave trade. Many people made a living from it, either directly or indirectly. Sailors, carpenters and bankers all worked directly with the trade making profits from slave labour. However, the growth of cities, whose populations consisted of those who worked in the new industries, led to a raised awareness of the political issues of the day. The French Revolution in 1789 highlighted to the working classes the power of the people and the ability of the masses to overcome their oppressors, albeit by violent methods. Word started to come back from the Americas that the raw goods used in the factories had been farmed by slaves. People in Britain were paid very little for working in the factories so could empathise deeply with those kept in servitude and earning nothing. Many factory workers began to refuse to work with goods farmed by slaves.

In 1787 the Society for the Abolition of the Slave Trade was set up to try to end the slave trade. It did not aim to end slavery because they wanted to tackle one problem at a time – they thought if the slave trade could be ended then slavery itself might follow soon after. Further, they knew it would take more than gentle persuasion to change the minds of those in Parliament; most were avid supporters of the slave trade. Different people became involved in the campaigns to end the slave trade, one of the most notable figures being William Wilberforce, MP.

The first group to publicly oppose the slave trade were the Society of Friends, or the Quakers. They were a religious group who decided that no one who was involved in the slave trade could be a member of their group. Many Christians also promoted the idea of equality among the races – the Bible taught that God created all men as equals and

📖 **Key Word**

- **Abolitionist**
The abolitionists wanted to end the *slave trade* rather than *slavery* itself.

that people should treat each other with kindness, love and respect. For this reason, slavery should not be allowed to continue.

Source I: John Wesley, arguing against slavery in 1774:

> To the captains employed in the slave trade, every merchant who is engaged in the slave trade and every gentleman that has an estate in our plantations – Is there a God? Is he a just God? Then there must be state of retribution. Then what reward will he render you? Think now, 'He shall have judgement without mercy that showed no mercy.'

The principle that slavery allowed merchants to make maximum profit by not paying their work force also came under criticism. Adam Smith, an economist, promoted the idea that by paying your slaves they would have an incentive to work and therefore production would increase. This, in turn, would mean that profits would in fact be better than if the workers were not being paid.

Source J is from Adam Smith, *The Wealth of Nations*, 1776.

> Work done by slaves, though it appears to cost only their maintenance, is in the end the dearest of any. A person who can acquire no property, can have no other interest but to eat as much, and to work as little, as possible. Whatever work he does beyond what is enough to meet his own basic needs, must be squeezed out of him by violence.

Furthermore, sugar was now being produced elsewhere in the British Empire for much less – in India sugar was being produced at a reduced rate compared to the costs of production in the Caribbean. It seemed unlikely the Caribbean trade could continue if the same product could be produced elsewhere for less.

The humanitarian arguments were probably the most compelling to those who listened to the abolitionists. It was the evidence of the cruel treatment of the slaves as described in testimonies like that of Olaudah Equiano and the extensive research conducted by some abolitionists, that led to the argument to end the slave trade receiving support inside and outside Parliament.

Source K: Granville Sharp writing in 1769:

> The claim to own a negro like a horse or a dog, is defective. It cannot be justified unless you can prove that a slave is neither man, woman nor child. The poor negro has not been guilty of any offences for which he might lawfully lose his humanity. Therefore it must be recognised that he differs from a horse or a dog in this essential point – he is a human being.

Make the Link

You may learn more about a motivated work force in Business Management or Economics.

Hint

Adam Smith is often considered the 'father of modern economics' and a leading thinker of the Enlightenment, an eighteenth century movement that promoted the ideas of rational thought and challenging traditional authority. He wrote about the benefits of a free market economy.

GO! Activity 11

1. Using the information in this section find at least two arguments for the abolition of the slave trade under the following headings:

   - religious arguments
   - economic arguments
   - humanitarian arguments.

   Include information from one source under each heading as well as information from the text.

2. Using the summary of arguments why the slave trade should end, write a speech to be delivered in Parliament asking for the slave trade to be abolished. Your argument must contain five well explained points.

   (Unit outcomes: National 5: Outcome 1.2)

Exam style question

3. Evaluate the usefulness of **Source K** to a historian studying the reasons the abolitionists gave to try to end the slave trade. **SH 5**

   (You may want to comment on who wrote it, when they wrote it, why they wrote it, what they say or what has been missed out.)

The methods of the abolitionists

The abolitionists used a variety of methods to try to win support for the abolition of the slave trade. Meetings were held where speakers could deliver evidence on the cruelty of the trade. Petitions were signed and submitted to Parliament – once people became better informed of the slave trade they sympathised with the slaves and helped to protest against it. Several people lobbied Parliament including Olaudah Equiano – no mean feat in the eighteenth century considering he had previously been a slave. Further, *The Interesting Narrative of the Life of Olaudah Equiano* was very influential as it detailed his capture in Africa, the Middle Passage and life on the plantations. Publicity was key to promoting the message of the abolitionists. The Wedgwood Cameo was inscribed: 'Am I not a man and a brother?' It was produced in its thousands and given away free to promote the cause.

Figure 22: *The Wedgwood Cameo.*

Make the Link

You will learn about the methods used by pressure groups today in Modern Studies.

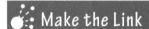

Make the Link

You will learn about how new laws are created today in Modern Studies.

Although certain figures such as William Wilberforce and Thomas Clarkson were definitely the driving force behind the campaign, it must be remembered that the support of ordinary people was vital in getting the bill passed in Parliament. Moreover, the action of the slaves themselves was fundamental to the passing of the Abolition Act. The threat of rebellion and actual rebellions did much to cast doubt in the minds of those involved in the slave trade as to whether it should continue.

The key abolitionists

William Wilberforce is generally regarded as the key figure of the abolition movement. He was a Member of Parliament and used his position to introduce bills to end the slave trade. He was friends with William Pitt, who was Prime Minister and encouraged Wilberforce to introduce the bills on a regular basis as he knew the other parliamentarians would take a lot of persuading to pass the bill into law. Wilberforce used evidence gathered by Thomas Clarkson among others to persuade other MPs that the trade was cruel and against humanitarian and religious principles. It took him almost 20 years, but in 1807 the Abolition of the Slave Trade Act came into being and the slave trade was outlawed in the British Empire. However, Wilberforce's role in abolition has been questioned by historians. They claim he was only a figurehead for abolition and that the work of others, such as Thomas Clarkson, was more influential.

Figure 23: *William Wilberforce.*

Thomas Clarkson is considered as the 'forgotten hero' of abolition. He worked tirelessly to gather evidence proving that the slave trade was cruel and that slaves were treated no better than animals. He helped set up the Society for the Abolition of the Slave Trade. He collected physical evidence such as shackles and thumbscrews and visited the slave ships while they were in Liverpool and Bristol harbours to look at the conditions aboard. He talked to over 20 000 sailors and dockworkers and found that they too could be considered victims of the slave trade – many were in indebted servitude and treated no better than slaves. He even suffered an attack on his life – some captains of slave ships were so worried about the evidence he was gathering they pushed him into the dock. The attempt to take his life failed. Clarkson probably worked the hardest out of all the abolitionists to provide the evidence necessary to end the slave trade.

Figure 24: *Thomas Clarkson.*

Figure 25: *Slave shackles used as evidence by Thomas Clarkson to prove the horrors of the Middle Passage.*

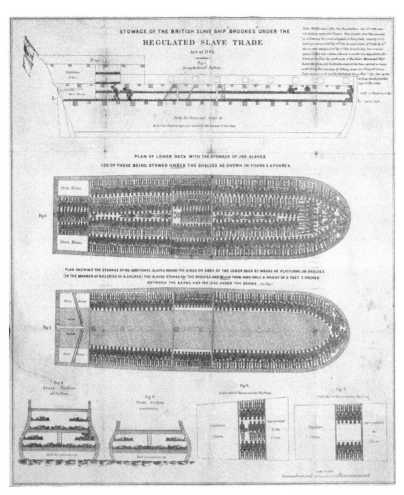

Figure 26: *Drawing of the slave ship the Brookes. Clarkson used it to demonstrate how overcrowded the slave ships could be. In the case of the Brookes, it was supposed to carry 482 slaves but carried 609.*

Figure 27: *Granville Sharp.*

Granville Sharp's interest in slavery began in 1765 after he befriended Jonathan Strong, a slave who had been badly beaten by his master. When Strong's former owner attempted to sell him back into slavery in the Caribbean, Sharp took the case to the lord mayor and Strong was freed. He was involved in securing the famous 1772 ruling by Lord Chief Justice William Mansfield, which concluded that slave owners could not legally force slaves to return to the colonies once they were in Britain. This was regarded by many as effectively abolishing slavery within Britain.

Figure 28: *Granville Sharp befriending Jonathan Strong.*

Figure 29: *John Newton.*

 Hint

John Newton wrote the hymn 'Amazing Grace' which has become a celebrated African American hymn.

Figure 30: *James Ramsay.*

Figure 31: *Hannah More.*

📖 Key Word

- **Boycott**
To refuse to use a service or buy particular goods in protest.

John Newton had been an active member of the slave trade and worked aboard many slave ships including the *Duke of Argyll*. Even after he gave up working on slave ships he continued to invest in the slave trade. In 1788, thirty four years after he had retired from the slave trade, Newton published *Thoughts Upon the Slave Trade,* in which he described the horrific conditions on the slave ships during the Middle Passage, and apologised for ever having had a role in the slave trade. A copy of the pamphlet was sent to every MP, and sold so well that it required reprinting. Newton was also friends with William Wilberforce.

Source L: John Newton regrets participating in the slave trade in *Thoughts Upon the Slave Trade*, 1788.

> a confession, which ... comes too late ... It will always be a subject of humiliating reflection to me, that I was once an active instrument in a business at which my heart now shudders.

James Ramsay witnessed the suffering of the enslaved people as a ship's doctor in the Navy. In 1759, his ship, *HMS Arundel*, was stationed in the West Indies when a slave ship, the *Swift*, approached seeking help. The ship had been struck down with dysentery. Many of the slaves and crew were dead. Ramsay treated over 100 victims packed close together in the most inhuman and filthy conditions. He published *An Inquiry into the Effects of Putting a Stop to the African Slave Trade* in 1784. These were the first anti-slavery works by someone who had personally seen the suffering.

Hannah More helped give the abolition movement a public voice. In 1788, she wrote *Slavery, a Poem*, to coincide with Wilberforce's parliamentary campaign for abolition. The poem described a mistreated, enslaved female separated from her children and it questioned Britain's role in the slave trade. She encouraged other women to boycott sugar – many persuaded grocers to stop selling sugar produced by slaves. By 1792, 400 000 people were boycotting slave-produced sugar and grocers reported that sales had dropped by one third.

🔵 Activity 12

In groups of three, each take an abolitionist. Produce a presentation on the life of that abolitionist and their contribution to the abolition of the slave trade. You will need to complete further research online.

You must include:

- background information on the person
- their religious beliefs
- their contribution to the abolition of the slave trade.

(Unit outcomes: National 4/5: Outcome 1.2)

Arguments for the slave trade

Many people did not want the slave trade to end. They were worried that Britain had built up a considerable amount of wealth because of slavery and they did not want to sacrifice this. Further, many people had jobs connected with slavery – the dock workers, blacksmiths and sailors were worried they could be put out of a job. Many MPs in Parliament had investments in the slave trade and had become wealthy merchants. They did not want to lose this.

Some MPs were also planters and tried to say that the evidence of the abolitionists about life on the plantations was untrue. MPs were wealthy and could afford to bribe other MPs to support them.

Source M: View of the Assembly of Planters of Jamaica in 1789

> The plan to abolish the slave trade is based on false information. It is based on prejudice, and on a few examples of bad treatment of slaves. We planters have worked hard and taken risks, and our success has poured wealth into Britain. It is unfair that we have our property, the slaves, taken away from us.

The French Revolution had scared MPs in Britain. The population of France had risen up and overthrown the King. Rather than take this as a sign that perhaps enforcing the slave trade would lead to rebellion amongst slaves, MPs were certain that the continuation of the slave trade and slavery, and tightening control, would keep them safer.

In 1792 an agreement was reached in Parliament to abolish the slave trade slowly. It would take another fifteen years before it was abolished entirely.

GO! Activity 13

1. Write down three reasons why there were many people who did not want to see the end of the slave trade.

Exam style question

2. Evaluate the usefulness of **Source M** when examining the reasons why some people were against abolition.   **SH 5**

   (You may want to comment on who wrote it, when they wrote it, why they wrote it, what they say or what has been missed out.)

Why did the abolition campaign eventually succeed?

There are many different theories about why the slave trade was abolished.

Religious reasons

There was a great feeling of religious revival in the eighteenth century and many people felt that, as Christians, the enslavement of Africans should not be allowed to continue. Most of those who were abolitionists were Christian and many like John Newton were converted to the cause for abolition as part of their new found religious beliefs.

Economic reasons

Britain no longer needed the slave trade by 1807. The goods produced in the industrial revolution did not have to be traded in West Africa because they had buyers elsewhere – the European market had grown considerably. Also, sugar was being produced by free labour in India so there was no need to buy it from the West Indies. Many people boycotted sugar from the West Indies in support of abolition.

Political reasons

William Wilberforce was able to use his position as a politician to convince other MPs in Parliament that abolition was necessary. His friendship with William Pitt, the Prime Minister, meant that he could safely introduce abolition bills regularly until the Abolition of the Slave Trade Act was eventually passed in 1807. However, he would not have been able to do this without the extensive work of other abolitionists such as Thomas Clarkson.

Slaves themselves

Slaves had grown in number and plantation owners were always very aware that a revolt could happen at any time. This often meant the punishments would become harsher and rather than make the slaves submit it just emphasised that slavery in the West Indies was cruel and unjust. Continued slave resistance on the islands, even on a small level, showed that the slaves were not ever willing to fully submit to their white masters.

GO! Activity 14

1. Discuss with a partner the four reasons detailed above explaining why slavery ended. Number your reasons in order of importance – number 1 being the most important. For each reason, explain why you think it contributed to the end of the slave trade.

Exam style question

2. To what extent can the abolition of the slave trade be attributed to the work of William Wilberforce?   **KU 9**

   (Unit outcomes: National 5: Outcome 2.3)

Summary

In this topic you have learned:

- the details of the triangular trade route
- how slaves were captured in Africa
- about conditions on the Middle Passage and life on the plantations
- why slavery helped the British economy to grow
- the effect of slavery on British towns and the Caribbean

- the slave revolts
- why the abolitionists wanted the slave trade to end
- why many did not want to see slavery end.

You should have developed your skills and be able to:

- evaluate the usefulness of a source
- put a source into context by saying how fully it describes an issue.

Learning Checklist

Now that you have finished **The Atlantic Slave Trade, 1770–1807,** complete a self-evaluation of your knowledge and skill to assess what you have understood. Use traffic lights to help you make up a revision plan to help you improve in the areas you identified as red or amber.

- Describe and explain the triangular trade route.

- Explain why slaves were desirable to British merchants.

- Describe how slaves were captured in Africa.

- Describe the conditions on the Middle Passage.

- Describe slave auctions in the Caribbean.

- Describe life on the plantations for the slaves.

- Explain why slavery helped the British economy.

- Describe the effect of the slave trade on British towns like Liverpool.

- Describe and explain the effects of slave resistance on the West Indies.

- Describe the religious, economic and humanitarian arguments for abolishing slavery.

- Explain who the abolitionists were and what they wanted to achieve.

- Describe the methods of the abolitionists.

- Describe the role of William Wilberforce in the abolition campaign.

- Explain why many people did not want to see the end of the slave trade.

- Explain why slaves themselves had a large role to play in abolition.

This topic looks at the reasons for and impact of industrialisation on life in Britain. It will focus on the social, economic and political developments which transformed life across Britain in the late eighteenth and nineteenth centuries.

You will develop your skills and be able to:

❖ evaluate the usefulness of a source

❖ compare two sources by saying what they agree or disagree about

❖ put a source into context by saying how fully it describes an issue.

This topic is split into four sections:

❖ Health and housing

❖ Industry—textile factories and coal mines

❖ Transport—canals and railways

❖ Pressure for democratic reform up to 1867

Level 4 experiences and outcomes relevant to this topic:

I can evaluate conflicting sources of evidence to sustain a line of argument. **SOC 4-01a**

I have developed a sense of my heritage and identity as a British, European or global citizen and can present arguments about the importance of respecting the heritage and identity of others. **SOC 4-02a**

By studying groups in past societies who experienced inequality, I can explain the reasons for the inequality and evaluate how groups or individuals addressed it. **SOC 4-04a**

I can make reasoned judgements about how the exercise of power affects the rights and responsibilities of citizens by comparing a more democratic and a less democratic society. **SOC 4-04c**

I can present supported conclusions about the social, political and economic impacts of a technological change in the past. **SOC 4-05a**

I have investigated a meeting of cultures in the past and can analyse the impact on the societies involved. **SOC 4-05c**

I can assess the impact for those involved in a specific instance of the expansion of power and influence in the past. **SOC 4-06d**

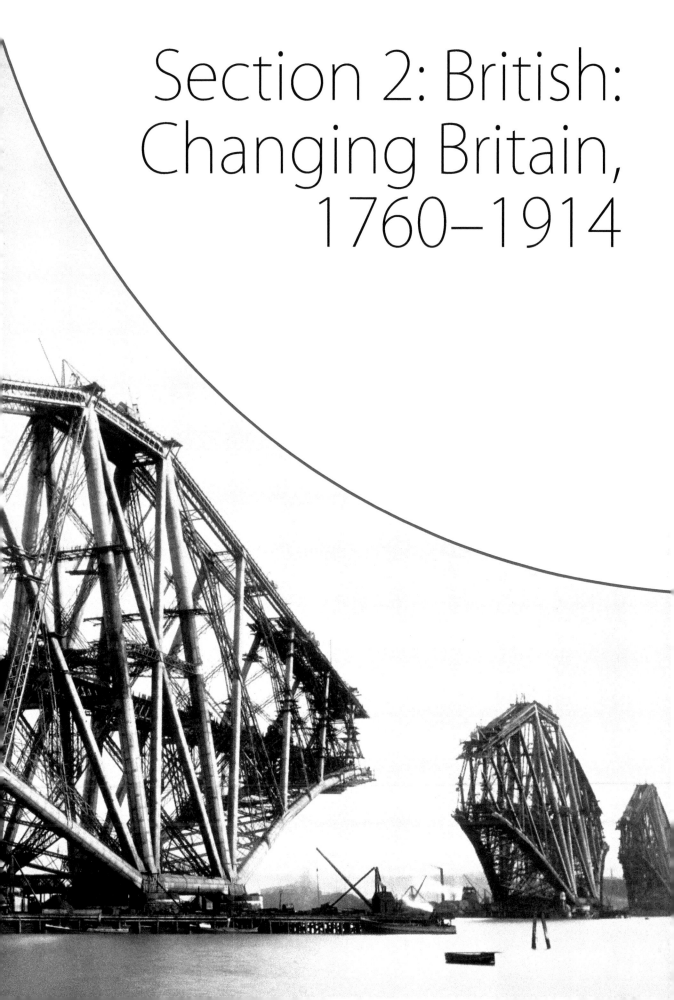

Section 2: British: Changing Britain, 1760–1914

Background

Make the Link

If you take Geography you will study population in detail.

Throughout the course of the latter half of the eighteenth century and the whole of the nineteenth century Britain's population grew substantially. The population of Scotland grew from about 1 250 000 in 1755 to almost 4 500 000 by 1900. The rise in population accompanied a change in the way people worked. By 1850, it is estimated that 80% of the population lived and worked in towns rather than in the countryside whereas a century earlier the reverse had been true. Health and housing became an issue as towns quickly grew in population and often did not have appropriate accommodation. Overcrowding led to the spread of disease and, for most of the working classes, living conditions were appalling. Slowly, improvements were made to living conditions.

Figure 1: *Glasgow Bridge, 1850. The bridge was built to accommodate the large volume of traffic carrying goods and people to factories in Glasgow from the docks and back again.*

The new industries like coal mining and textile production offered employment opportunities but the working conditions were dangerous and entailed working long hours for little pay. Parliamentary investigations led to improvements in working conditions and new industries brought a need for better transport to enable manufacturers to sell their goods throughout Britain and beyond. Canals grew out of a demand to be able to transport goods to the coast and railways opened up vast travel networks within Britain and transformed the way people lived, travelled and worked. The coming of the railways is often hailed by historians as one of the most important events to occur in the last 150 years as the impact and legacy it had on British history was so significant. The rise in population and change in living and working conditions prompted political reform. At the beginning of the nineteenth century few but the upper classes had the vote. The rise of the middle class meant that Parliament had to increase the franchise and many protests supported the idea of universal suffrage.

Key Word

- **Reform**

To improve or amend. In the case of this unit, reform means to change and improve the political, economic or social conditions for the people of Britain.

GO! Activity 1

Write down 'Changing Life in Britain, 1760–1914' in the middle of a piece of A3 paper. On separate branches of your mind map write down the following headings:

- **Health and housing**
- **Factories and coal mines**
- **Canals and railways**
- **Political reform**

You have 10 minutes to work with a partner to come up with anything you know about the headings above. Discuss your answers with the class to build a picture of what life was like in 1760 and what had changed by 1914.

1 Health and housing

In this section you will learn about:

- The reasons for problems of overcrowding, poor quality housing and subsequent medical problems.
- The improvements in housing and living conditions including slum clearances.
- The improvements in health including medical advances, piped water supply and public health.

Overcrowding, poor quality housing and subsequent medical problems

Between 1760 and 1914, the towns and cities of Britain grew rapidly. With the coming of the industrial revolution people favoured working in the towns and cities because of higher wages offered in the new industries. There were also fewer jobs in the countryside because of changes to technology in agriculture. Many people migrated from the Highlands to Lowland towns in search of work after the Highland Clearances. The Irish potato famine of 1845 had left thousands in need of food and work and many Irish families moved to Scotland to seek employment.

📖 Key Word

- **Industrial revolution**

The industrial revolution took place in eighteenth and nineteenth centuries and saw Britain change from an agrarian (farming) society where work was done by hand to a society that relied on machines and industry.

⁂ Make the Link

If you study 'Migration and Empire, 1830–1939' in Unit 1 you learn more about the movement of the rural population.

Figure 2: *Overcrowding quickly became a problem in the cities. This is an image of a Glasgow slum from 1868.*

Figure 3: *Overcrowding and poor conditions in tenement housing continued well into the 20th century.*

By 1851 more people lived in the towns than in the countryside. The houses that were provided for the new industrial workforce had been built in tenement style to accommodate as many people as possible and families would occupy just one room. As demand for housing grew, landlords often subdivided the rooms to rent out to other families. Rents stayed the same and living space got smaller. Landlords were not regulated by anybody and had no duty of care for their tenants. It did not matter to them if the conditions were not very good. Streets were narrowed so more houses could be built and people lived in damp and dirty conditions. Landlords could charge what they wanted and threatened tenants with eviction if they did not pay.

Figure 4: *Drawing of needy children going to the distribution of food in Sheffield in the mid-nineteenth century. Rubbish, excrement and household waste was just thrown into the street. There were no underground sewers, nor running water.*

Due to poor living conditions, disease was rife. In the nineteenth century the most common diseases were influenza, typhoid and TB (tuberculosis). Infant mortality was extremely common and life expectancy for most working class people would be between forty and fifty. Houses had been poorly planned and had little ventilation. They were damp and had no supply of running water. Any toilets would have been outside in the courtyard and could be shared by at least sixty other people. They were sometimes cleaned but there was no flush so the excrement would just sit in a hole in the ground. Water pumps were often built next to the toilets and middens (rubbish heaps), so water became contaminated with disease. In the early nineteenth century, no one had really made the connection with cleanliness and health so doctors were baffled by the high rate of illness among the working classes. They reported that it was a result of poverty but many

Make the Link

In Geography you will look at the conditions in slum housing in the developing world today.

middle and upper class people felt that the poor deserved no help. Food was also an issue – it was not only expensive but fresh, healthy food was in short supply.

Source A is from *Oliver Twist* by Charles Dickens, written in 1836.

> The filthiest, the strangest, the most extraordinary of the many localities that are hidden in London … maze of close, narrow, and muddy streets, thronged by the roughest and poorest of waterside people. Coal-whippers, brazen women, ragged children, and the very raff and refuse of the river.

GO! Activity 2

1. Account for the problem of overcrowding in the towns and cities in Britain by 1850.

Exam style questions

2. Describe, in detail, the reasons why diseases were common in nineteenth century industrial towns. **KU 4**

   (Unit outcomes: National 5: Outcome 2.1)

3. Evaluate the usefulness of **Source A** as a description of poor living conditions in London in the nineteenth century. **SH 5**

   (You may want to comment on who wrote it, when they wrote it, why they wrote it, what they say or what has been missed out.)

Of all the diseases none had the devastating effect of cholera. Cholera epidemics hit throughout the course of the nineteenth century, the most devastating being in 1831 and 1848.

A COURT FOR KING CHOLERA.

Figure 5: *This drawing shows the Punch cartoon, 'A Court for King Cholera'.*

Make the Link

In Health and Food Technology you will learn about a balanced, healthy diet.

GO! Activity 3

With a partner, discuss what the artist has drawn. What does he think are the main reasons for the spread of cholera?

Cholera was no respecter of social class. It caused the victim to suffer severe diarrhoea which led to dehydration and for most victims, death, within a matter of days.

Figure 6: *Cartoon about the contaminated water supply during a cholera outbreak.*

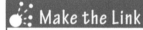

It spread throughout the towns and cities in Britain like wildfire. No one knew what to do – they burned the clothes of the victims, quarantined the bodies of those that had died from cholera and buried them together but nothing worked. When rich people began to die from the disease, the government took notice. There was a realisation that the unsanitary conditions many lived in could have something to do with the spread of disease. In fact, the disease was spread by cholera infected water. The disease had come over on merchant ships from Asia and spread from the docks of the north east. As it was spread through the water supply, cess pits and toilets full of excrement from cholera victims seeped through and contaminated the water supplies.

Activity 4

Imagine that you would like to be elected as a town councillor to the health and housing department.

Write a speech that you would give to encourage town dwellers to support you.

You should include information on the following:

- The main problems of living conditions in the town, with reference to **overcrowding** and **lack of sanitation**.
- The kind of problems these living conditions are giving rise to – **diseases** and **infant mortality**.
- What you propose to do about the appalling living conditions.

(Unit outcomes: National 4/5: Outcome 1.2)

Improvements in housing and living conditions

Cholera highlighted the extent of the poor living conditions for those in the towns and cities. Houses had been built so quickly that the authorities were sometimes unprepared and could not respond fast enough to the demand for proper sanitation and running water. There was no building regulation so conditions quickly deteriorated and no intervention from local authorities was required by law.

Source B is from John Robertson, *Report of the Committee on the Health of Towns*, 1840.

> Manchester has no building Act, and hence, with the exception of certain central streets, over which the police Act gives the commissioners power, each proprietor builds as he pleases … A cottage row may be badly drained, the streets may be full of pits, brimful of stagnant water, the receptacle of dead cats and dogs, yet no-one may find fault.

The government also took a 'laissez-faire' approach to people's lives.

Many people began to take an interest in the social reform of the poor. They wanted to improve the standards of living for the working classes and the prevention of disease. One such man was Edwin Chadwick.

Chadwick wrote a report in 1834 which looked at why people became sick in the tenements and slums. He concluded that sickness and disease caused poverty and that the way to prevent sickness would be to get rid of the filth. In 1842 the *Report on the Sanitary Conditions of the Labouring Population* was published under Chadwick's name. 10 000 copies were distributed and it was so popular another 20 000 had to be printed. The report highlighted conditions but also made recommendations about how to resolve the problems.

 Key Word

- **Laissez-faire**

This means that the government did not want to interfere and regulate people's lives. It means 'to do nothing'.

Figure 7: *Edwin Chadwick, social reformer.*

Source C is from the *Report on the Sanitary Conditions of the Labouring Population of Great Britain,* 1842.

> The most important measures to put in place] are drainage, the removal of all refuse of habitations, streets, and roads, and the improvement of the supplies of water … That for the prevention of the disease occasioned by defective ventilations, and other causes of impurity in places of work and other places where large numbers are assembled, and for the general promotion of the means necessary to prevent disease, that it would be good economy to appoint a district medical officer independent of private practice, and with the securities of social qualifications and responsibility to initiate sanitary measures.

Despite Chadwick's report, little was actually done by the government to introduce laws to help clean up Britain. Local authorities did put some measures in place. Manchester had a water supply by 1847 and Liverpool and London appointed medical inspectors in 1847 and 1848 respectively.

In 1848 there was another cholera epidemic and the government responded with the Public Health Act. This stated that local health boards could be set up if the demand was great enough. The boards could appoint an officer of health and could raise money to pay for proper sewerage systems and clean water supplies. However, local authorities did not actually have to enforce anything by the Act. Many people opposed the health boards. They saw it as unnecessary intervention in people's lives and did not want to pay higher taxes to pay for the changes.

Below is a list of some of the other Acts to be put in place over the course of the nineteenth century:

- 1855 Nuisance Removal Act. Overcrowded housing was made illegal.
- 1867 Public Health Act. Local authorities were responsible for sewers, water and street cleaning.
- 1868 Torrens Act. This Act encouraged the improvement of slum housing or its demolition.
- 1875 Artisans' and Labourers' Dwellings Act. House owners had to keep their houses and dwellings in good order, particularly if they were landlords. If they did not follow these conditions local authorities could buy and demolish the houses.
- 1875 Public Health Act. Medical officers were put in charge of public health. Slaughterhouses had to be looked after by local sanitary inspectors to ensure contaminated food was not sold. Sewers had to be looked after, fresh water supplied, rubbish collected and street lighting provided.

Activity 5

1. Take a sheet of A3 paper. Write down the following title:

   'Edwin Chadwick and Improvements in Public Health'

   - Write a short summary of Edwin Chadwick and how he was able to bring to public attention the problems with the living conditions in Britain.
   - Write down the details of each of the Acts.
   - In a different coloured pen, underneath each of the Acts, write down the difference you think the Act would have made to housing and living conditions of people in the nineteenth century.

   (Unit outcomes: National 4/5: Outcome 1.1)

Exam style question

2. Evaluate the usefulness of **Source C** to a historian investigating the reasons why Acts which aimed to improve public health were introduced in the nineteenth century.　　**SH 5**

   (You may want to comment on who wrote it, when they wrote it, why they wrote it, what they say or what has been missed out.)

Improvements in health

Health improved thanks to medical advances. Doctors took a long time to make the connection between dirt and disease but over the course of the nineteenth century advances in medical treatment including vaccines for smallpox were introduced. The use of antiseptics in hospital treatments and higher levels of cleanliness meant that people had a better chance of surviving illness.

Better training for doctors, nurses and midwives meant that people who entered hospital had a better chance of survival.

The improvements in public services and provisions made for better sanitation and clean water helped to improve the health of the nation.

Outbreaks of cholera in London in the nineteenth century, along with the Great Stink of 1858 (the Thames was so clogged with filth Parliament called it a crisis), meant a solution to London's unhealthy living conditions was required. Bazalgette engineered a new type of sewer – he designed it in the shape of an upturned egg so that the effluence would run away from the streets and could be deposited out of the city. Modern sewerage systems were based on this design.

The need for a clean water supply became important. Water pumps that were not in any way connected to the sewerage system became an increasing feature throughout towns and cities. Town councils became more involved in people's lives to ensure such provisions could be made.

📖 Key Word

- **Antiseptic**

Antiseptics prevent wounds from becoming infected and aid the healing process.

Figure 8: *Joseph Bazalgette designed London's modern sewerage system.*

Activity 6

Exam style question

Explain the reasons why public health was able to improve over the course of the nineteenth century.　　**KU 6**

(Unit outcomes: National 4/5: Outcome 2.2)

⚬ Make the Link

If you study Design and Manufacture you may learn about the theories behind practical designs such as this.

2 Industry—textile factories and coal mines

In this section you will learn about:

- The impact of technology and legislation on textile factories and coal mines.
- The impact of the Factory Acts and Mines Act.
- Improvements to working conditions.

Figure 9: Over London by Rail *by Gustave Doré shows the factories and living conditions of London, 1870.*

The impact of technology and legislation on textile factories and coal mines

Many people worked in the textile factories and coal mines. The working conditions in the factories and mines were generally regarded as being poor and often dangerous. Men, women and children worked in harsh conditions for little pay. Often the whole family would work to try to make ends meet.

Textile factories

In 1831 a Royal Commission was set up by Parliament to investigate the working conditions and child labour in the factories of Britain. Below is some of the evidence given to the Royal Commission and other sources about factory life in the early nineteenth century.

Source D: rules in a north of England factory:

> Doors will be closed 10 minutes after the engine starts and no weaver will be admitted until breakfast time.
>
> Weavers leaving the room without the permission of the overseer while the engine is running, fined 3d.
>
> All shuttles, wheels, brushes, oilcans, windows found broken will be paid for by the weaver.
>
> Any worker found talking, whistling or singing will be fined.
>
> Any worker opening a window will be fined.

Source E: evidence of a Leeds factory worker to the Royal Commission in 1832.

> Q: How were the children kept working?
>
> A: Sometimes the overseers would tap them over the head, or nip them over the nose, or give them a pinch of snuff, or throw water in their faces, or pull or jab them about.

Source F: evidence of Samuel Coulson to the Royal Commission in 1832.

> Q: At what time, when it was busy, did the girls go into the mill?
>
> A: At the busy time, for about six weeks, they have gone at 3 o'clock in the morning, and ended at ten, or nearly half past at night.
>
> Q: What intervals were allowed for rest and refreshment?
>
> A: Breakfast, a quarter of an hour, and dinner, half an hour, and drinking, quarter of an hour.

Source G: Elizabeth Bentley, evidence to the Royal Commission, 1832.

> Q: Did [working in the factory] affect your health?
>
> A: Yes, it was so dusty, the dust got on my lungs, and the work was so hard; I was middling strong when I went there, but the work was so bad; I got so bad in health, that when I pulled the baskets, I pulled the bones out of their places.

📖 Key Word

- **Royal Commission**

A parliamentary group which conducted investigations into, for example, the working conditions in factories. Their findings would often shape future legislation on the issue they had investigated.

Key Words

- **Scavenger**

A child employed to pick up scraps of material or loose threads from underneath the machinery.

- **Piecer**

An older child or woman employed to keep the spinning thread tied together.

Figure 10 and Source H: *An illustration of* scavengers *and* piecers *at work, 1840.*

GO! Activity 7

Using the evidence in this section, imagine you work for the Royal Commission and have been asked to produce a report into the working conditions and child labour in Britain's factories. You need to include:

- Details of the conditions in the factories.
- One piece of evidence from each **source, D–H** to illustrate the conditions.
- Your recommendations to Parliament about what needs to be done to improve conditions.

(Unit outcomes: National 4/5: Outcome 1.2)

Coal mines

Coal mining had existed in Scotland for hundreds of years and by 1760 at least 500 000 tons of coal were being produced annually. As the industrial revolution gathered pace, the demand for coal increased.

GO! Activity 8

1. With a partner write down all the things you think coal was, and is, used for.
2. Share your ideas with the rest of the class.
3. Add any answers from the text below to your notes.

Coal was used in the industrial revolution as a source of energy – for driving the steam engines of the new machinery of the factories as well as powering trains and steam ships. Coal was also used for domestic purposes – to heat homes. Coal became one of Scotland's largest exports with coal being transported for sale in Europe. Most coal was cut by hand.

Once the mine was dug the main job was to cut the coal. This was done by hewers, normally adult males who cut the coal by hand, using pick axes. It was back breaking work and so hot in the mine shaft that hewers would often work naked. Working in the mine shafts brought dangers such as suffocation, the risk of drowning from flooding, death by inhalation of carbon monoxide and explosions from a build-up of methane gas. Roof falls were common.

Figure 11: *Illustration of a hewer.*

Different kinds of dangerous gases were given different nicknames.

- Black damp: not poisonous or flammable but reduced the amount of oxygen in the mines. In earlier mines, small fires would be lit to create ventilation in the form of a draft to reduce black damp.

- Fire damp: methane gas, highly flammable and caused many explosions.

- White damp: carbon monoxide. No smell and no colour, difficult to detect. Miners took canaries into the shafts to help detect carbon monoxide as they would die quite quickly and alert the miners of the presence of this dangerous gas.

Figure 12: *Illustration of a bearer.*

Bearers carried the coal from the hewers to the coal surface and were mostly women and older children. It was heavy and dangerous work – there was a risk that coal could fall onto the person below. Bearers were expected to carry up to 170 lb on their backs from the bottom of the coal shaft to the top. Disfigurement and dislocated shoulders were common.

Children also worked in the mine. Older children would carry the coal and transport it along the mine shafts in carts but even the youngest at age three or four were put to work as trappers, opening and closing the doors of the mine shafts to keep them ventilated. The youngest children would be scared as they spent their time in the dark alone. Their health also suffered. They developed rickets due to lack of sunlight and also breathing problems which were associated with working in the mines – the 'black spit' affected many coal workers.

Figure 13: *A bearer with falling coal.*

🔍 Hint

170 lb is about 12 stones or 77 kilos. Do you think you could carry this?

📖 Key Word

- **Black spit**

So called because of a build-up of coal dust in the lungs.

Figure 14: *The trapper is opening the door.*

GO! Activity 9

Copy and complete the following table using the information on the previous page.

JOB	DETAILS OF WORK	DANGERS
Hewer		
Bearer		
Trapper		

(Unit outcomes: National 4/5: Outcome 1.2)

The 1842 Royal Commission on Children's Employment set out to investigate the conditions of the children working in the mines.

Source I is from the 1842 Royal Commission on Children's Employment: Ellison Jack, 11 years old, coal-bearer:

> I have been working below three years on my father's account; he takes me down at two in the morning and I come up at one and two next afternoon. I go to bed at six at night to be ready for work next morning … I have to bear my burthen up four traps, or ladders, before I get to the main road which leads to the pit bottom. My task is four to five tubs; each tub holds 4·25cwt. I fill five tubs in twenty journeys. I have had the strap when I did not do my bidding.

Source J is also from the 1842 Royal Commission on Children's Employment: Jane Duncan, sixteen years of age, coal-bearer:

> Began to carry coals when twelve years old. Went to school prior and can read and write. Do not like the work, nor do the other women, many of whom have wrought from eight years of age and know no other. My employment is carrying coals from wall-face to the daylight up the stair-pit. I make forty to fifty journeys a day and can carry 2 cwt as my burthen. Some females carry 2·5 to 3 cwt, but it is overstraining.

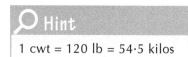

🔍 Hint

1 cwt = 120 lb = 54·5 kilos

GO! Activity 10

Exam style questions

1. Evaluate the usefulness of **Source I** when investigating the working conditions in the mines in the nineteenth century.　　　　**SH 5**

   (You may want to comment on who wrote it, when they wrote it, why they wrote it, what they say or what has been missed out.)

2. Compare **Source I** and **Source J** about the working conditions in the mines in the nineteenth century.　　　　**SH 4**

   (Compare the information overall and/or in detail.)

3. How fully does **Source J** describe the jobs done in the mine in the nineteenth century?　　　　**SH 6**

   (Use **Source J** and recall.)

The impact of the Factory Acts and Mines Act

Factory Acts

In response to the Royal Commission the Factory Act of 1833 came into being. The details were as follows:

- The working day was to start at 5.30 a.m. and finish at 8.30 p.m.
- A young person (aged 13 to 18) might not be employed beyond any period of twelve hours, less one and a half for meals.
- Children (aged 9 to 13) could not work beyond any period of nine hours.
- Children were not allowed to work overnight:
  from 8.30 p.m.–5.30 a.m.

The Act was not always welcomed by families. Reducing the working hours of children meant less money for the family.

Further Acts passed included:

1844 Labour in Factories Act:

- Factories were to have inspectors and surgeons appointed.
- Machinery was required to be guarded.
- The age at which children may be employed was reduced from nine to eight years.

The Factory Act of 1847:

- Women and children between the ages of 13 and 18 could work only 63 hours per week.
- From 1848, women and children aged 13–18 could work only 58 hours per week, the equivalent of 10 hours per day.

1850 Factory Act:

- Working day increased to 10 and a half hours.

1878 Factory Act:

- No child under 10 to be employed.
- 10–14 year olds on half-days only.
- Women restricted to 56 hours work per week.

1891 Factory and Workshop Act:

- Extended safety and sanitary regulations.
- Raised the minimum age for employment in factories to 11 years.
- Prohibited the owner of a factory from knowingly employing a woman within four weeks of giving birth.

Mines Act

In the coal mines, the main Act passed was the 1842 Mines and Collieries Act, usually known as the Mines Act.

1842 Mines Act:

- No female was to be employed underground.
- No boy under 10 years old was to be employed underground.

There were other changes made to the mines. In 1864 the 'Gartsherrie' coal cutter was introduced meaning not all coal had to be cut by hand. Originally the mine shafts were held up with wooden props; these were replaced by metal ones and the winding gear of the lifts was refined for safety. The introduction of steam power meant that coal carts were pulled by steam engines and steam operated pumps kept the pits free of excess water. The Davy Safety Lamp was introduced in 1815 by Humphrey Davy and was designed to allow the flame within to burn a different colour should it detect inflammable gas. However, it did not give off a great deal of light so many miners continued to used naked flames despite the dangers.

GO! Activity 11

1. a) Research online the safety methods that were introduced over the course of the nineteenth century to improve the conditions in the mines.

   b) Work in groups of four. Create four separate posters, one covering each of the following areas for 'improvement':
   - cutting the coal and roof falls
   - ventilation and gas
   - transporting the coal
   - flood prevention.

   c) Each person should produce an information poster, including pictures, on their chosen heading. Once complete, together you will have a visual representation of the safety improvements in the mines.

   (Unit outcomes: National 4/5: Outcome 1.2)

Exam style questions

2. Explain the reasons why there was a need to improve the safety of working conditions in the mines. **KU 6**

   (Unit outcomes: National 4/5: Outcome 2.2)

3. Describe, in detail, the changes made to safety in the mines. **KU 4**

   (Unit outcomes: National 4/5: Outcome 2.1)

Limitations of the improvements to working conditions

Despite the fact that Acts were passed in both factories and mining, by 1900 working conditions in both remained difficult and dangerous. Innovations in factories such as the change from water-powered machinery like Arkwright's water frame and Crompton's spinning mule to the new steam-powered machines only brought more complications and dangers. The Acts put in place to improve the conditions in factories were circumvented and the need to earn money put many families in a difficult position if their children could not work.

Mining remained dangerous well into the twentieth and twenty-first centuries. Although many mines were closed throughout the twentieth century, culminating in mass closures in the 1980s, the same safety problems of dangerous gas, roof falls and explosions remained.

> ### Hint
>
> The UK miner's strike of 1984–85 was in direct response to government proposals to close twenty mines which would put 20 000 miners and whole communities out of work. The struggle between the National Union of Miners and the government lasted until 1985 when the government won and the mine closures went ahead. The power of the NUM was significantly reduced and further closures followed until by 2013, there were only three deep-pit mines left in the whole of the UK. Further pit closures are scheduled.

3 Transport—canals and railways

In this section you will learn about:

- The reasons for the decline of canals.
- The building of the railways and the development of the railway networks.
- The impact of these transport networks on society and the economy.

Reasons for the decline of canals

The period between 1770 and 1830 is often known as the 'Golden Age' of canals. Canals used man-built waterways to transport goods. They were run by companies who competed to control key industrial areas so they could make money out of the need to transport goods around Britain. Canals were built by navigators (navvies) who were often Irish immigrants. Many were single men but many also worked and travelled with their families. In Scotland the main canals were the Forth and Clyde Canal and the Union Canal which linked Edinburgh and Glasgow allowing quick transport of goods from the industrial west to the east for sale or export to Europe. However, as industry grew, the need to transport goods quickly necessitated the rise of a quicker method of transport.

The rise of the steam engine eclipsed the capability of water power in the factories and it did the same in transport. Trains were quicker, cheaper and less reliant on the weather. Further, although both canals and railways were dependent on there being a canal or rail network at their chosen destination, it became clear that railways had much greater potential for increased network size than canals. Those that had invested in canals turned their investments into rail instead.

GO! Activity 12

Write down the heading 'Reasons for the decline of the canals'.

1. What advantages did canals give to the industrialists?
2. What was a navvy?
3. Why was the building of the Union canal such an important event in Scottish industrial history?
4. Give 2 well explained reasons for the decline in canals.

The building of the railways and the development of the railway networks

THE BRIDGE AS SEEN FROM THE WEST.

Figure 15: *The iconic Forth Rail Bridge under construction in the 1880s.*

The idea of putting a carriage on rails was not new. Trucks and rails had been used in mines for years and with the introduction of the steam engine the idea grew that steam engines could pull trucks on land to transport goods. It would be quicker, more reliable and cheaper than the canals. Richard Trevithick first demonstrated the idea of putting a steam engine on rail tracks in 1808. George Stephenson revealed his now infamous 'Rocket' in 1829. He had already designed the first public rail service between Stockton and Darlington a few years earlier.

Figure 16: *Stephenson's 'Rocket'.*

In 1830, the Manchester to Liverpool line was opened and carried over 1000 passengers a day. It could travel at 30 m.p.h. – very fast for its time. New investors saw that this method of transport would return big profits. Landowners could charge large sums of money for any track laid on their land. However, this new introduction was not welcomed by everyone. Many people were afraid of the new high-speed travel – there was concern over what such speeds could do to the human body. Those who ran coaches and canals quickly realised they were going to lose out to this new method of transport and transferred investments to the railways. Farmers disliked the railways because they thought the smoke the steam engines billowed as they passed the fields would ruin crops and livestock.

Make the Link

You may learn more about steam power in Science.

GO! Activity 13

1. Divide your page into two. On the left hand side write the heading 'Reasons why railways were welcome' and on the other write 'Reasons why railways were not welcome'.

2. Using the information from this section, divide the reasons into the appropriate column.

3. Add in any extra reasons you can think of that have not been mentioned above.

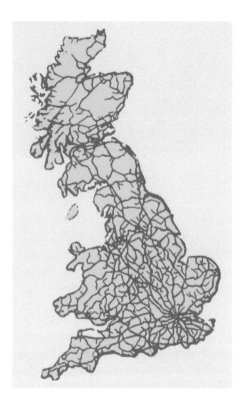

Figure 17: *British Rail Network, c. 1900.*

Hint

Railway transport is as popular as ever with the 2012 figure estimating that around 1 460 000 000 passengers used the British railway service network that year.

The network of railways in Britain grew rapidly throughout the nineteenth century. Everyone could travel by rail – even the working class, as third class fares were available. They did have to travel in open carriages though with no protection from the smoke or the rain. The 1844 Railway Act changed conditions for third class rail travellers making sure the rail companies provided shelter and seats. This meant that many working class people could now travel for work as it was affordable and so the idea of 'commuting' began. Smaller towns were linked with larger lines meaning that smaller industrial towns like Hawick in the Scottish Borders could have raw goods, such as wool, transported to the town and they could export knitwear in high numbers to other British towns and to the ports for export abroad. Small towns could offer employment opportunities to their inhabitants without them having to leave for the bigger cities to find work. Railway gauges were standardised so that trains could operate on any line in the country – the standard of 4 feet 8·5 inches was set by the Railway Act of 1846. Further, Greenwich Mean Time was established so that trains could run on time throughout Britain.

MIDLAND RAILWAY, ROWSLEY AND BUXTON EXTENSION.
CONTRACT No. 1.

THE BIG CUTTING, SOUTH ENTRANCE TO DOVE HOLES TUNNEL.

Figure 18: *Navvies in the cutting at the south entrance to Dove Holes tunnel on the Midland Railway.*

Being a navvy was a dangerous job – rails could only be built in relatively straight lines so hills, mountains, rivers all had to be navigated successfully. The work was largely done by hand with pick axe and shovel. The navvies laid extensive tracks for the railway engines and also built railway embankments, tunnels, viaducts and bridges to allow the trains to travel over naturally occurring obstacles as well as rail stations for passenger safety.

Being a navvy was dangerous work but it was often well paid. Navvies often had a reputation for spending their money on alcohol and creating trouble wherever they set up camp. However, although this was true in many cases, many navvies were not young, single men and often had their families travelling with them wherever they worked on the railway. It may be that the navvy has been given a bad reputation in history whereas perhaps they should be celebrated for the achievement of laying the railway network of Britain which allowed the country to be so industrially successful.

> **🔍 Hint**
>
> Railways were also built by 'navvies'. They were normally Irish immigrants, especially after 1845 when they immigrated to Scotland to find work after the Irish potato famine.

> **⁛ Make the Link**
>
> If you study Modern Studies you will learn more about stereotypes of social classes.

MIDLAND RAILWAY. EXTENSION TO LONDON
CONTRACT No. 1.
BRICK MAKING MACHINE.

Figure 19: *Navvies using a brickmaking machine during the construction of the Midland Railway's extension.*

🔵 Activity 14

Write the heading 'The Rise of the Railways' and answer the following questions in full sentences.

1. What was the purpose of the 1844 Railway Act?

2. Why were these changes necessary?

3. Give an example of a small town which benefited from the coming of the railways and explain how it benefited.

4. What did railway gauges do?

5. Why was Greenwich Mean Time introduced?

6. What were the railway navigators responsible for building?

7. Why did the navvies often have a bad reputation?

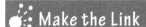

Impact of these transport networks on society and the economy

Both the coming of the canals and the railways had a large impact on society and the economy of Britain.

Canals were invested in at a rapid rate and many people became rich from the profits made from charging industrialists to use their canals. Canals could transport goods in large quantities quicker than could be done by horse-drawn cart so manufacturers increased their export network within Britain quickly. Further, goods could be easily transported to the coast for export abroad. Items in high demand could be transported quickly. Coal could be transported easily and as such after the introduction of the canals the price of coal in Manchester fell by two thirds. Between 1770 and 1830, considered the Golden Age for the canals, rival companies competed heavily for business. The Worcester and Birmingham Canal Company and the Birmingham Canal Navigations Main Line Company both ran their canals so close to each other that at one point they only ran seven feet apart. Canals meant industrial goods could be transported quicker and in larger numbers which fuelled the rise of industry even further. However, the transportation of coal and development of steam power meant that the canals eventually fell in favour of the railways.

Railways benefited the coal and iron companies when they were being built, and other industries like shipbuilding became reliant on the railways to transport quantities of iron to the shipyards for them to use. The bridges, viaducts and extensive tracks of rail all used raw goods like iron in their construction. The construction of the railways themselves employed about 60 000 people and afterwards jobs like train drivers, station masters and porters provided employment for thousands. Other industries like the Border woollen mills benefited as well, as they could transport their goods elsewhere in Britain and to the coast for export to Europe. Farmers and fishermen could now transport their goods quickly so fresh fish, milk, vegetables, fruit and meat were available to the new industrial towns. Farmers could also sell their livestock easily as they could be transported by rail. Shopping facilities improved in the towns. The spread of news increased rapidly. The post could be delivered quickly and the newspaper industry boomed. People could go on holiday. For many, it may only have been for a day but outings to Portobello and North Berwick meant that those previously denied leisure time away from the home could now enjoy this because of cheap rail fares.

> ### Make the Link
>
> In Business Management you will learn about how goods are transported now.

Figure 20: *Portobello sands.*

Figure 21: *Poster produced for London & North Eastern Railway (LNER) to promote rail travel to North Berwick.*

GO! Activity 15

1. Take an A3 piece of paper. On one side, create a mind map with 'Social changes brought by the canals and railways.' Find the social changes brought by the canals and railways and write them down.

2. On the other side of the paper write down 'Economic changes brought by the canals and railways.' Find the economic changes brought by the canals and railways and write them down.

   (Unit outcomes: National 4/5: Outcome 1.1)

Exam style question

3. Complete one of the following N5 style essay questions:
   - To what extent did Britain benefit from the social and economic impact of the railways? **KU 9**
   - To what extent did the rise of British industry depend on the development of the railways?

     KU 9

   (Unit outcomes: National 5: Outcome 2.3)

4 Pressure for democratic reform up to 1867

In this section you will learn about:

- Radical unrest at Peterloo.
- The 1832 Reform Act.
- The work of the Chartists.
- Reasons for the 1867 Reform Act and the extent of democratic change it brought.
- Reasons for the 1884 Reform Act and the extent of democratic change it brought.

Radical unrest, 1815–1822

In 1760, few people could vote. Voting was the reserved right of upper class males. This meant that in Britain very few people had a political voice. The old political system was unfair and corrupt and only benefited the rich landowners. Demands for change came from the working class whose spokesmen were Radicals like Henry Hunt and William Cobbett. The new middle classes also wanted the vote. They felt that because they had made money in the industrial revolution which had benefited Britain then they should have a say in the governing of the country. Some politicians favoured political reform. The French Revolution had shown them the political power of the masses and they worried that lack of reform could lead to revolution in Britain. Changes were generally favoured by the Whigs (Liberals). The Conservatives (Tories) were generally against reform. Most were landowners and the existing system suited them. They believed that no other class of person other than the landowners was fit for government.

However, protests between 1815 and 1822 showed that people's attitude towards political reform had hardened and many believed that change could only be achieved by force or by an Act of Parliament. The period of time between 1815 and 1822 was known as a period of Radicalism.

In 1815 the Corn Laws were passed, which raised the price of bread. This was very unpopular with the working classes but also the middle classes who claimed that trade and industry would suffer. It was the perfect example of a few people in a position of power making decisions on behalf of the masses. The Radicals, led by Henry Hunt and William Cobbett, began to form an opposition. They organised meetings, marches and rallies. The Spa Field riot in 1816 was one of the first examples of Radical action and, although it did not come to much, it highlighted to Parliament the level of discontent at the lack of political reform. One extreme case was the Cato Street conspiracy – a plot to blow up the Prime Minister and the cabinet and take over the

📖 Key Word

- **Radical**
Anyone who wanted to change the existing system of government.

Figure 22: *William Cobbett, Radical reformer.*

☄ Make the Link

In Modern Studies you learn about who has the right to vote today.

country by force. However, they were found out and their leader, Arthur Thistlewood and four conspirators, were executed.

The Peterloo Massacre, 1819

Some of the protests that took place ended up in violence and were known as the radical wars. A famous example is the Peterloo Massacre, a protest meeting that ended in tragedy. On 6 August 1819 over 50 000 people had come to St Peter's Field in Manchester to hear Radicals like Henry Hunt speak. The local authorities were worried about the size and scale of the protest so sent in the cavalry to break it up. However, instead of being members of the actual army the 'cavalry' were made up of local shop workers and merchants. Over 400 people were injured and an estimated eleven people died. It was very clear that the government was worried that political protests might develop into a more dangerous situation or a revolution.

Source K is from Samuel Bamford, *Passages in the Life of a Radical*, 1864.

> On the cavalry drawing up they were received with a shout of goodwill, as I understood it. They shouted again, waving their sabres over their heads; and then, slackening rein, and striking spur into their steeds, they dashed forward and began cutting the people.

Figure 23: *Execution scene of the Cato Street conspirators.*

Key Words

- **Massacre**
An indiscriminate killing of many people.

Many people were shocked by what happened at Peterloo – a peaceful protest had ended in massacre. Following the massacre, despite the outcry, the authorities did not issue any reforms that made politics fairer but instead made it more difficult for people to protest.

Activity 16

1. Describe three reasons why the Radicals wanted political change in Britain.
2. Explain why those in power were reluctant for change to take place.
3. Give the details of the Spa Field riot and the Cato Street conspiracy and explain how they showed political unrest.
4. Describe the details of Peterloo.
5. What was the effect of the Peterloo Massacre?

Exam style question

6. Evaluate the usefulness of **Source K** to a historian studying the events at Peterloo.   **SH 5**

   (You may want to comment on who wrote it, when they wrote it, why they wrote it, what they say or what has been missed out.)

The 1832 Reform Act

Despite the protests and harsh treatment of protesters it took until 1832 before any real political change was implemented with the Great Reform Act of 1832.

Before the Act, Scotland had 45 MPs in total and voters numbered about 4500 out of a population of 2 500 000. The rules for voting in the countryside and the towns were different and depended on a property qualification.

The Whigs (Liberals) introduced the bill for change in 1830 and despite Tory opposition won support elsewhere. It was passed in 1832.

The Act did the following:

- Seats were distributed more fairly – the new industrial towns became better represented and the number of rotten burghs (towns that had few people but still returned MPs to Parliament) was significantly reduced.
- The number of those who could vote in Scotland increased to 65 000 – the vote was largely given to the new middle classes and merchants.
- In the counties (countryside) the vote was given to owners of land worth £10 per annum or £10 long-term leaseholders and £50 short-term leaseholders.
- In the burghs (towns) the vote was given to householders of property worth £10 per annum.

The changes that the Act made seem pretty moderate but at the time they were radical. However, the Act failed to achieve:

- votes for the working class
- votes for women
- abolition of rotten burghs
- an end to voting in public, leaving elections still open to bribery and corruption.

Radicals felt that the Act did not go far enough. Much of the unrest in Britain had been caused by people's appalling living and working conditions and the Radicals believed the only way to resolve this was by gaining representation for the working classes in Parliament and giving working class men the vote.

The work of the Chartists

The Chartist movement was founded in 1838. They came up with the 'People's Charter'.

It outlined six simple points for parliamentary reform:

1. Voting rights for every man over twenty one.
2. A secret ballot so voting would not have to be public.
3. No property qualifications for MPs.
4. Payment of MPs.
5. Constituencies of equal size.
6. Yearly elections for Parliament.

> **GO! Activity 17**
>
> 1. Describe the political situation in Britain before 1832.
> 2. Give two reasons why the Reform Act may have been put in place.
> 3. Make a note of the changes the Act brought.
> 4. What did the Act fail to do?

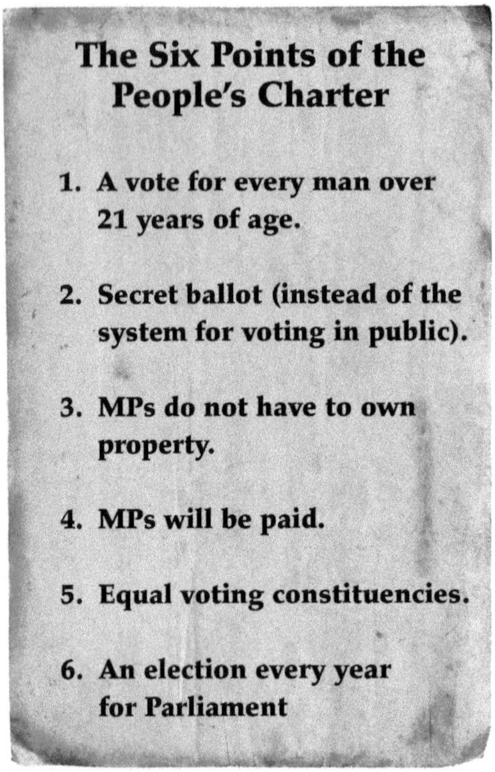

The Six Points of the People's Charter

1. **A vote for every man over 21 years of age.**

2. **Secret ballot (instead of the system for voting in public).**

3. **MPs do not have to own property.**

4. **MPs will be paid.**

5. **Equal voting constituencies.**

6. **An election every year for Parliament**

Figure 24: *The six points of the People's Charter.*

GO! Activity 18

For each of the points of the 'People's Charter' explain how you think this would make Britain more democratic.

(Unit outcomes: National 4/5: Outcome 1.1)

Figure 25: *William Lovett, leader of the Chartists.*

Protests occurred throughout the nineteenth century to try to have the changes outlined by the Chartists put in place. Petitions were submitted on a regular basis but were always rejected by Parliament.

The Chartists had some good ideas for reform, most of which were implemented throughout the course of the nineteenth century. However, they largely failed to have these reforms implemented sooner because of in-fighting. Some Chartists, such as William Lovett, were in favour of peaceful protests but others like Fergus O'Connor were in favour of more violent methods. In Glasgow, the campaigns were often violent, for example the Bread Riots of 1848 where five people were shot after demanding 'bread or revolution'.

Reasons why the Chartists failed to have parliamentary reform implemented sooner include:

- Lack of being able to agree on the best method of protest – some believed in violence, some in peaceful protest.

- Too many leaders – Chartist movements all over the country suffered from too many leaders and too many ideas about how to achieve change.

- Too radical. What they proposed was extreme for the time and it would take years of persuasion for some of the changes to be made.

- Economic improvement – the Chartists had been popular during times of economic difficulty but when the economic situation improved, support for Chartism disappeared.

- The Third Petition submitted to Parliament protesting for change contained 6 000 000 signatures. However, it was discredited as many of the signatures had been forged.

Figure 26: *Fergus O'Connor, Irish leader of the Chartists.*

> ###  Activity 19
>
> **Exam style question**
>
> 'The Chartists were too ambitious for their time.'
>
> To what extent is the above statement the main reason why the Chartist campaign failed? **KU 9**
>
> **(Unit outcomes: National 5: Outcome 2.3)**

The 1867 Reform Act

Reasons for the 1867 Reform Act

In 1866 the Whigs introduced a new reform bill. They were swiftly defeated in Parliament and the Tories took over at the next election. The Tories knew there was a mood for change in Britain so they decided to 'dish the Whigs' by 'stealing the Liberals' clothes'. This meant the Tories were going to steal and use the Liberals' policies to their political advantage. The Act was passed in 1867 and became known as the Second Reform Act.

What democratic change did the 1867 Reform Act bring about?

1867 Reform Act achieved the following:

- Vote was given to male adult householders but also to lodgers paying £10 or more in rent.

- In the counties owners of land worth £5 per year and tenants paying £14 per year got the vote.

- Representation was balanced – thirty five boroughs lost one of their MPs, seventeen boroughs lost both MPs. The counties were given twenty five extra MPs and large cities were given a third MP.

- The number of MPs in forty five burghs with a population under 10 000 went from two to one.

- The number of Scottish constituencies rose from fifty three to sixty.

The main effects were:

- Some working class men now had the vote.
- The electorate doubled in number to 2 500 000.

It failed to:

- give all working class men the vote
- give any women at all the vote
- introduce a secret ballot.

In spite of its shortfalls, the 1867 Act was more radical in its changes than probably either the Whigs or the Tories had intended. The Conservative Prime Minister Benjamin Disraeli had called the Act a 'leap in the dark' as he was unsure about what the effects of the Act might be. Although it did not revolutionise the political landscape, the 1867 Act paved the way for future reform as more men in Britain had a political voice.

Figure 27: *This Punch cartoon from 1867 shows the 'leap in the dark'.*

The 1884 Reform Act

Reasons for the 1884 Reform Act

By 1884 it became apparent that there was still a desire for further reform. Protests in Scotland in 1884 advocated for further extension of the franchise and better representation in parliament. Also, there was increasing demand that voting rights in the towns should be the same as in the countryside. The Prime Minister, William Gladstone (Liberal) was very aware that extending the franchise further would possibly reward him and his party with votes in future elections. Popular support for the Liberal party, therefore, was a driving reason behind the 1884 Reform Act.

The 1884 Act achieved the following:

- All male adult householders and men who rented unfurnished lodgings to the value of £10 a year were given the vote in both the boroughs and the counties.

The main effects were:

- Franchise extended to 5.5 million men – about 60% of men had the vote.
- The vote went to householders and lodgers: the middle classes and many working class men had the vote for the first time.

It failed to:

- Give women the vote
- Redistribute seats.

Overall the 1884 Act responded to a population growth and protestors asking for a further extension in the franchise and better representation. Importantly, the franchise was no longer considered a class privilege. Although women were ignored, the change to increase the right to vote and to equalise the voting qualification in the boroughs and counties at least showed the government were open to the ideas of change and responding to protests, even if it only seemed like it was inching very slowly towards universal suffrage.

> **GO!** **Activity 20**
>
> 1. Explain what is meant by the terms 'dishing the Whigs' and 'stealing the Liberals' clothes'.
> 2. Describe the changes brought in by the 1867 Reform Act and the 1884 Reform Act.
> 3. Explain the effects of the 1867 Reform Act and the 1884 Reform Act.
> 4. What still needed to be done to make Britain more democratic after 1867?
> 5. What still needed to be done to make Britain more democratic after 1867?
>
> **Exam style questions**
>
> 6. To what extent did the radical wars improve the political landscape of Britain? **KU 9**
> 7. To what extent did the Reform Acts of 1832, 1867 and 1884 make Britain more democratic? **KU 9**
>
> **(Unit outcomes: National 5: Outcome 2.3)**

Summary

In this topic you have learned:

- the reasons for overcrowding in the towns and cities
- the reasons for the spread of disease in the towns and cities
- the role of Edwin Chadwick
- the improvements made to towns and cities and their impact
- the working conditions in the mines and factories
- the improvements made in the mines and factories
- the effects of the improvements made in the mines and factories
- the reason for the decline in the use of the canal network
- the economic and social benefits of the railways
- the events of the radical wars
- the effects of the 1832, 1867 and 1884 Reform Acts.

You should have developed your skills and be able to:

- evaluate the usefulness of a source
- compare two sources by saying what they agree or disagree about
- put a source into context by saying how fully it describes an issue.

Learning Checklist

Now that you have finished **Changing Britain, 1760–1914**, complete a self-evaluation of your knowledge and skills to assess what you have understood. Use traffic lights to help you make up a revision plan to help you improve in the areas you identified as red or amber.

- Describe the problems of overcrowding and unsanitary conditions in the towns and cities.

- Explain the reasons why poor housing occurred.

- Describe how men like Edwin Chadwick worked to improve conditions.

- Explain the improvements that were made and their effects.

- Describe the working conditions inside the mines and the factories.

- Explain the effects of the improvements that were made in the mines and the factories.

- Explain why the need for the canals was replaced with a need for railways.

- Describe the building of the railways.

- Describe the social and economic benefits of the railways.

- Describe the events of the period of Radicalism at Peterloo.

- Explain why the Chartist movement was so important.

- Explain the effects of the 1832, 1867 and 1884 Reform Acts.

Studying this topic will provide you with a good understanding of the collapse of imperial rule in Russia and the establishing of communist government. It will focus on the different political ideas that began to emerge in Russia in this period, as well as the conflict between those who had been in power for many years and those who had little power in Russian society. Above all, this course will allow you to investigate the ways in which social and economic changes in society often lead to major political changes, using Russia in this period as an example.

You will develop your skills and be able to:

❖ evaluate the usefulness of a source

❖ compare two sources by saying what they agree or disagree about

❖ put a source into context by saying how fully it describes an issue.

This topic is split into four sections:

❖ Imperial Russia—government and people

❖ The 1905 Revolution—causes, events and effects

❖ The February Revolution—causes, events and effects

❖ The October Revolution—causes, events and effects

Level 4 experiences and outcomes relevant to this topic:

I have developed a sense of my heritage and identity as a British, European or global citizen and can present arguments about the importance of respecting the heritage and identity of others. **SOC 4-02a**

By studying groups in past societies who experienced inequality, I can explain the reasons for the inequality and evaluate how groups or individuals addressed it. **SOC 4-04a**

I can describe the main features of conflicting world belief systems in the past and can present informed views on the consequences of such conflict for societies then and since. **SOC 4-04b**

I can make reasoned judgements about how the exercise of power affects the rights and responsibilities of citizens by comparing a more democratic and a less democratic society. **SOC 4-04c**

Having critically analysed a significant historical event, I can assess the relative importance of factors contributing to the event. **SOC 4-06a**

I can express an informed view about the changing nature of conflict over time, appreciate its impact and empathise with the experiences of those involved. **SOC 4-06b**

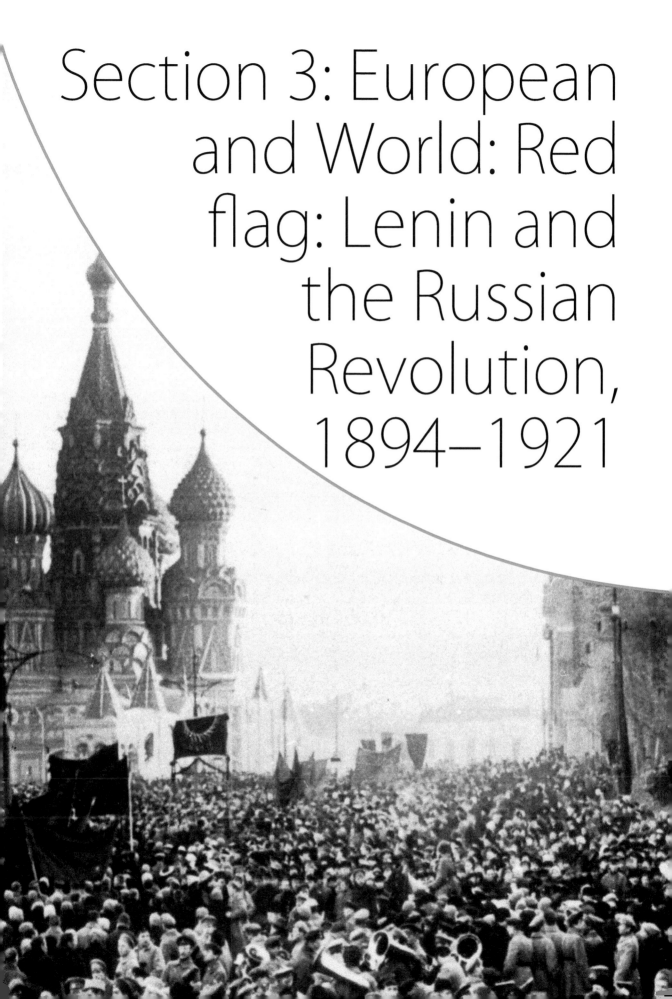

Section 3: European and World: Red flag: Lenin and the Russian Revolution, 1894–1921

Background

 Make the Link

In Modern Studies you may study Russia in detail in Unit 3.

Figure 1: *Vladimir Lenin addresses a crowd, with the red flag of the Bolsheviks below him. The Bolsheviks, led by Lenin, seized power in Russia in the October Revolution of 1917.*

GO! **Activity 1**

Read the information on this page. Create a poster/ illustrated mind map/ presentation that summarises what each paragraph says. Also, you will notice that there are **seven** key words/ names in **bold** throughout the text. You must write these down in your piece of work, with an explanation of what the word means or who the person or group was. You should use words and pictures in your piece of work.

In 1894 the Russian Empire covered one sixth of the world's surface. It was a massive country with approximately 120 000 000 people living in it. Although Russia's size made it look like a strong, powerful nation, the reality was quite different. For example, the sheer size of Russia made it difficult for its ruler to control. Also, Russia did not have good transport or communication networks, or an advanced industry or economy. This meant that most people in Russia were poor peasants who generally worked the land to survive. Most of the money that was made in Russia was controlled by the people at the top, especially Russia's ruler, the Tsar.

Russia was ruled by **Tsar Nicholas II**. A **Tsar** is an emperor, the ruler of an empire. His family, the Romanovs, had ruled Russia for over 300 years. Tsar Nicholas II ruled Russia as an **autocrat**. An autocrat is someone who rules with absolute power. As far as the Tsar was concerned, this was completely normal and acceptable. In fact, for the vast majority of people living in Russia, autocratic rule by the Tsar was how it had always been and they accepted it. However, as Russia's economy began to grow, so did the way its people lived and where they lived. These changes in Russia brought problems for the Tsar, as many Russians now began to question why they had so little money and power over their own lives. In the years before 1917 various groups emerged that challenged his power.

Political parties were illegal in Russia before 1905 but that did not stop people joining them. Many of these political parties and groups were very unhappy with the way people in Russia were treated by the Tsar and his government. They called for the overthrow of the Tsar so that a new, fairer society, where the workers had the power, could be created. These groups generally believed in the political idea of **communism**. Communism is when the workers control the country and economy, and wealth is equally shared among everyone. Some people in Russia did not want to overthrow the Tsar. Instead, they wanted a parliament and a democracy, led by the Tsar, similar to the system in Britain. These people were known as **Liberals.** By February 1917, the Tsar had been overthrown, and the Liberals were in power. However, in October 1917, one of the main communist groups called the **Bolsheviks** seized power. The leader of the Bolsheviks was a man called **Vladimir Lenin**. Between 1917 and 1921 the Bolsheviks, led by Lenin, established their control over Russia. In the process of doing so, Russia became the first country in the world to be run using communist ideas.

In summary, the economic changes that Russia went through between 1894 and 1921 meant that the country changed politically too. However, as we will see, there were many different events in this period, such as World War One, that contributed to the political changes that took place. What will become clear as you go through this topic is that Russia changed a lot during this period and that, by 1921, Russia was a very different country than in 1894. You can decide for yourself if it had changed for the better or for the worse.

1 Imperial Russia—government and people

In this section you will learn about:

- How the Tsarist government controlled Russia.
- Class divisions in Russia.
- Reasons for the backwardness of Russian agriculture and industry.
- Why the peasantry and industrial workers were unhappy.
- The Russification of national minorities.

How did the Tsarist government control Russia?

The Tsar's personal authority

In 1894 Tsar Nicholas II took the throne. His family, the Romanovs, had ruled Russia for centuries. The Tsar wasn't a natural leader, and disliked politics. His father had been a powerful, feared and respected Tsar, yet Nicholas was seen as likeable and pleasant, hardly the character traits needed to rule an empire! Despite going so far as to say that he 'never wanted to rule' Nicholas nonetheless did so and, as an autocrat, he had the power to rule as he saw fit. The Fundamental Laws of 1832 clearly stated that the Tsar, as 'Emperor of all the Russians, is an autocratic and unlimited monarch'. It also said that 'God himself ordains that all must bow to his supreme power'. In short, the Tsar could appoint his own government, his own advisors, make new laws whenever he wanted to, and he had the final say on every issue.

Figure 2: *A portrait of Tsar Nicholas II at the time of his coronation in 1894.*

The role of the army

The Tsar relied heavily on the loyalty of his large army. He appointed men he knew and could rely upon to the top positions. This sometimes meant that they were not the best men for the job, but for the Tsar loyalty was more important than ability. For ordinary soldiers, loyalty was ensured through very strict discipline. Russian citizens respected and feared the army, especially the Cossacks, the elite cavalry who would break up riots and strikes with brute force. The loyal, often brutal army certainly helped the Tsar control Russia.

The role of the Okhrana

The Tsarist government relied on the Okhrana, its secret police force, to spy on any enemies of the Tsar. The Okhrana kept files on anyone who they considered dangerous, usually focusing on revolutionary

Figure 3: *Russian Cossacks in 1915.*

groups. Because political parties and groups were illegal and had to meet in secret, the government didn't always know what they had been discussing or planning. It was the Okhrana's job to make sure the government knew what opposition groups were up to.

The role of the Russian church

The Orthodox Church played a significant role in ensuring that the peasants, and others, did not challenge the autocratic Tsarist system.

In 1894 the vast majority of Russians were members of the Russian Orthodox Church. They were also peasants who had little or no education and were barely literate. These peasants had no access to alternative information and simply believed what they were taught in church.

Orthodox priests would preach that the Tsar had been appointed by God and that Russians should therefore obey the Tsar without question. Russians would go to church from an early age, hear priests talking about the Tsar in such a way, and grow up believing that to disobey or oppose the Tsar was the same as challenging God. The Tsar himself actually appointed the chief bishops and the Holy Synod who ran the church.

Censorship

Source A was written by a modern historian.

 **Make the Link**

You may learn more about censorship in English or Media.

> The Tsarist government controlled the information that ordinary Russians had access to. They did this by censoring all books and newspapers so that people would not be influenced by liberal or socialist ideas. Any material that the government felt was dangerous was banned. Also, the Okhrana would arrest anyone who tried to distribute banned newspapers or books.

Activity 2

Exam style question

How fully does **Source A** describe the ways that the Tsarist government controlled Russia? **SH 6**
(Use **Source A** and recall.)

(Unit outcomes: National 4/5: Outcome 1.1)

The law

The Tsar was able to make laws so as to maintain his power. Anyone who opposed the Tsar could be exiled to remote Siberia or conscripted to the army where they would be treated terribly. It was very difficult for any opposition to oppose the Tsar when he controlled the police and the laws they enforced.

Figure 4: *This painting of 1894 shows Russian Poles who have been exiled to Siberia.*

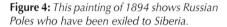

Activity 3

Using all the information in this section, create a comic strip or presentation that explains how the Tsar was able to control Russia. Include at least six detailed, clear points.

(Unit outcomes: National 4/5: Outcome 2.2)

Class divisions in Russia

The **ruling and upper classes** were those people who helped the Tsar rule and who, in return for their loyalty, benefited from his rule. These people were usually members of the **nobility**, meaning that they had some royal blood and owned a lot of land.

The **middle class** were a very small part of Russia's population. They lived in the cities, working as civil servants or in professions such as law, education and medicine. Many were unhappy that they didn't have any political power in Russia. Many openly called for Russia to be a democracy and were Liberals. Liberals believed in reforming the system but wanted the Tsar to remain as head of state.

The Russian census of 1897 found that approximately 82% of Russian population were **peasants**. Peasants worked the land, usually didn't own it, had very little money and lacked an education. Their living conditions were basic and their lives were hard. These peasants were called the 'dark masses' by the ruling classes, because they were considered uneducated and resistant to change.

By 1900 there was a growing number of **industrial workers** who had moved to the major cities from the countryside searching for work. However, conditions in the towns and cities were terrible and by 1900 the Tsarist government had become increasingly worried about this group because many had joined revolutionary groups. There was a real division between this group and the ruling class.

Figure 5: *This is drawing of the Russian class divisions and social structure in 1900. It was drawn by someone who wanted the Tsar overthrown: how can you tell this?*

Activity 4

Create or draw your own diagram describing the class divisions (words in **bold** above) in Tsarist Russia. Make sure you label and explain each section.

(Unit outcomes: National 4/5: Outcome 2.1)

Reasons for the backwardness of Russian agriculture and industry

The large number of peasants in Russia showed that Russia's economy relied mainly on agriculture. However, agriculture in Russia was extremely backward because the soil in Russia was generally not ideal for farming and most land lay too far north. What was left of the good land had to be shared among over 100 000 000 peasants. Peasant families were therefore left with small pieces of land which usually provided only enough crops to survive on. Also, peasants used old farming tools and systems that other European nations had long since abandoned. On the whole, agriculture barely provided enough to feed Russia, and as a result famine was never far away.

Figure 6: *Russian peasants had a low standard of living and by the twentieth century had grown increasingly unhappy.*

By 1894, Russia had not gone through the industrial revolution as fully as other major European nations like Britain and Germany had. Russia did have large industrial cities such as Moscow and St Petersburg that contained large textile factories and growing populations, but nowhere near as many as industrialised nations did. One of the main problems in Russia was the lack of investment in industry, mainly because the banking system had not modernised. Also, the lack of an effective transport network restricted the growth of industry and the movement of goods. Russia's underdeveloped and backward industry meant that Russia, despite its size, was actually quite poor.

🔵 Activity 5

Exam style question

Explain why the Russian economy was so backward in 1900.

KU 6

(Unit outcomes: National 4/5: Outcome 2.2)

Why were the peasantry and industrial workers unhappy?

Russian peasants lived in basic and often terrible conditions but it was the land issue that really angered them. Since 1861 they had been allowed to buy land but they had to take out big loans to do so. These loans were called redemption payments and would have to be paid back annually over 49 years. Even when they bought land, it was often not of great quality as the landowners would keep the best for themselves. Even worse, the land peasants bought was sometimes overpriced and too small to suit their needs.

Source B was written by John Simkin on the History website *Spartacus Educational*.

Conditions in Russian factories were well below those enjoyed by industrial workers in Europe. They worked on average an 11 hour day (10 hours on Saturday). Conditions in the factories were extremely harsh and little concern was shown for the workers' health and safety. Trade Unions were illegal in Russia and industrial workers found it difficult to improve their standard of living. Strikes were also prohibited and when they took place the Russian Army was likely to be called in to deal with the workers.

Source C is adapted from *The Origins of the Russian Revolution, 1861–1917*, by Alan Wood.

Living and working conditions were generally appalling, with long hours, low pay, inadequate accommodation and safety procedures and punitive code of labour laws which heavily penalised breaches of industrial discipline. Trade unions and political parties were of course banned … [and they worked in] dangerous and insanitary conditions.

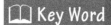 Key Word

- **Redemption payments**

Redemption payments were like large mortgages.

 Make the Link

In Business Management you will learn about working conditions and laws today.

GO! Activity 6

Exam style questions

1. Compare the views of **Sources B** and **C** on the reasons why industrial workers were so unhappy.   **SH 4**

   (Compare the sources overall and in detail.)

2. Explain why peasants and industrial workers were so unhappy in Tsarist Russia.   **KU 6**

   (Unit outcomes: National 4/5: Outcome 2.2)

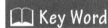

Key Word

- **Pogroms**

Organised attacks on Jews that usually saw homes being set on fire and Jews being murdered.

Make the Link

If you study RMPS you will learn more about Judaism.

Make the Link

Russian Jews and Lithuanians left the empire in this period because of Russification, with many settling in Scotland. In the Scottish topic 'Migration and Empire, 1830–1939' you learn about the impact these groups made on Scotland.

The Russification of national minorities

In 1894 the Russian Empire was massive, containing many different nations with their own cultures, languages and religions. The Tsar wanted everyone to be Russian, so that the Empire would be united and stronger, so he continued the centuries old policy of Russification.

Russification tried to restrict the influence of national minorities within the Russian Empire. Russian was made the official first language of the Russian Empire, and all government business and law enforcement was to be conducted in Russian. This was also the case in some countries when it came to education. In Poland, for example, it was illegal to teach children in Polish. The Orthodox Church supported Russification as they wanted all Russians to join their church. Religious persecution was also, therefore, an aspect of Russification.

Perhaps the worst victims of Russification were the Jews. They were denied the same job or educational opportunities as others. The Tsarist government used Jews as scapegoats for Russia's problems, leading to violent pogroms. Russian nationalist groups like the 'Black Hundreds' were well known for their attacks on Jews but the government did little to stop them.

Figure 7: *This postcard from 1905 shows a violent pogrom against Jews in the town of Odessa.*

Russification was designed to wipe out the individual cultures of the minority groups in the Russian Empire and unite everyone behind the Tsar. In reality, it did the opposite. Many people from these national minority groups left Russia to escape persecution, while others formed or joined opposition groups. Many historians, such as Michael Lynch, have argued that Russification created enemies for the Tsar right at the point when he needed all the friends he could get.

Activity 7

1. Imagine you are a Jew living in Poland in 1903. Write a letter to a friend describing the effects Russification has had on you and your family's lives. Also, explain what actions you are taking in response to Russification and why.

   (Unit outcomes: National 4/5: Outcomes 2.1 and 2.2)

Exam style question

2. To what extent was the loyalty of the army responsible for maintaining the Tsarist state before 1905? **KU 9**

   (Unit outcomes: National 4: Outcome 1.2; National 5: Outcomes 1.2, 1.3 and 2.3)

2 The 1905 Revolution— causes, events and effects

In this section you will learn about:

- Challenges to the Tsar's power from revolutionary groups.
- The main causes of the 1905 Revolution.
- How the Tsar dealt with the 1905 Revolution.
- The political changes in Russia after 1905: the Dumas.
- The political changes in Russia after 1905: Stolypin's reforms.

Challenges to the Tsar's power from revolutionary groups

Although all political parties were illegal in Russia in 1900, many did exist. They all wanted change, but they differed as to what these changes should be.

Social Revolutionaries (the SRs)

The SRs wanted a full-scale revolution in Russia, which would see the Tsar removed from power and society reorganised in a more equal fashion. They mainly represented the peasants and hoped that it would be this group who would spearhead the revolution. The SRs had no problem in using violence and terror and between 1901 and 1905 they were responsible for over 2000 political assassinations, including the Tsar's uncle.

The Kadets

The Kadets did not want a revolution that would overthrow the Tsar. They wanted the government to introduce a Duma (a parliament) and to legalise political parties, but to keep the Tsar as the head of the Russian state. For the Kadets, changes were necessary to help reform Russia and make it more modern like Britain, USA and Germany.

Figure 8: *A French newspaper depicting the Social Revolutionaries' assassination of the Tsar's uncle, Grand Duke Sergei, in 1905.*

> **📖 Key Word**
>
> - **Revolution**
>
> When there is an attempt to overthrow the current political system.

> **Make the Link**
>
> You may learn more about revolutionaries around the world in recent times in Modern Studies.

Social Democrats (the SDs)

Hint

Karl Marx had set out his ideas in a famous publication called 'The Communist Manifesto' (1848)

The Social Democrats wanted a revolution that would overthrow the Tsar and completely change the way Russia was run. They believed in the ideas of Karl Marx. Marx believed that the living and working conditions of industrial workers throughout the industrialised world were so bad that they would rise up in revolution and overthrow their rulers. In this new society the workers would run the country fairly and equally. This idea was known as communism and the Social Democrats wanted communism in Russia. They believed that Russia could be run by workers' groups called Soviets, who would represent ordinary people. However, there were some differences of opinion within the SDs as to how this communist revolution would take place. This caused the SDs to split into two groups in 1903: the Bolsheviks and the Mensheviks.

Figure 9: *Lenin addresses a crowd in 1920. By 1920 Lenin's Bolsheviks ruled Russia.*

Hint

The proletariat is another name for the industrial workers.

The Bolsheviks were led by Lenin. Lenin and his supporters believed that the revolution would only succeed if it was led by a small group of professional revolutionaries. Lenin called this the 'Dictatorship of the Proletariat'. The Mensheviks, on the other hand, wanted the revolution to be more democratic, with all workers having an equal say.

GO! Activity 8

Imagine it is 1904 and you are in advertising. You have been approached by the SRs, the Kadets and the Bolsheviks and Mensheviks to design small A5 posters for each of them. They must explain the aims of each group in a clear, catchy way.

(Unit outcomes: National 4/5: Outcome 2.2)

The main causes of the 1905 Revolution

Long term causes: The four discontented groups

Four main groups in Russia had been unhappy with their position in society for many years: **peasantry; industrial workers; national minorities; middle classes**.

> ### GO! Activity 9
>
> Based on what you learned in the previous section, work with a partner to bullet point all the reasons each group (above, in **bold**) was unhappy, including the economic problems some of them experienced. See how many you can come up with but aim for at least **six** to begin with.
>
> **(Unit outcomes: National 4/5: Outcome 2.2)**

Short term causes 1: Russo-Japanese War, 1904–1905

In 1904 the long term problems in Russia were coming to a head. Plehve, the Tsar's Minister of the Interior, believed that a short, successful war would distract the Russian people from their problems and unite them behind the Tsar in a wave of patriotism. In 1904 Russia went to war with Japan, hoping for a quick, morale boosting victory, but it did not quite go to plan.

The Russo-Japanese War was unpopular from the beginning. It was too far away for most Russians to care and the first battles went badly. Russia lost its naval base of Port Arthur to the Japanese in early 1905 and was well beaten in the Battle of Tsushima in May 1905. Also, there was a mutiny on the Russian battleship Potemkin when sailors were fed rotten food. They rebelled, seizing control of the ship from their officers. The Tsar and his ministers were blamed for the mutiny and the defeats in the war. At the same time there were severe food shortages in the cities and prices had gone up. Russians didn't like the fact that they were starving when money was being wasted on a war they were losing. Far from uniting Russians behind the Tsar, the war actually convinced many to rise up against him in 1905.

> ### 📖 Key Words
>
> - **Patriotism**
>
>   Caring deeply for your country.
>
> - **Mutiny**
>
>   A rebellion by a group, usually sailors or soldiers, to overthrow whoever has authority.

Short term causes 2: Bloody Sunday, 22 January 1905

In early 1905 many workers in the Russian cities were deeply unhappy. For the industrial workers in Moscow and St Petersburg, their living and working conditions were terrible and many were struggling to buy food. It was in this atmosphere of discontent and desperation that a Russian Orthodox priest called Father George Gapon led a large group of workers to the Tsar's Winter Palace to present a petition to him.

Figure 10: *An artist's impression of the events of Bloody Sunday.*

The petition was signed by 150 000 people and called on the Tsar to use his powers to help ordinary people. It did not call for a revolution or for the Tsar to step down.

Despite the peaceful nature of the march, when the crowd reached the Winter Palace they were met by the army and police. As ever with issues of public order the first response of the Tsarist government was to send out the army as a show of strength. However, in this case the army and police were not well organised and there was widespread confusion. In this confusion, troops fired shots into the crowd. As the crowd panicked the Cossacks moved in to restore order, using their swords. Hundreds of marchers were left dead, with many more injured. Although the Tsar had not issued the order to fire, Russians blamed him for the way his army had behaved. The image of the Tsar as the 'Little Father' of the Russian people was destroyed as news spread of 'Bloody Sunday'.

Throughout Russia, people took to the streets in protest against the Tsar. In the countryside peasants seized property from their landlords and openly called for his overthrow. What had started out as a city-wide reaction to a massacre soon spread throughout the country. The Tsarist government had lost control. Bloody Sunday was the spark that ignited the 1905 Revolution.

Figure 11: *A barricade erected by workers in Moscow during the 1905 Revolution.*

Activity 10

1. Create either a comic strip or presentation that describes the two short term events that helped cause the 1905 Revolution.

    (Unit outcomes: National 4/5: Outcome 2.1)

Exam style questions

Source D is an extract from the petition that Father George Gapon hoped to present to Nicholas II on 22 January 1905.

> We workers, our children, our wives and our old, helpless parents have come, Lord, to seek truth and protection from you. We are impoverished and oppressed, unbearable work is imposed on us, we are despised and not recognised as human beings. We are treated as slaves, who must bear their fate and be silent. We have suffered terrible things, but we are pressed ever deeper into the abyss of poverty, ignorance and lack of rights.

2. Evaluate the usefulness of **Source D** for investigating the causes of the 1905 Revolution. **SH 5**

    (You may want to comment on who wrote it, when they wrote it, why they wrote it, what they say or what has been missed out.)

3. To what extent was the discontent of the industrial workers the main cause of the 1905 Revolution? **KU 9**

    (Unit outcomes: National 4: Outcome 1.2; National 5: Outcomes 1.2, 1.3 and 2.3)

How the Tsar dealt with the 1905 Revolution

By October 1905 the revolution was in full swing. There was widespread disorder in the countryside that saw landlords murdered and land seized. The SRs assassinated Plehve. Workers went on strike and the transport system ground to a halt. National minorities got in on the act, with Georgia announcing its independence. The Kadets united all the liberal groups into a 'Union of Unions' that openly called for major political reforms. Also, industrial workers had begun to organise themselves into elected Soviets (workers councils) so that they could call for better working and living conditions. The Tsar was in real trouble but, under the advice of his ministers, regained his nerve and issued the October Manifesto.

Key Word

*   **Manifesto**

    A set of ideas.

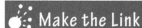

Make the Link

In Modern Studies you will look at both trade unions and civil liberties.

The October Manifesto was cleverly designed to split the revolutionary forces. The Manifesto promised the liberals that a Duma would be set up and political parties and trade unions made legal. It also established a wide range of civil rights such as freedom of speech. For the liberals it was enough to convince them to call an end to their part in the revolution. The Tsar had successfully bought off one group.

The peasants had not joined the revolution in the hope of establishing a new political order; their main issue was that of land, and their massive redemption payments. The Tsarist government recognised this so in November they announced that all redemption payments would be reduced immediately and eventually abolished in 1907. Upon hearing the news, peasants generally returned to their homes. The countryside had now been restored to order.

The industrial workers had been right at the heart of the revolution and, unlike peasants and liberals, could not be bought off. With this in mind the government simply decided to use the army to suppress the workers. The St Petersburg Soviet was stormed and shut down and revolutionary leaders were imprisoned or exiled to Siberia. The army's loyalty was key to dealing with the industrial workers.

GO! Activity 11

Imagine it is December 1905. Create a front page newspaper announcing the end of the revolution. You must use words and pictures to explain how the Tsarist government survived the revolution.

(Unit outcomes: National 4/5: Outcome 2.2)

The political changes in Russia after 1905: the Dumas

The October Manifesto of 1905 established a Duma. For the first time, ordinary Russians had the opportunity to vote for Deputies (members of the Duma) who would represent their interests. However, just when the first Duma was about to meet, the Tsar issued his Fundamental Laws. These stated that the Tsar still had 'Supreme autocratic power', that no law could come into being without the Tsar's approval and that the Tsar could close the Duma whenever he wanted. The Tsar clearly had no intention of allowing Russia to become a proper democracy.

There were four Dumas between 1906 and 1914, when the Great War began. **The First Duma** (April–June 1906) was shut down on the Tsar's orders because many Deputies were calling for further reforms and restrictions to his power.

Figure 12: *This is a painting of the opening of the first Duma. The Tsar, in the centre of the painting, did not plan on it limiting his power.*

The Second Duma (February–June 1907) was no more successful. SR and SD Deputies opposed most of the plans brought forward by the Tsar and his Prime Minister, Peter Stolypin. As a result the Tsar became frustrated and annoyed, and within three months closed it down.

The Third Duma (1907–1912) was much more successful but was even less democratic than before. Stolypin wanted to make some changes to Russia but knew this would never happen if the Duma was full of Deputies who annoyed the Tsar. With this in mind, he changed the rules so that only the richest and therefore most pro-Tsar Russians could vote. This meant that the Deputies who were elected were pro-Tsar, and the Duma functioned because the Tsar was happy to work with men who supported him. With Stolypin leading it, this Duma actually did make an impact on Russia, modernising the armed forces and expanding national insurance schemes for workers. Improvements were also made to primary school education.

The Fourth Duma (1912–1914) was not as successful as the third, mainly because Stolypin had been assassinated in 1911 and his successors as Prime Ministers were not very good. During the Fourth Duma the number of strikes in Russia rose dramatically, a clear sign that all was not well.

> **GO!** **Activity 12**
>
> Produce a presentation or A5 booklet which explains the following:
>
> - how the Tsar planned to control the Duma from the beginning
> - how effective each Duma was and why.
>
> **(Unit outcomes: National 4/5: Outcome 2.2)**

The political changes in Russia after 1905: Stolypin's reforms

Figure 13: *Peter Stolypin, Prime Minister of Russia, 1906–1911.*

Make the Link

If you study Economics you may learn about theories like Stolypin's.

Peter Stolypin firmly believed that for the Tsarist state to survive, it needed to reform. However, before any reforms could take place he set about ensuring that those who posed the biggest threat to the Tsar were dealt with once and for all.

Between 1906 and 1909, Peter Stolypin had over 3000 people hanged because he believed them to be a threat to the Tsar. His use of this method of execution earned the hangman's noose the nickname 'Stolypin's necktie'. Stolypin used the powers that the Tsar had given him to convict these people quickly, usually without juries, and simply hang them there and then. Stolypin used the army, Okhrana and police to round up these 'enemies of the state'. By 1911 the number of revolts and protests in the cities and countryside had dropped dramatically.

Stolypin also ensured the loyalty of the army by reforming the way it was run. He improved the training of soldiers, their working conditions and certain pay conditions too. The army now became an even stronger ally of the Tsar in keeping opponents suppressed.

Stolypin's desire to reform Russia came from his belief that if the people of Russia felt that they had a stake in Russia's success and were treated fairly then they would be more likely to support the Tsar. First, redemption payments were to be cancelled by 1907. Secondly, he set up a Land Bank that offered peasants loans at low rates so that they could buy their own land. Lastly, Stolypin encouraged peasants to produce more grain than they needed so they could sell it and make more money. Previously, peasants had not been encouraged to treat their farms and land as businesses but Stolypin wanted to change this. Stolypin believed that richer peasants, known as kulaks, would be more likely to support the Tsar.

Stolypin also introduced reforms in industry, such as better working conditions and a scheme of national insurance for workers. By 1912 there were signs of a more content workforce.

Overall, these reforms could have been more successful if Stolypin had had more time to implement them fully. Also, an economic slump made life difficult for many and affected the success of his reforms, as did many peasants' reluctance to change centuries of tradition and adopt his reforms.

GO! Activity 13

1. Create a Facebook page for Peter Stolypin, explaining all his achievements and reforms, and describing how he dealt with enemies of the Tsar.

   (Unit outcomes: National 4/5: Outcomes 2.1 and 2.2)

Exam style question

2. Describe the main political changes in Russia after 1905. **KU 4**

   (Unit outcomes: National 4/5: Outcome 2.1)

3 The February Revolution— causes, events and effects

In this section you will learn about:

- Russia and the First World War: effects of military defeat and economic hardship.
- Rasputin and the growing unpopularity of the regime.
- The February Revolution of 1917.
- The Dual Authority.

In 1914 the Tsar's position seemed secure. The nobility, the church and the army remained loyal and the Tsar was well in control of the weak Duma. Most of the opposition leaders who were a threat to the Tsar were in prison, in exile or had fled to other countries. However, beneath the surface, Tsarist Russia was still not stable and the stresses and strains of fighting the Great War in 1914 would highlight this. By February 1917, the Tsar had become very unpopular and he was forced to abdicate.

> ## 📖 Key Word
> - **Abdicate**
> To give up your throne.

Russia and the First World War: effects of military defeat and economic hardship

Effects of military defeat

The Tsar's decision to go to war with Germany and Austria-Hungary in August 1914 was actually very popular in Russia. The city of St Petersburg changed its name to Petrograd, a much less German and more Russian sounding name! Many people rallied behind the Tsar and his government and millions of men volunteered to join the army. The first battles of the war went well but the tide soon began to turn, and the Germans began to inflict heavy defeats on Russia. Terrible losses at Tannenberg and the Masurian Lakes greatly affected the army's morale and ordinary Russians lost enthusiasm for the war. By the end of 1914 there had been over 1 000 000 casualties. What is more, Russia lost control of Poland in 1915, which was a huge blow to Russian unity and morale.

The Russian army was nowhere near as well equipped or well led as the Germans, and this became clear to soldiers very early on. For example, there were not even enough rifles for every soldier to have one each, and machine guns and artillery would often not work properly. Although historians debate the extent of the shortages, with some historians arguing that front line troops actually were well equipped, it is clear that across the whole army, there was a shortage of equipment. There were some instances of Russian troops going into battle armed with farming implements alone. The defeats, heavy losses

>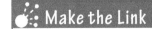
> ## ⁂ Make the Link
> The Scottish topic 'The Era of the Great War, 1900–1928' goes into a lot of detail about the weapons and warfare of the First World War.

and lack of equipment led to low morale within the army, and many soldiers began to question the tactics of their leaders. Revolutionaries were beginning to make their voices heard in the trenches, calling for soldiers to abandon their weapons and return home. Many did. By 1915 it was clear that the Russian army was falling apart.

Figure 14 and Source E: *This photo shows two Russian soldiers deserting, and one loyal soldier trying to force them to stay. By 1917 desertions had become common.*

In September 1915, the Tsar travelled to the front to take charge of the armed forces. However, the Tsar was not a military tactician or leader, and as defeats and casualties mounted, he became the focal point of soldiers' anger. The Tsar's decision to take control of the army was a big mistake as he could now be personally blamed for all the defeats and the war's effects on Russia.

Figure 15: *The Tsar, seated on his horse, inspects his troops during the First World War.*

GO! Activity 14

1. Imagine you are a Russian soldier fighting in the Great War. Write a detailed diary entry explaining why Russia is doing so badly in the war and what you think about the Tsar taking control. You can add drawings below your diary entry.

   (Unit outcomes: National 4/5: Outcome 2.2)

   Exam style question

2. Evaluate the usefulness of **Source E** as evidence of the problems Russia was experiencing by 1917.   **SH 5**

Economic hardship

The war was very costly and it was the people who paid. Taxes were raised at the same time as the price of food went up, meaning ordinary Russians struggled to survive. Also, the war put a massive strain on the already fragile Russian economy.

Going to war meant that peasants and their horses were conscripted into the army. This reduced the productivity of farms. Also, as the German army continued to win battles and advance into Russia, so Russia lost a lot of its agricultural land to Germany. To make matters even worse, the food that was produced often did not even make it to the major cities and towns. The rail network was not large or advanced enough to cope with the war and there were cases where trains full of food were pushed off the line to make way for military trains. Often these trains full of food would be left to rot beside the tracks as no one was free to get them back on the tracks again.

The terrible food shortages that occurred as a result of all these factors saw Russians become increasingly unhappy with the war and their leader. Queues for food became commonplace in the cities and inflation increased. Wages may have doubled during the war but prices quadrupled! Winters were harsh due to fuel shortages. The price of bread increased by 300% leading to riots in the major cities and workers began to go on strike in protest.

GO! Activity 15

1. Make up five questions on the way the war affected Russia's economy. In groups of three, ask one another questions and see how well you do by keeping a tally of the questions you answer correctly.

   Exam style questions

2. Explain why the Russian army struggled in the First World War.   **KU 6**

   (Unit outcomes: National 4/5: Outcome 2.2)

3. Describe the effects the war had on the Russian economy.   **KU 4**

   (Unit outcomes: National 4/5: Outcome 2.1)

Figure 16: *Rasputin, centre, with two army officers who were appointed by the Tsar on Rasputin's advice.*

Hint

Tsarina Alexandra was in fact German. She was also the grand-daughter of Queen Victoria of Great Britain.

Figure 17 and Source F: *A Russian political cartoon from 1916.*

Rasputin and the growing unpopularity of the regime

When the Tsar took command of the army in September 1915 he left his wife, the Tsarina Alexandra, in charge. This angered many politicians who felt that they should have been left in charge. However, perhaps the biggest consequence of leaving the Tsarina in charge was that it allowed a man whom the Tsarina trusted and greatly relied on to gain power and influence in Russia. That man's name was Rasputin.

Rasputin was a mystic who some people believed had the power to heal. He managed to gain such influence over the Tsarina because she believed that he was able to heal her son, Alexei, the heir to the throne. Alexei had haemophilia, a disorder that stops blood clotting and is potentially fatal. Alexandra kept Rasputin close by so that he could be called on to heal her son, and grew close to him. She began to consult Rasputin on government matters and in two years twenty one government ministers were sacked and replaced by friends of Rasputin. Rasputin even used his influence to interfere in military matters and tactics, and lived a lavish lifestyle that the Tsarina paid for. He was a drunken womaniser and stories soon got out about his often outrageous behaviour. Ordinary Russians were angered by these stories and by the fact that a man like this, who had no experience or skill in politics, now had such power and influence. Rumours began to spread that Rasputin and the Tsarina were having an affair and that the Tsarina was a German spy.

In December 1916 Russian noblemen lost patience with the Tsarina and, led by the Tsar's cousin, took matters into their own hands, murdering Rasputin. By this point, however, the damage to the Tsar and Tsarina's reputations had been done. The Rasputin affair, as it became known, had highlighted the worst, most corrupt aspects of the Tsarist state and had shown the Tsar to be a weak and incompetent leader.

Following the Rasputin affair, the Tsar was advised by his ministers to introduce reforms in Russia. People were calling out for political power to be shared more equally, and for changes to be made in the way the war was being handled. The Tsar ignored the advice and completely failed to see how serious the situation had become.

Activity 16

1. Create a newspaper article, complete with a picture, which explains why the Tsar had become so unpopular by 1917.

   (Unit outcomes: National 4/5: Outcome 2.2)

Exam style question

2. Evaluate the usefulness of **Source F** as evidence of the reasons the Tsar was so unpopular by 1917.　　　　**SH 5**

   (You may want to comment on who created it, when they created it, why they created it, what they say or what has been missed out.)

The February Revolution

By February 1917 the Tsar had lost the support of all sections of society. Even the army was questioning his authority. There were bread riots on the streets of Petrograd, strikes in factories and even anti-war marches. In the Duma, liberals and socialists were beginning to work together to oppose the Tsar.

Throughout February the situation worsened. On 23 February workers at the Putilov steelworks went on strike, demanding and then being refused a wage increase. The workers took to the streets and were soon joined by over 200 000 people, protesting about food and fuel shortages. The army and police used force to disperse the crowds but soon police stations and prisons were attacked and set on fire. The government was slowly losing control.

Figure 18: *Putilov workers on strike in St Petersburg, February 1917.*

Source G is a telegram from Michael Rodzianko, President of the Duma, to Nicholas II on 26 February 1917.

The situation is serious. The capital is in a state of anarchy. The government is paralysed; the transport service has broken down; the food and fuel supplies are completely disorganised. Discontent is general and on the increase. There is wild shooting in the streets; troops are firing at each other. It is urgent that someone enjoying the confidence of the country be entrusted with the formation of a new government. There must be no delay. Hesitation is fatal.

On 27 February army regiments mutinied and joined the strikers. The Duma, frustrated by the Tsar's inaction, formed a Provisional Government. Hours later, workers and revolutionaries set up the Petrograd Soviet. On 28 February the Tsar was told by his generals that they no longer supported him and railway workers prevented him from entering Petrograd. On 2 March, having lost the support of his army, the Tsar abdicated, offering the throne to his brother. His brother refused and the rule of the Romanovs was over.

GO! Activity 17

1. Create either a comic strip or an illustrated timeline that describes the Tsar's fall from power.

   (Unit outcomes: National 4/5: Outcome 2.1)

Exam style question

2. Evaluate the usefulness of **Source G** as evidence of the reasons why the Tsar fell from power in February 1917. **SH 5**

   (You may want to comment on who wrote it, when they wrote it, why they wrote it, what they say or what has been missed out.)

The 'Dual Authority'

When the Tsar abdicated, a group of politicians took control of Russia. They had been members of the Duma, were generally middle class liberals, and called themselves the Provisional Government. Provisional means temporary so these politicians were saying that they would rule Russian temporarily, until elections took place in November to elect a permanent government. At the same time as the Provisional Government took control, workers' Soviets were set up in Petrograd and the other major cities. The Soviets said that they should have a share of power in Russia because they had been elected by the workers. In the months to come, the Soviets and the Provisional Government ruled Russia together in an uneasy alliance that came to be known as the 'Dual Authority'.

At the beginning, the Provisional Government, with the support of the Soviets, made some positive changes. It introduced the 8 hour working day, legalised trade unions, and banned capital punishment and exile to Siberia. This made them quite popular and the Dual Authority worked for a while. Perhaps the main reason it worked was because both groups were quite simply glad to be rid of the Tsar and were making a real effort to get along. This would not last for long.

GO! Activity 18

1. Create an A5 poster showing who ruled Russia after the February Revolution and some of the changes that were made early on. You can use twenty words maximum.

Exam style questions

2. To what extent was the First World War responsible for the downfall of the Tsar? **KU 9**

   (Unit outcomes: National 4: Outcome 1.2; National 5: Outcomes 1.2, 1.3 and 2.3)

3. Describe the events of February 1917 that led to the abdication of the Tsar. **KU 4**

   (Unit outcomes: National 4/5: Outcome 2.1)

4 The October Revolution—causes, events and effects

In this section you will learn about:

- The failure of the Provisional Government under Kerensky.
- Lenin's return and the April Theses.
- The July Days and the Kornilov Revolt.
- Bolshevik leadership.
- The Civil War, 1917–1921 and why the Reds won.
- The nature of the Soviet state.

Cause 1: The failure of the Provisional Government under Kerensky

Despite promising early signs of cooperation, the Dual Authority did not function well for long. The Provisional Government did not deal with many major issues and before long the Soviets, and the Russian people, lost faith in them.

The Provisional Government was faced with many problems when it took over control of Russia: the war, the land issue and conditions in the cities, most notably food shortages.

The Russian people were sick of the war, yet the Provisional Government chose to continue it. To make matters worse, the Provisional Government decided to launch a major attack on Germany in June 1917 (the June Offensive) when only months before they had promised to fight only a defensive war. Kerensky, Minister of War in June, and leader of the Provisional Government from July 1917, became very unpopular because of the way he dealt with the war issue.

The Provisional Government also failed to deal with the land issue. Peasants wanted land distributed among them and taken away from the ruling classes and landowners. However, the Provisional Government said that this task was simply too big to deal with at the time, as there were over 100 000 000 peasants and millions of square miles of land to divide up. They therefore did nothing. Before long peasants had taken matters into their own hands, attacking landowners in the countryside, and seizing land from them.

Figure 19: *Kerensky, in his office, 1917.*

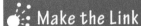

Make the Link

In the Scottish topic 'The Era of the Great War, 1900–1928', pupils learn about how the British government dealt with food shortages and other problems caused by the war.

Key Word

• **Exiled**

When someone is sent out of their country by its leader or government, usually because they are seen as a political threat.

As we have seen, the terrible conditions in the cities had contributed to the Tsar's fall from power, and they would do the same to the Provisional Government. The cities had become overcrowded as refugees flocked there from areas that the Germans had invaded. Food shortages worsened and by September bread, meat, grain, potatoes, milk and sugar were scarce. People waited in queues for hours, street robberies and housebreakings increased and in some areas there were food riots and looting. Kerensky and his Provisional Government failed to improve the conditions and citizens lost faith in them. Many viewed Kerensky and his government as no better than the Tsar.

Cause 2: The return of Lenin and the April Theses

At the beginning of 1917 Vladimir Lenin, the Bolshevik leader, was living in Western Europe, having been exiled by the Tsar for his radical beliefs. Lenin may not have been in Russia but he was well aware of what was going on and had maintained links with the Bolsheviks. When Lenin learned of the Tsar's fall from power, he was desperate to get back to Russia and approached the German government for help. The Germans were keen to do anything to upset their enemy, and put Lenin on a private train bound for Petrograd. In April 1917 Lenin returned to Russia and within the year would make history.

Figure 20: *Lenin addressing a crowd in Red Square, Moscow, October 1917.*

Lenin returned to Russia having thought long and hard about how to seize control of Russia and begin a revolution. He wrote all his ideas down in a book, which was called the April Theses. The April Theses called for the removal of the Provisional Government and for all power to be transferred to the Soviets, who were, in Lenin's mind, the true representatives of the workers. Lenin's April Theses also said that the Bolsheviks would deliver 'Peace, Bread and Land'. This was clever because these were the three areas that the Provisional Government were failing in and it meant Russians saw the Bolsheviks as the main alternative to Kerensky's government. Lenin's slogans 'All power to the Soviets' and 'Peace, Bread and Land' were soon appearing on red flags and posters throughout Petrograd.

Cause 3: The July Days and the Kornilov Revolt

In July 1917 the Bolsheviks tried to seize power from the Provisional Government but failed. These July Days showed that the Bolsheviks were not yet strong enough and that the Provisional Government still commanded some loyalty from the army. After the July Days Kerensky had many Bolshevik leaders imprisoned and Lenin fled. It looked like the Bolsheviks were done for.

Figure 21: *Soldiers loyal to the Provisional Government shoot down Bolshevik protestors during the July Days, 1917.*

In August 1917 General Kornilov, one of the top army generals, tried to seize power. He was unhappy with the way Kerensky was running Russia. Kerensky knew he had to stop Kornilov's revolt so asked the Soviets to help defend the city. The Soviets agreed to help but said that they would need weapons and demanded that the Bolsheviks be released. Kerensky agreed and, with the Soviets' help, the Kornilov Revolt was stopped. However, Kerensky had now armed the Bolsheviks, the very group who had tried to overthrow him only a month earlier.

Figure 22: *The Provisional Government armed Bolsheviks, like those above, during the Kornilov Revolt.*

Cause 4: Bolshevik leadership and organisation

During October 1917 the Bolsheviks began to organise and plan their seizure of power. This would have been very difficult had it not been for the strong leadership of Lenin. By October 1917 the Bolsheviks dominated the Soviets, mainly because Lenin had insisted that Bolshevik members attend every meeting to ensure they won important votes. Also, Lenin's charisma and will had convinced the Bolshevik leadership to support his plan to seize power. Lenin relied on his second in command, Trotsky, to actually plan the revolution.

Figure 23: *Painting of Lenin addressing a Soviet meeting. Lenin's effective leadership ensured that, by October 1917, the Bolsheviks dominated the Soviets.*

Figure 24: *Lev Trotsky was crucial in the Bolshevik's seizure of power in October 1917.*

Lev Trotksy had helped set up the St Petersburg Soviet in 1905 as a Menshevik, but in 1917 joined the Bolsheviks. He was very bright, a brilliant organiser and a tireless worker. In October 1917, he came up with the idea, and then led, the Military Revolutionary Committee (MRC). The MRC instructed the army to only obey orders that came from the Soviet and essentially planned the revolution of October 1917.

Figure 25: *Organised and armed Red Guard units ensured that the Bolsheviks were able to seize power easily in 1917.*

In the days before the actual seizure of power, Trotsky and the MRC ensured that Bolshevik soldiers, known as Red Guards, were in place to seize important positions. Red Guards took over important government buildings, railway stations, the post office, bridges and telephone and telegraph exchanges. By 25 October, the day the Bolsheviks had planned to take power from the Provisional Government, Trotsky and his MRC had control over the army and city of Petrograd. When Red Guards stormed the Winter Palace in Petrograd on 25 October and arrested the remaining members of the Provisional Government, it was because Lenin and Trotsky had led and planned it so well. The Bolsheviks were now in power.

Activity 19

1. Working in pairs, your challenge is to deliver a lesson to other members of the class that:
   - explains why there was a revolution in 1917
   - describes the events of October 1917
   - explains why the Bolsheviks were successful.

   You should produce a teaching aid (a presentation or poster) and an information sheet that focuses on the four main causes discussed in this section.

   (Unit outcomes: National 4/5: Outcome 2.2)

Exam style questions

2. Explain why the Provisional Government failed to win the support of the Russian people.   **KU 6**

   (Unit outcomes: National 4/5: Outcome 2.2)

3. To what extent was Trotsky responsible for the Bolsheviks' success in the October Revolution?   **KU 9**

   (Unit outcomes: National 4: Outcome 1.2; National 5: Outcomes 1.2, 1.3 and 2.3)

The Civil War, 1917–1921

📖 Key Words

- **Civil war**

A war between different groups within one country.

- **Ideology**

A set of ideas that a person or group firmly believes in.

🔵 Make the Link

If you study Modern Studies or even just watch the news, you may be aware of countries around the world where brutal and bloody civil wars are taking place.

🔵 Make the Link

If you take RMPS you will learn more about different ideologies.

Following the October Revolution the Bolsheviks, led by Lenin, ruled through a small committee called the Council of People's Commissars. They were not yet in control of the whole of Russia, though. The other revolutionary groups, like the SRs and the Mensheviks, wanted to rule Russia and overthrow the Bolsheviks, as did the liberals, many of whom also wanted the Tsar back. Until 1921, the Bolsheviks were engaged in a brutal and bloody civil war with these opposition forces.

In Russia the civil war was fought between the Reds (the Bolsheviks) and the Whites (the opposition forces). The Reds were made up of communists, workers, peasants, soldiers and sailors. The Whites were a collection of various opposition groups, including troops from foreign countries like the USA and Britain. By 1921, millions of Russians had died, the Whites were defeated and the Reds had emerged victorious. There were various reasons for this.

Why the Reds won: ideology and unity

The Reds shared the common ideology of communism. With every soldier fighting for the same cause the Reds were united in battle. Morale could be maintained by constantly focusing on this shared ideology. The Whites on the other hand, did not share an ideology. The SRs and Mensheviks simply wanted to get rid of the Bolsheviks and establish a more democratic Russia whereas ex-Tsarist generals wanted the Tsar restored. Other Whites, like the Kadets and liberals, wanted to re-establish the Duma. With no common ideology, there was no real unity to the White's cause, making it harder for each group to work together and for morale to be maintained.

Why the Reds won: Trotsky's leadership

The Whites had three main armies, all of whom were led by different commanders. Admiral Kolchak led forces in Siberia, General Yudenich in the north-west and General Denikin in the south. Each wanted to have total control and did not fully trust one another. The Reds, on the other hand, were led by Trotsky who coordinated all attacks and was brilliant at inspiring his troops. He introduced compulsory military service for all men between eighteen and forty, boosting the Red Army's numbers. He also recruited around 50 000 former officers of the Tsar's army, whose choice was to fight for the Reds or be sent to a prison camp. Discipline in Trotsky's Red Army was strict and the death penalty was restored. In terms of leadership, Trotsky may not have had the military experience of his White counterparts, but he was a supreme war leader who united the Red Army in battle.

Why the Reds won: geography and resources

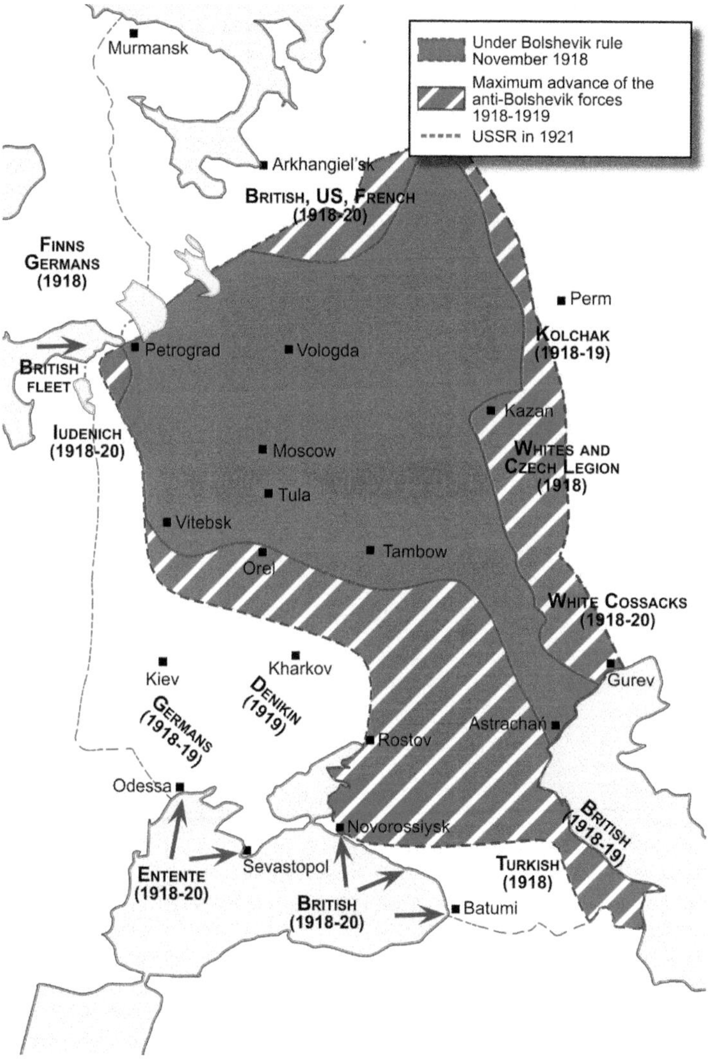

Murmansk

Under Bolshevik rule
November 1918

Maximum advance of the
anti-Bolshevik forces
1918-1919

USSR in 1921

Arkhangiel'sk

**BRITISH, US, FRENCH
(1918-20)**

**FINNS
GERMANS
(1918)**

Perm

**KOLCHAK
(1918-19)**

Petrograd   Vologda

**BRITISH
FLEET**

Kazan

**IUDENICH
(1918-20)**

**WHITES AND
CZECH LEGION
(1918)**

Moscow

Tula

Vitebsk

Tambow

Orel

**WHITE COSSACKS
(1918-20)**

Kharkov

Kiev

**DENIKIN
(1919)**

Gurev

**GERMANS
(1918-19)**

Astrachan

Rostov

**BRITISH
(1918-19)**

Odessa

**ENTENTE
(1918-20)**   Sevastopol   Novorossiysk

**TURKISH
(1918)**

**BRITISH
(1918-20)**   Batumi

Figure 26: *The Reds controlled the central region of Russia whereas the White forces were scattered around Russia.*

The Reds controlled central Russia which gave them numerous advantages. First, this area contained the major cities where many large factories and munitions works could produce weapons. Also, this area was well connected by railways, telegraph and telephone. This meant Trotsky and his commanders could easily communicate and transport resources (soldiers, weapons) to wherever they were needed most. The Whites, on the other hand, were cut off from one another meaning they could not communicate easily or share resources. This made it easy for the Reds to pick off the White armies one by one.

Why the Reds won: propaganda

Lenin and Trotsky used propaganda in various ways to gain support from Russians. First, they continually told the peasants that the Whites wanted a return to the Tsarist state which would see landlords take back land. Secondly, propaganda focused on the atrocities that the Whites had committed against peasants. Lastly, the Reds focused their propaganda on the fact that the Whites had help from foreign powers.

Make the Link

You may learn about propaganda in English or Media.

Figure 27 and Source H: *This Bolshevik propaganda poster shows the three White generals under the control of the USA, France and Britain.*

Posters, like the one here, made the Whites out to be under the control of foreign powers and therefore not fighting in the interests of Russia. The Reds, by contrast, always showed themselves as the saviours of Russia. Bolshevik propaganda certainly helped the Reds gain support in the countryside and cities.

War communism

Lenin introduced war communism to ensure that the Reds had all the food and equipment they needed to defeat the Whites, which in practice meant that the Bolsheviks controlled all aspects of the economy. In agriculture, peasants had to sell any grain they had left over to the government at a fixed rate. They were no longer allowed to sell grain privately and if they hid any then they could be sent to prison or even executed. In industry, workers were conscripted into factories, strikes were banned and discipline was harsh. War communism may have provided the Red Army with food and resources but it was a disaster for Russia, as you shall see later.

GO! Activity 20

1. In pairs, discuss all the reasons the Reds won. Now, using scrap paper, make up your own card sort with one reason on each. Decide as a pair which is the most important factor and put this at the top. Put the one you think is least important at the bottom.

2. Create a poster/presentation that reflects your card sort decision but this time add in details about each factor using words and pictures.

   (Unit outcomes: National 4: Outcome 1.2; National 5: Outcomes 1.2, 1.3 and 2.3)

Exam style questions

3. To what extent was Trotsky's leadership responsible for the Red victory in the Civil War?   **KU 9**

   (Unit outcomes: National 4: Outcome 1.2; National 5: Outcomes 1.2, 1.3 and 2.3)

4. Evaluate the usefulness of **Source H** as evidence of the reasons why the Reds won the Civil War.   **SH 5**

   (You may want to comment on who created it, when they created it, why they created it, what they say or what has been missed out.)

The nature of the Soviet state

When the Bolsheviks came to power they had no intention of sharing power. When the first elections to the Constituent Assembly were held, the Bolsheviks only gained a third of the votes. Lenin ordered it to be shut down and had his new secret police, the Cheka, crush any opposition to his rule. Lenin then set about creating a communist state in Russia, where, under his leadership, Soviets would run the country.

The Treaty of Brest-Litovsk

In March 1918, Lenin made a peace with Germany, taking Russia out of the Great War. This resulted in Russia losing a lot of land, resources and money, but Lenin was not concerned. He believed there would be a worldwide communist revolution soon anyway, and in the meantime he had to create a Soviet state in Russia. Importantly, by making peace with Germany, Lenin delivered on his earlier promise of ending the war and so gained support from Russian soldiers who could now return home.

Creating a communist society

Communists saw religion as a way for the rich to control the poor. Lenin banned religion, priests were sometimes killed and churches were destroyed. Workers were given an 8 hour day, unemployment pay and pensions. Education was focused on, with literacy rates improving under Bolshevik rule. Also, abortion and divorce were legalised, providing women with more control over their lives. The idea of equality ran through all these policies, yet if a Russian disagreed with anything the Bolsheviks did, the penalties were severe.

The economy and the effects of war communism

The Bolsheviks took control of all banks and factories and land was redistributed among the peasantry. Soviets were established throughout Russia, and they were given the task of ensuring that Bolshevik policies and ideas were put into place.

Lenin and his Bolshevik party controlled all aspects of the Russian economy through war communism. The effect on Russian industry was terrible, as factories were being run by people who lacked the experience and skills to do the job properly. By 1921 industrial production was lower than in 1917.

In the countryside peasants produced less grain than ever before because there was no incentive to sell surplus grain to the government at such low prices. Also, they slaughtered their own livestock rather than let the government seize them. All this meant that agricultural production declined rapidly and, with more and more grain being seized by the Red and White armies, there was famine in Russia. Millions of Russians died and there were even cases of cannibalism. The biggest killers of the Russian civil war were not soldiers, but famine and disease. In 1920, over 1 000 000 are thought to have died from typhus and typhoid alone.

The Cheka and 'Red Terror'

By the summer of 1918 Lenin had banned all other political parties and censorship was in place, but there was still much opposition to Bolshevik rule, as the civil war showed. Lenin established the Cheka almost immediately when he came to power. The Cheka, led by the fearsome and ruthless Felix Dzerzhinsky, was the Bolshevik secret

Figure 28: *A Bolshevik poster from 1920 which says: 'Comrade Lenin Cleanses the Earth of Filth'. Lenin believed there would be a worldwide revolution.*

Make the Link

If you study RMPS you might learn about religious discrimination.

Figure 29: *A Ukrainian family suffering from typhus. War communism led to famine, and with it diseases like typhus spread quickly.*

Hint

In dictatorships today, secret police forces often exist to control the population.

police. It soon gained a reputation for violence and intimidation. Its aim was to crush any opposition to the Bolshevik revolution and it was certainly effective. In the summer of 1918 the Cheka murdered the Tsar and his family. In September 1918 an attempt was made on Lenin's life. In response, the Cheka began the 'Red Terror', arresting, torturing and even killing anyone who it considered to be a danger to the revolution.

Source I: Felix Dzerzhinsky interviewed in a communist newspaper, 14 July 1918.

> We stand for organised terror – this should be frankly admitted. Terror is an absolute necessity during times of revolution. Our aim is to fight against the enemies of the Soviet Government and of the new order of life. We judge quickly. In most cases only a day passes between the apprehension of the criminal and his sentence.

GO! Activity 21

1. It is 1921 and you are living and working in Moscow. Write a set of three diary entries describing your life and all you see and hear, over the course of a week.

Exam style questions

2. Explain why the Bolsheviks were successful in seizing power in October 1917. **KU 6**
   (Unit outcomes: National 4/5: Outcome 2.2)

3. Describe the effects of war communism on Russia and its people. **KU 4**
   (Unit outcomes: National 4/5: Outcome 2.1)

4. How fully does **Source I** describe the nature of the Soviet state? **SH 6**
   (Unit outcomes: National 4/5: Outcome 1.1)

Summary

In this topic you have learned:

- how the Tsar controlled Russia
- what life was like for peasants and industrial workers in Tsarist Russia
- why there was a revolution in 1905
- how the Tsar managed to remain in power after 1905
- why the Tsar fell from power in the February Revolution of 1917
- why the Bolsheviks were able to seize control from the Provisional Government in October 1917
- why the Reds won the Civil War
- what the Soviet state was like in 1921.

You should have developed your skills and be able to:

- evaluate the usefulness of a source
- compare two sources by saying what they agree or disagree about
- put a source into context by saying how fully it describes an issue.

Learning Checklist

Now that you have finished **Red flag: Lenin and the Russian Revolution, 1894–1921,** complete a self-evaluation of your knowledge and skills to assess what you have understood. Use traffic lights to help you make up a revision plan to help you improve in the areas you identified as red or amber.

- Explain how the Tsar controlled Russia.

- Describe the role of the Orthodox Church in the Tsar's control of Russia.

- Describe the class divisions in Tsarist Russia.

- Explain why the Russian economy was so backward.

- Explain why the peasantry and the industrial workers were so unhappy.

- Describe the policy of Russification.

- Explain the effect of Russification on national minorities.

- Describe the main revolutionary groups in Russia before 1905.

- Evaluate the main causes of the 1905 Revolution.

- Explain how the Tsar dealt with the revolution.

- Evaluate whether the Dumas made any real change to the Tsar's power.

- Explain what Stolypin did to try and maintain the Tsar's power.

- Evaluate whether the Tsar was stronger in 1914 than he had been before the 1905 Revolution.

- Describe the effects of the First World War on Russia.

- Explain why the Tsar was becoming increasingly unpopular during the war.

- Describe the events of the February Revolution of 1917.

- Explain what the Dual Authority was.

- Explain why the Provisional Government failed to retain power.

- Describe Lenin's return and the April Theses.

- Describe the July Days and the Kornilov Revolt.

- Explain the importance of the Bolshevik leadership in the October Revolution.

- Explain why the Reds won the Civil War, 1917–1921.

- Describe the nature of the Soviet state in 1921.

Studying this topic will provide you with a good understanding of the vast changes Germany underwent between the years 1918 and 1939. You will learn how the failures of the democratic Weimar Republic, set up in the wake of Germany's catastrophic defeat in 1918, led to the formation of the Nazi state under the leadership of Adolf Hitler. You will also learn how, once in power, the Nazi regime controlled the population through intimidation and propaganda, as well as developing social and economic policies that appealed to many Germans.

You will develop your skills and be able to:

❖ evaluate the usefulness of a source

❖ compare two sources by saying what they agree or disagree about

❖ put a source into context by saying how fully it describes an issue.

This topic is split into four sections:

❖ Weimar Germany, 1919–1929

❖ Nazi rise to power, 1929–1933

❖ Nazi control of Germany

❖ Nazi social and economic policies

Level 4 experiences and outcomes relevant to this topic:

I can evaluate conflicting sources of evidence to sustain a line of argument. **SOC 4-01a**

By studying groups in past societies who experienced inequality, I can explain the reasons for the inequality and evaluate how groups or individuals addressed it. **SOC 4-04a**

I can describe the main features of conflicting world belief systems in the past and can present informed views on the consequences of such conflict for societies then and since. **SOC 4-04b**

I can make reasoned judgements about how the exercise of power affects the rights and responsibilities of citizens by comparing a more democratic and a less democratic society. **SOC 4-04c**

I have investigated a meeting of cultures in the past and can analyse the impact on the societies involved. **SOC 4-05c**

Having critically analysed a significant historical event, I can assess the relative importance of factors contributing to the event. **SOC 4-06a**

I can assess the impact for those involved in a specific instance of the expansion of power and influence in the past. **SOC 4-06d**

Section 3:
European and
World: Hitler and
Nazi Germany,
1919–1939

📖 Key Words

- **Kaiser**

German word for Emperor.

- **Stalemate**

A position or situation where no action or progress can be made.

- **Armistice**

A ceasefire and suspension of hostilities.

🔍 Hint

The First World War was fought between the Triple Alliance (Germany, Austria-Hungary and Italy) and the Triple Entente (Great Britain, France and Russia, often called 'the Allied powers' or 'the Allies').

⁘ Make the Link

If you study 'The Era of the Great War, 1900–1928' you will learn more about the trench system on the Western Front and how it led to a stalemate.

🔍 Hint

In 1923, Adolf Hitler used the heroic status of General Ludendorff to gain popularity and support for his Munich Putsch.

🔵 Activity 1

Write a short summary that gives a detailed and clear view of what Germany was like at the end of the war. Your summary should be at least 150 words long.
(Unit outcomes: National 4/5: Outcome 2.1)

Background

Germany in 1914 was ruled by Kaiser Wilhelm II. The Kaiser led Germany into the First World War (1914–1918), after Austria-Hungary's heir to the throne, Franz Ferdinand, was shot in Sarajevo by a Serbian terrorist group. German soldiers rushed to join the war after being assured it would only last a few months, but by 1916 the stalemate and horrific trench conditions had taken their toll on the men.

By the summer of 1918 it was clear that Germany would not win the war. Bulgaria, Turkey and Austria-Hungary, Germany's allies, were now devastated by war and wanted peace. The USA had entered the war in April 1917 in support of the Allied powers, resulting in an influx of fresh troops. Ultimately, the failure of Germany's final push at winning the war, the Ludendorff offensive, meant Germany had to face an inevitable defeat. On the German home front, in January 1918 over a million workers took part in the biggest strike Germany had experienced during the war.

The final weeks of the war were devastating for Germany. British Navy ships had successfully blocked German ports halting all supplies of food, medicine and fuel. The situation was made even worse when a terrible bout of Spanish flu swept through the country, lowering morale even further and leading to more pleas for peace. The growing economic crisis, the realisation of having lost the war and the sense of loss and betrayal, led to revolutionary feelings growing among both civilians and soldiers. As the Kaiser had been responsible for leading Germany into the war, he was the prime target for blame.

In November 1918, an armistice was signed between Germany and the Allies and the Kaiser abdicated. An elected parliament was set up called the Reichstag under the leadership of a socialist, Friedrich Ebert. The new system of government was to be known as the Weimar Republic. This was closely followed by economic crises that crippled the country financially and socially. These financial crises would be one of the fundamental reasons for the rise to power in 1933 of Adolf Hitler and the National Socialist (Nazi) Party.

Figure 1: *Kaiser Wilhelm II, the last Emperor of Germany*

1 Weimar Germany, 1919–1929

In this section you will learn about:

- How Germany was affected by the Great War.
- The peace settlements Germany had to agree to.
- How Germany was affected by the Treaty of Versailles.
- Why the Weimar Republic was established and how.
- Attempts to overthrow the Weimar Republic.
- The economic problems that weakened the Weimar Republic between 1919 and 1933.

How was Germany affected by the Great War?

Kaiser Wilhelm II had led Germany into war in 1914 but by 1918 the Germans had lost faith in their leader. The human cost of war had been terrible for Germany, with 2 000 000 dead and 6 300 000 injured. In October 1918 the German Navy based at the port of Kiel mutinied. Many soldiers also felt the war was now pointless and this, along with dwindling resources, led them to stop fighting for the Kaiser, who they felt had failed them. By November 1918 many ships would fly a red flag to show their desire for revolution.

📖 Key Word

- **Mutiny**

A revolt by soldiers or sailors.

Figure 2: *Exhausted German soldiers on the frontline.*

Key Word

- **Abdicate**

To give up the throne.

Make the Link

If you study Modern Studies you will learn in detail about what makes a democracy.

Figure 3: *Friedrich Ebert*

Soldiers were seeking peace, women wanted their men back from the war and many civilians were joining revolutionary groups who were hoping for peace and reform. By 6 November 1918, Workers' and Soldiers' Councils had taken over in many cities and there was civil unrest. In an effort to restore order German politicians sent messages to the Kaiser to inform him they were losing control fast and urged him to abdicate. The politicians felt that if the Allies could see that Germany now had a solid democratic foundation on which to build a new government then there was a chance they would be more lenient when drawing up the peace settlement.

On 9 November 1918, a new provisional government was established under the initial leadership of Prince Max of Baden, who immediately announced the Kaiser's abdication. Prince Max was the last imperial Chancellor. He quickly resigned and handed the Chancellorship to Friedrich Ebert of the Social Democrats (SPD). On the same day, Ebert's deputy, Philip Scheidemann, announced, from a balcony of the Reichstag, that Germany would become a democratic republic. On 11 November 1918 an armistice was signed and Germany awaited the terms of the peace settlement. The Kaiser agreed to the abdication and went into exile in Holland.

After 1918 many German civilians started to believe the 'Stab in the Back' myth, branding the new government as the 'November criminals'. This was the belief that Germany did not lose the war but instead were betrayed by the provisional government who signed the armistice.

GO! Activity 2

1. Using the information above write the Kaiser's letter of abdication. State clearly at least four reasons as to why you feel you have to give up your throne. Hint: *soldiers, sailors, women, war*.

   (Unit outcomes: National 4/5: Outcome 2.2)

Exam style question

Source A describes the effects of the end of the First World War on Germany.

> In November 1918, when the Kaiser fled to Holland, German soldiers retreated in disarray. They were in a state of shock. The streets were full of lorries with sailors, soldiers and workers brandishing red flags. There was fighting and gunfire in the streets around my home. Families kept close together, often afraid to venture out in fear of stray bullets.

2. How fully does **Source A** describe the effects of the end of the First World War on German people? **SH 6**

   (Use **Source A** and recall.)

   (Unit outcomes: National 4/5: Outcome 1.1)

The Treaty of Versailles

The peace settlement

In June 1919 the terms of the peace settlement, to be known as the Treaty of Versailles, were announced. The discussions had been dominated by 'The Big Three': David Lloyd George, Prime Minister of Britain, Woodrow Wilson, President of the USA and George Clemenceau, Prime Minister of France.

- Britain was split between public opinion, which supported Germany being punished, and the government's belief that Germany shouldn't be completely ruined. Newspaper headlines demanded Germany should pay for the whole cost of war, but the British government wanted to ensure future trade with Germany and did not want Germany to be so harshly punished that it would look for revenge or turn to communism.
- The French were determined to take revenge for what Germany had put them through during the war and demanded humiliation and harsh punishment.
- The USA were unwavering in their desire not to be pulled into future European issues and so hoped they could come to a peaceful settlement.
- The Italian Prime Minister, Vittorio Orlando, was also present but had little say on the terms.

At the palace of Versailles in France the following terms were agreed and put to Germany:

Military

- Army had to be cut to 100 000 men.
- Navy had to reduce their battleships to just six.
- Airforce and submarines were forbidden.
- Heavy artillery and weapons were to be destroyed.
- The German Rhineland that borders France was to be demilitarised for fifteen years.

Territorial

- All colonies were divided up among the Allies.
- Alsace and Lorraine were returned to France.
- Eupen and Malmedy were given to Belgium.
- West Prussia, Upper Silesia and Posen were given to Poland; this included the industrial hub of Port Danzig, which meant that Germany was now split in two.
- Northern Schleswig was given to Denmark.

Reparations

- Germany was ordered to pay for the cost of the war, a final sum of £6 600 000 000 being decided in 1921.

 Hint

Germany only finished paying off First World War reparations in September 2010, with a final payment of £59 000 000.

War Guilt Clause (Article 231)

- Germany had to accept full responsibility for the war, which included all damages and losses.

Germany was instructed that they had to accept these terms or the Allies would resume the war. The new German government were left with no choice and the treaty was signed on 28 June 1919.

Figure 4: *The Treaty of Versailles*

Activity 3

Produce a poster to outline the four areas of the Treaty of Versailles and how they affected Germany. Use images to give your poster more detail and ensure that it is bright and colourful. All terms of the treaty should be shown on the poster. Make sure any written work is big and can be read clearly from a distance.

(Unit outcomes: National 4/5: Outcome 2.1)

How did the Treaty of Versailles affect Germany?

The German people were furious at the terms of the treaty and called it a 'Diktat' (a dictated peace treaty that was forced on them). In June 1919 a German newspaper declared:

'Vengence! German Nation! Today in the Hall of Mirrors the disgraceful treaty is being signed. Do not forget it. The German people will with unceasing labour press forward to reconquer the place among nations to which it is entitled. Then will come vengence for the shame of 1919.'

Activity 4

Come up with a slogan for how the German people felt towards the Treaty of Versailles. No more than ten words!

The Weimar Republic

Why was the Weimar Republic established and how?

In January 1919, elections were held for a new National Assembly. Berlin was in ruins and there was a danger of rioting so, on 6 February, the National Assembly constituted itself in Weimar, a town in Saxony known over the centuries as a cultural hub for many German poets, artists and composers. The new government drew up the new German constitution in Weimar and would choose to keep the name after they returned to Berlin. Friedrich Ebert was elected as first President of the new Republic with Philip Scheidemann as Chancellor.

The Weimar government wanted to ensure democracy in Germany, which they felt was the best way to represent the people fairly. The German people would have the right to elect the politicians who would represent them and guarantee their basic rights.

In August, the new 'Weimar' constitution became law:

- The government was elected using proportional representation.
- All men and women over twenty could vote.
- All Germans were entitled to civil rights, with freedom of speech and freedom of religion.
- The President was to be elected every seven years and he was responsible for appointing the Chancellor.
- The Chancellor was in charge of day to day government affairs.

Attempts to overthrow the Weimar Republic

Revolutions and putsches, 1919–1923

Spartacist (communist) Revolt

Germany was not united in its support for the Social Democrats and the provisional government, and in January 1919 an armed communist (Spartacist) uprising occurred, led by Rosa Luxemburg and Karl Liebknecht, which attempted to seize power.

The Spartacists believed that the German parliament would never pass acts to benefit the workers, so they would have to take power for themselves. Ebert was expecting the violent attack from the Spartacists and enlisted the German army to help him keep control. He appointed as a minister of defence Gustav Noske, whose first task was to bring together war-hardened ex-soldiers (Freikorps) who firmly believed the war had been lost because of the communists and revolutionaries.

The Spartacist revolt began on 5 January 1919, with a workers' demonstration in the centre of Berlin which quickly became violent. The next day the Communists joined in and Liebknecht called for a

Figure 5: *Rosa Luxemburg*

📖 Key Word

- **Communism**

When the workers control the country and economy, and wealth is equally shared among everyone.

Figure 6: *Karl Liebknecht*

general strike which prompted the government to send in Noske and the Freikorps. The Freikorps used great violence in crushing the Spartacists and used artillery to recapture buildings in Berlin. On 15 January, leaders Karl Liebknect and Rosa Luxemburg were arrested by the Freikorps and and were executed for their part in the uprising.

Kapp Putsch

On 13 March 1920 Wolfgang Kapp attempted a putsch in Germany. His aims were to:

- make the German army stronger
- give Germany back its pride
- get back the land that had been given to Poland in the Treaty of Versailles.

Wolfgang Kapp was an extreme nationalist who hated the 'November criminals'. Kapp had secured the support of several influential groups in Germany, including:

- the Berlin police
- the Freikorps
- a large portion of the army.

Kapp marched on Berlin with 5000 supporters and was quick to gain control of the city. The German government quickly escaped to Dresden. However, he had failed to gain the support of the German workers who, instructed by the Weimar government in Dresden, organised a strike against Kapp. This strike paralysed Berlin and led to the loss of water, food, gas, coal, trains and buses. It was at this point Kapp realised he had made an error and fled to Sweden. After a little over 100 hours Friedrich Ebert returned as if nothing had happened.

Political assassinations

There were 356 political murders between 1919 and 1922. Most politicians were excuted by right-wing extremists. One example was the murder of Walter Rathenau on 22 June 1922. The group called Organisation Consul murdered him while he drove to work in an open top car. When questioned years later, one of the assassins, Ernst von Salomon, spoke about that day and his desire to eliminate all the politicians that had accepted the Treaty of Versailles.

Munich Putsch

In November 1923 another putsch was attempted in Germany, this time led by Adolf Hitler. Hitler, who had recently taken over the National Socialist German Workers' Party (later to be known as the Nazis), tried to seize power in Munich, Bavaria. By the time of the Munich Putsch the party had thousands of members, who had started to become restless and craved an attempt to overthrow the government. The party became aware of a government meeting that was going to be attended by three important individuals: Gustav von Kahr (a Bavarian politician), General Otto von Lossow (head of the Bavarian army) and Colonel Hans von Seisser (head of the Bavarian State Police). The meeting, held in a beer hall, was interrupted by Hitler, announcing he would be taking over

Figure 7: *Hitler surrounded by Nazi Party members at the Munich Putsch, 1923.*

the Weimar Republic, with the support of General Ludendorff (a general who led the German army during the First World War). Hitler then stated that they would march on Berlin. However, he and his 600 supporters failed to gain the support of the three men and were met by armed police. The following day sixteen supporters of Hitler were killed in the streets. He was later caught, put on trial and imprisoned in Landsberg prison.

 Activity 5

Create a front page newspaper article that outlines the Spartacist uprising, Kapp Putsch and Munich (Beerhall) Putsch that happened in Germany between 1919 and 1923. Describe each event in detail, being specific about locations and individuals involved. Explain how each event affected the Weimar Republic and what caused the events to fail.

(Unit outcomes: National 4/5: Outcome 2.1)

Economic problems, 1919–1933

Passive resistance in the Ruhr

The reparation payments set out in the Treaty of Versailles had had a devastating effect on the German economy. A huge number of industrial areas had been given away to neighbouring countries, making it very difficult for Germany to recuperate after the First World War. This also affected unemployment in the country as thousands returned from war to find they no longer had a job and this placed the German economy under yet more strain. By the end of 1922, when Germany failed to honour an instalment of the reparations, France took drastic action. French and Belgian troops entered the German area of the Ruhr, taking over factories, coal mines and railway yards to try to force Germany to pay up. The Weimar Republic instructed the German people to use 'passive resistance', which meant the German people would refuse to work for the French and Belgian troops. As the workers went on strike, industrial production ground to a halt and some incidents of violence and industrial sabotage occurred. In order to cope with the situation and pay the striking workers the Weimar government simply printed more money. This very quickly led to hyperinflation.

Hyperinflation

The face value of money became virtually worthless and the German economy was on the brink of collapse. In 1922 a loaf of bread cost 163 German marks, by September 1923 it was 1 500 000 and by November 1923 it was 200 000 000 000. The hyperinflation crises meant people were paid every hour. Bartering became common with people trading in the streets. Elderly and middle class people with savings were worst affected as their pensions and savings disappeared. Small business owners were ruined and factories closed. Hyperinflation

 Hint

An illustration of the devastating effect of hyperinflation was that people bought two cups of coffee at a time because by the time they had finished the first one the price of coffee had doubled.

Make the Link

If you take Economics you will learn about the control of inflation.

was also responsible for a large degree of psychological trauma in the nation. There were bonuses, however, as many huge debts were now wiped out completely.

Many people lost all faith in the Weimar Republic and at this stage joined the more extremist parties.

Figure 8: *Children were allowed to play with worthless German marks.*

Figure 9: *Women would use money to light their fires as it was cheaper than buying the wood or coal.*

Activity 6

1. Write a letter as if you were living in Germany at the time of hyperinflation. Talk about how the crisis has affected your day to day life and what it has done to the people around you.

   (Unit outcomes: National 4/5: Outcome 2.2)

Exam style questions

Source B is about hyperinflation in Germany in 1923.

> During 1923, hyperinflation gripped Germany. On Friday afternoons, workers deperately rushed to the nearest store, where a queue had already formed. It was soul-destroying. When you arrived a pound of sugar cost 2 000 000 marks but, by the time your turn came, you could only afford a half pound. In the chaos, people pushed prams loaded with money. Life became nightmarish. We were devastated as life savings became worthless.

2. How fully does **Source B** describe the effects of hyper-inflation?   **SH 6**

   (Use **Source B** and recall.)

   (Unit outcomes: National 4/5: Outcome 1.1)

3. Describe the political problems faced by the Weimar Republic between 1919 and 1923.   **KU 4**

   (Unit outcomes: National 4/5: Outcome 2.1)

2 Nazi rise to power, 1929–1933

In this section you will learn about:

- How discontent against the Weimar Republic grew between 1929 and 1933.
- How the National Socialists (Nazis) came to power in 1933.
- Why the Reichstag fire helped the Nazis.
- Nazi consolidation of power: how Hitler made Germany a dictatorship.

Background: Weimar 1924–1929

Democracy in the Weimar Republic was always fragile due to attacks from extreme right and left, in addition to major economic problems. However, the years between 1924 and 1929 are often referred to as a high point in German history (the 'Golden Age of Weimar').

Gustav Stresemann was Chancellor for a year in 1923 before becoming Foreign Minister and in this time he managed to stabilise a fractured German economy with the introduction of the rentenmark to replace the collapsed mark. He also arranged for huge loans from America as part of the Dawes Plan in 1924, which led to increased wages in Germany and prosperity. Another crucial part of the Dawes Plan was the agreement to have Germany's reparation payments reduced and extended over a longer period of time, giving them a lot more time to pay. The Belgian and French troops agreed to leave the occupied Ruhr after the Locarno Pact was signed in October 1925, in which Germany agreed to again follow the terms outlined by the Treaty of Versailles. This, along with the monetary boost from America, meant that German industry also recovered. Stresemann even made huge steps towards bringing Germany back into international favour with the country being welcomed into the League of Nations.

Figure 10: *Berlin during the Golden Age.*

How discontent against the Weimar Republic grew between 1929 and 1933

After the brief period of prosperity between 1924 and 1929 Germany suffered an economic crisis that would, ultimately, bring it to its knees and lead to a second, political, crisis. In October 1929, the New York stock exchange on Wall Street collapsed, and within days businesses were ruined and the value of shares plunged. The USA had no choice but to stop loan payments going to Germany and demand immediate repayment. It was at this point that it became very clear that Germany's recovery was heavily based on the hand-outs it had been receiving. The financial crash in America had an effect worldwide with most countries slipping into a depression.

Figure 11: *Demonstrators with a poster that reads '2 million unemployed 1.2 billion for princes', Berlin 1930.*

> ### Make the Link
>
> In Modern Studies you will look at coalition governments today.

> ### Key Word
>
> • **Coalition**
>
> An alliance between organisations, governments or people.

The impact on Germany was devastating with the number of unemployed rocketing to 6 000 000 by 1932. Many lost their homes and livelihoods and looked to the Weimar government for assistance.

In 1929, the Weimar Republic was a coalition, made up of the Centre Party and the Social Democratic Party (SPD). However, at a time when cooperation was needed among the parties, they instead chose to clash over the unemployment benefit cuts the Centre Party believed were essential in the circumstances.

Between 1929 and 1931 the SPD Chancellor, Heinrich Brüning, tried to maintain the power of the Weimar government, but he was doing this without a majority in the Reichstag and so relied on the emergency Article 48 of the Constitution. Article 48 enabled laws to be issued by the President, Paul von Hindenburg, who was also a member of the SPD. Hindenburg had replaced Friedrich Ebert after Ebert died in 1925 and, being a member of the SPD himself, was sympathetic to Brüning's efforts.

Figure 12: *Heinrich Brüning.*

Decrees issued under Article 48 of the Constitution, 1930–1932	
Year	Decrees issued
1930	5
1931	44
1932	60

Timeline of events 1929–1932

September 1929 – Reichstag election sees a large boost in Nazi seats from 14 to 107.

October 1929 – Wall Street Crash in America sends the world into a Great Depression – Germany's unemployment soars.

May 1930 – Unemployment reaches 4 000 000 in Germany due to Depression.

April 1932 – Hindenburg is re-elected.

May 1932 – Franz von Papen is made Chancellor of Germany.

July 1932 – Nazis win 230 of 608 seats in Reichstag; they are now the largest party.

August 1932 – Hitler declares in public that he will not accept any role in the Weimar Republic, other than Chancellor.

October 1932 – Franz von Papen is not able to govern and forced to hold another election.

November 1932 – The Nazis retain their majority in the election.

December 1932 – Hinderburg appoints Kurt von Schleicher as Chancellor to replace Franz von Papen.

January 1933 – Hindenburg sacks Kurt von Schleicher and appoints Adolf Hitler as Chancellor.

Between 1929 and 1932 the Reichstag met less frequently and appeared to be growing ever weaker due to the growing popularity of the Nazis. Hitler was a dynamic and confident leader who promised to restore German pride and crush the Treaty of Versailles, something every German wanted. This weakness was highlighted further when Brüning was replaced twice – by Franz von Papen in 1932 and Kurt von Schleicher in 1933. These changes were desperate attempts by Hindenburg to prevent the growing strength and influence of the Nazi party. He also wanted to avoid giving Adolf Hitler the power he demanded in the Reichstag.

Hitler had worked hard to organise his party; for example, he created youth organisations, he established the SD (Sicherheitsdienst), an intelligence gathering division of the SS (Schutzstaffel) and he delivered speeches to thousands of dedicated Nazi supporters at the Nuremberg Rallies. Only too aware of how influential Hitler was becoming, von Papen convinced Hindenburg to remove von Schleicher in 1933, and replace him with Adolf Hitler. When Hitler became Chancellor on 30 January 1933 it was with von Papen as his Deputy Chancellor.

Figure 13: *Franz von Papen and General von Schleicher in Berlin, 1932.*

Figure 14: *President Hindenburg, President of Germany from 1925–1934.*

Hindenburg despised Hitler and feared he would be a dangerous man given the power of the Reichstag. However, he agreed to the Chancellorship because von Papen had convinced him that, as his Deputy, he would be able to keep control of Hitler.

Although the Nazis' popularity had grown during the economic crisis in Germany by 1932 they had, in fact, lost some of their seats. It was for this reason that Hindenburg and von Papen felt Hitler's popularity could be manipulated to their advantage. How wrong they were.

GO! Activity 7

1. Take a large sheet of paper (A3) and draw a crumbling building being held up by two huge pillars. The pillars should be large enough to write in a lot of information. The crumbling building signifies the weakening Weimar Republic and should be labelled as such. The two pillars are the two crises that hit the Weimar Republic between 1929 and 1933. One pillar should be headed **'Economic crisis'** and the other should be headed **'Political crisis'**. Each of the pillars should be filled with the information that will lead to the ultimate downfall of the Weimar Republic. Be sure to enter in your information in an organised and chronological manner. It would also be of benefit to fill the crumbling building with all the initial problems the Weimar government had to deal with after the end of the Great War (you will find this information in the first part of this topic).

(Unit outcomes: National 5: Outcome 2.3)

Exam style question

2. Describe political problems faced by the Weimar Republic between 1929 and 1933. **KU 4**

(Unit outcomes: National 4/5: Outcome 2.1)

Appeal of Hitler and the Nazis

One of the reasons the Nazis were able to come to power was because of their popular appeal. Their name, National Socialist German Workers Party tried to appeal to broad sections of society, those with differing political beliefs and both the middle and working classes. Hitler was good at gauging what people wanted to hear and adapting his policies at will. Even when the name of the party NSDAP was shortened to 'Nazis' as a joke, Hitler capitalised on it and instead of getting angry went with the flow and claimed the name for himself. He promised work and bread to those hugely affected by the Great Depression of the early 1930s and vowed to stabilise the economy which appealed to the middle classes. He promised to rip up the hated Treaty of Versailles and to reclaim Germany's position as a leading country on the world stage. His speeches and effective propaganda won him attention, and in turn votes.

How the National Socialists (Nazis) took power in 1933

Immediately after the 1933 March elections Adolf Hitler was swift to request a new law that would give him complete power in Germany. He knew he would need three quarters of the Reichstag to vote in favour of this new law so made a deal with the Catholic Centre Party. Hitler's intimidating elite bodyguard, the SS, lined the entrance to the Kroll Opera House where all members of the Reichstag would vote on Hitler's proposal that he be able to govern for four years without further consultation with the Reichstag. As the SPD had twenty six of their members missing because they had been warned, restrained and attacked by the SS it was impossible to hold back the Nazi grip on the German government. On 23 March 1933 Hitler was able to successfully pass the Enabling Act. This new law gave Hitler the ultimate power and he was now able to freely pass laws without first consulting the Reichstag or President Hindenburg. This act would succeed in giving Hitler his dictatorial powers.

📖 Key Words

- **Enabling Act**

This Act meant Adolf Hitler could pass laws without consulting the Reichstag, giving him dictatorial powers.

Make the Link

In Modern Studies you will learn about how laws are created in Scotland and the United Kingdom today.

Figure 15: *Adolf Hitler and President Hindenburg at the Tannenberg Commemoration in 1933.*

📖 Key Words

- **Dictator**

A ruler who has absolute and unrestricted power in government.

- **Trade union**

An organisation that represents workers' rights.

- **Concentration camp**

A building or buildings created to detain and imprison people.

One of Hitler's first laws was a ban of trade unions in May 1933; any union officials who disagreed were quickly removed from society and sent to a concentration camp (for more on concentration camps, see pages 193–195). Strikes were banned and the Nazis said 'divisive organisations, setting Germans against Germans' were now outlawed, especially as all Germans would now be part of the new Nazi Labour Service. Furthermore, Hitler banned the KPD (Communists) and the SPD and, by July 1933, the NSDAP (Nazis) declared themselves the only party in the Reichstag.

Make the Link

You will learn more about trade unions in Business Management and Modern Studies.

GO! Activity 8

1. Create a ladder diagram that details how Hitler increased his power and the steps he took to gain more influence after becoming Chancellor. Each point should be developed and explain clearly how it led to the Nazis gaining more power in Germany. The diagram should contain the following: Enabling Act, trade unions, political opponents.

   (Unit outcomes: National 4/5: Outcome 2.2)

   Exam style question

2. Explain the reasons why Hitler was able to become Chancellor in 1933.   **KU 6**

   (Unit outcomes: National 4/5: Outcome 2.2)

Why the Reichstag fire helped the Nazis

The Reichstag fire was a major factor in helping Hitler and the Nazis rise to power in Germany. On 27 February 1933 the Reichstag building burned down, coincidently the week before the 1933 elections. Historians have debated the origin of the fire for many years, with some firmly believing that the Nazis started the fire themselves. When the authorities arrived at the burning Reichstag building they discovered a Dutch communist, Marinus van der Lubbe, with a packet of matches and firelighters. He claimed to have burned the government building in a protest against Nazi rule. However, it was subsequently discovered that the fire was started in at least twenty different locations. Is it likely one man was able to complete this task himself? Either way, Hitler seized this opportunity to extend his power, and he instantly accused the communists of starting the fire. Only hours after the fire 4000 communists were arrested.

🔍 Hint

The Reichstag building was reopened in 1999 after a four year renovation and controversy still lingered about its links to the turbulent history of Germany and its name, with some saying it should be renamed.

Figure 16: *The burning Reichstag building in 1933.*

Nazi consolidation of power: how Hitler made Germany a dictatorship

Make the Link

You study civil liberties in Modern Studies.

Hitler also used the Reichstag fire as an excuse to convince Hindenburg to pass the Decree for Protection of the People and the State (the Reichstag Fire Law), which suspended the basic rights given to people by the Weimar Republic, like freedom of speech and press. It also took away basic human rights for communists. Communist media and private correspondence were checked and censored.

On 30 June and 1 July 1934 an event occurred that showed how much control Hitler had over the Nazi Party and would help him on his road to dictatorship. Hitler instructed detachments of his personal bodyguard, the SS, to eradicate (get rid of) the leaders of the SA (Sturm Abteilung), the paramilitary wing of the Nazi Party. Hitler had been suspicious of the SA for some time and felt threatened by their power. He was concerned about the leader of the SA, Ernst Röhm, and his plans to break up the regular army and make all soldiers part of his SA. Hitler felt this would make the SA so powerful that they could possibly start a revolution against the Nazis. On this two day purge, several hundred SA members, including Röhm, were killed. This was to be known as the Night of the Long Knives.

Figure 17: *Hitler walkes up swastika-lined steps during a mass Nazi rally, Germany, 1934.*

The regular army were so grateful for this that, following Hindenburg's death, they swore an oath of loyalty to Hitler. By 1935 the German army was reorganised into the Wehrmacht and were under the total control of Hitler.

After Hindenburg died on 2 August 1934 Hitler combined the roles of Chancellor and President and from this point forward he would be known as Führer. This was the last step on his journey to creating a dictatorship.

Key Word

• **Führer**
German word for leader.

Activity 9

1. Create a front page newspaper article that details the Reichstag fire from the point of view of a Nazi party member.

   Include in your article:
   • outline of the day and reactions from Nazi witnesses
   • communist blame
   • reaction to the Decree for Protection of the People and the State
   • how this would secure Nazi power in Germany.

   (Unit outcomes: National 4/5: Outcome 2.1)

2. Create a six block cartoon strip on an A3 piece of paper that tracks Hitler's road to being a dictator.

   Box 1: Hitler planning the annihilation of the SA.
   Box 2: SS members killing SA members.
   Box 3: SS members killing Ernst Röhm.
   Box 4: Hindenburg dying.
   Box 5: The German army becoming the Wehrmacht and swearing an oath of loyalty to Hitler.
   Box 6: Hitler making himself Führer in front of a crowd of thousands.

   (Unit outcomes: National 5: Outcome 2.3)

(continued)

3. Write a summary of how Hitler came to power in 1933. Things to include:
   - weakness of the Weimar Republic
   - Reichstag Fire
   - Enabling Act
   - death of Hindenburg.

   (Unit outcomes: National 4: Outcome 1.1; National 5: Outcomes 1.1 and 2.3)

Exam style questions

Sources C and **D** are about the Night of the Long Knives.
Source C

> Hitler's courage in taking firm action has made him a hero in the eyes of many Germans. He has won approval and sympathy for the steps he took. People think his action is proof that he wants order and decency in Germany. Reports from different parts of the country are all agreed that people are expressing satisfaction that Hitler has acted against the serious threat posed by Röhm and the SA to Germany and her people.

Source D

> On the morning of 30 June 1934, Röhm and other SA leaders were arrested and eventually shot. Hitler's personal popularity soared as a result of the Night of the Long Knives. Most Germans disliked the corruption of the SA and welcomed the strong action against it. President Hindenburg's telegram to Hitler read: 'By your determined action and brave leadership, you have saved the German nation from serious danger.'

4. Compare the views of **Sources C** and **D** about the attitude of Germans to the Night of the Long Knives. (Compare the sources overall and/or in detail.) **SH 4**

5. To what extent was the weakness of the Weimar Republic the main reason for the Nazi rise to power between 1919 and 1933? **KU 9**

   Your essay should include the following:
   - An introduction that: (a) addresses the question, (b) outlines the factors, (c) a sentence that links the four factors back to the question.
   - A main body that contains four paragraphs that each has: (a) a topic sentence, (b) gives evidence and facts to support the factor, (c) a sentence that links the information back to the question.
   - A conclusion that: (a) answers the question, (b) prioritises the factors and how important they are in answering the question.

   (Unit outcomes: National 4: Outcome 1.2; National 5: Outcomes 1.2, 1.3 and 2.3)

3 Nazi control of Germany

In this section you will learn about:

- Formation characteristics of the National Socialist Government.
- The changes that were made to the German government.
- How the SS used intimidation to gain control of Germany.
- The treatment of the Jews and other minority groups.
- Nazi opposition and what happened to it.

Formation and characteristics of the National Socialist Government

Adolf Hitler secured ultimate control of Germany using a combination of organisation, intimidation, foreign and domestic policies. The Nazis had also used a powerful mixture of fear and propaganda.

Hitler's charm and charisma were far reaching. The following was printed in Britain's *Daily Express* in 1936 after the former Prime Minister, David Lloyd George, had paid Hitler and Germany a visit: 'The old trust him, the young idolise him. It is not popularity – it is the worship of a national hero who has saved his country from disaster.'

What many were unaware of was how Hitler used the Enabling Act to eradicate any opposition to the party and also to begin the removal of the 'unwanted' in society.

Figure 18: *Members of the League of German Girls performing at a Reichs Party Congress in 1938.*

The police state

When Hitler established the Third Reich he created a police state. Every element of German national and local life was to come under Nazi rule. Hitler's dictatorship was undemocratic which meant that no one could speak out or overrule him.

SS

Led by Heinrich Himmler the SS (Schutzstaffel) was set up in 1925, as Adolf Hitler's bodyguard. They represented the perfect Aryan Nazi ideal and each took an oath to be loyal to Hitler. They were split into three sections. The SD (Sicherheitsdienst) was responsible for looking for enemies of the state. The Waffen SS was the combat arm of the SS. The Death's Head Unit were the SS men who ran the concentration camps.

📖 Key Word

- **Aryan**

A term used by the Nazis to describe the pure blood master race: ideally northern European, tall, blonde, blue eyed, non-Jewish.

Gestapo

Set up in 1933 and led by Reinhard Heydrich, the primary focus of the Gestapo was to seek out any enemies of the state inside Germany.

What would happen to you if your name was on the list of 'enemies of the state'?

1. Woken by members of the Gestapo and instructed you had three minutes to pack a bag.

2. Taken to the nearest police station and held in a cell.

3. After spending a considerable time in the cell you would then be taken to a room and forced to sign a D-11 form, also known as a 'Order for Protective Custody'. Once this is signed you are agreeing to go to prison.

4. After receiving no trial you are then taken to a concentration camp, where you will stay indefinitely.

Many people found themselves to be on the 'enemies of the state' list: political prisoners, 'work-shy', religious people who followed the Bible, homosexuals and professional criminals. In 1936, Hitler passed the Gestapo Law, which meant that the organisation could operate without review from the courts of law. This law meant the Gestapo could do anything they wanted without judgement. By 1939, 162 000 Germans had been found by the Gestapo and sent to concentration camps.

GO! Activity 10

1. Create a visual display that shows how Hitler ran his police state in Germany. Your display should include details of the role of the SS and Gestapo.

   (Unit outcomes: National 5: Outcome 2.3)

Exam style question

Source E is taken from an interview with a former prisoner of one of the concentration camps from 1939.

> 8000 prisoners included first of all the 'politicals' (as, for example, the Communist members of the Reichstag), many of whom have been in various concentration camps ever since 1933 … In addition to the genuine political prisoners there are many poor devils at Buchenwald accused of having spoken abusively of the sacred person of the Führer.

2. Evaluate the usefulness of **Source E** as evidence of the kind of people who were targeted by the Gestapo and SS in Germany under the Nazi regime. **SH 5**

   (You may want to comment on who wrote it, when they wrote it, why they wrote it, what they say and what has been missed out.)

What changes were made to the German government?

After Hitler passed the Enabling Act in 1933 he was able to change the way the German government was run. Hitler prioritised the eradication of trade unions and opposition parties but following this he destroyed the previous legal system in Germany. The creation of the 'People's Court' meant that any enemies of the state could be charged with treason, imprisoned and eventually sent to a concentration camp.

The 1935 Nuremberg Laws formalised the segregation of non-Aryan Germans from society. Among other measures, non-Aryans lost their German citizenship and marriage between Aryans and non-Aryans was forbidden. As time progressed these laws changed and became more extreme in their clear victimisation of the untermenschen.

Propaganda was an inescapable part of life in Nazi Germany and sought to ensure that all German people accepted the party policies without question. Headed by Josef Goebbels, the Ministry of Popular Enlightenment controlled all Nazi propaganda. It took many forms, including controlling the mass media (broadcasting, films, the press), flags depicting the swastika, posters and huge rallies that were organised at Nuremberg each year in September. At the rallies, Germans were bombarded by Nazi symbols, while listening to drums, trumpets and the charismatic speeches of Hitler.

📖 Key Word

- **Untermensch (plural: untermenschen)**

A German word meaning 'sub human'. Nazis used it to describe those people they regarded as inferior.

✴ Make the Link

You may look at propaganda and persuasion in English or Media.

Figure 19: *Josef Goebbels making a radio broadcast, 1936.*

🔵 GO! Activity 11

1. Create a piece of Nazi propaganda. This can be a poster, leaflet or speech. The propaganda piece should promote the Nazi ideal and how pure blood Germans should act in Germany.

   (Unit outcomes: National 5: Outcome 2.3)

Exam style question

2. Explain the reasons why Hitler was able to increase his control over Germany in 1933–34. **KU 6**

   (Unit outcomes: National 4/5: Outcome 2.2)

Figure 20: *Example of Nazi propaganda. 'Hitler is building up. Help out. Buy German goods'.*

Figure 21: *Heinrich Himmler*

How did the SS use intimidation to control Germany?

By 1933 the SS numbered 52 000. Many Germans felt intimidated by them into accepting the Nazi Party aims and ideals. The SS were under the charge of Heinrich Himmler, which meant he was at the centre of the control of the population. The SS were easily identified by their black uniform with lightning flash insignia. They were Hitler's most trusted men and were put in charge of the police, security and intelligence.

The SS would also be put in charge of the concentration camps that would become a fundamental element of the Nazi regime, used first to imprison people but later turned into death camps. The first camp was set up in Dachau in 1933. Himmler was ultimately responsible for ensuring that the population of Germany was all pure blooded – he would be the man to oversee the extermination of over 6 000 000 Jews in German occupied Europe.

Source F is Heinrich Himmler explaining to the army what the job of the SS was in 1937.

> When we go to war, the Army will win on land, the Navy will win at sea, and the Air Force in the skies – but this time the SS will look after the home front. These are the grass roots which we must keep healthy by hook or by crook because otherwise the three others, the fighting parts of Germany, will be stabbed in the back again. This is not just a war against an army, but against a political enemy – communism, led by the Jews.

🔍 Hint

Between 1889 and 1902 during the Second Boer War, Britain was responsible for the deaths of 27 000 innocent people when they imprisoned South Africans in concentration camps.

🔵 Activity 12

1. Using **Source F** above and all the sections in this topic so far, explain how Himmler and the Nazi Party planned to control Germany. You should mention something about each of the following: SS, Gestapo, propaganda and the Enabling Act.

   (Unit outcomes: National 4/5: Outcome 2.2)

Exam style question

Source G was written by historians J.F. Corkery and R.C.F. Stone in *Weimar Germany and the Third Reich.*

> Government organisation of the workers gave opportunity for brainwashing them. In 1935 the Labour Service was established. This meant that every male between the ages of 18 and 25 had to do six months in public work camps. Camp discipline was semi-military. Camp leaders were given ranks. Men drilled with spades instead of rifles. The Labour Service was an opportunity for spread Nazi propaganda, building upon that already provided by the schools and Hitler Youth. Workers were urged to regard themselves as 'soldiers of work'.

2. Evaluate the usefulness of **Source G** as evidence about militarism in Nazi Germany. (You may want to comment on who wrote it, when they wrote it, why they wrote it, what they say or what has been missed out.)
   SH 5

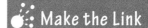

The treatment of the Jews and other minority groups

The Jews

- New laws victimised Jews:
  - ○ 1933 – Jews could no longer be members of sports clubs, signs were displayed in Jewish shops saying 'Germans! Do not buy from Jewish shops'.
  - ○ 1935 – Jews could not marry Germans, Jews were no longer German citizens and now could not vote (Nuremberg Laws).
  - ○ 1936 – Jews had to hand in their bikes and radios.
  - ○ 1938 – Jews could not use swimming pools or attend cinemas.
  - ○ 1940 – Jewish people could not use telephones.

- Kristallnacht (Night of Broken Glass) – On 9 November 1938 a Jew, Herschel Grynszpan, shot a German, Ernst von Rath, in Paris which gave the Nazis the perfect opportunity to attack the Jews in Germany. The SS destroyed Jewish owned shop windows, giving the night its name. They burned Jewish literature in the streets and synagogues were also burned. Approximately 30 000 Jews were sent to concentration camps.

- Anti-Jewish propaganda – Goebbels tried to ensure that all Germans understood that Jews were evil and were to blame for the loss of the First World War. In anti-Jewish propaganda the Jews were shown as evil people with large noses who would try to kidnap children.

- The Final Solution – In 1942, the Nazis decided that all Jews should be exterminated. This is when many concentration camps became death camps. These death camps, often built for the sole purpose of extermination, such as Auschwitz Birkenau, were equipped with huge gas chambers. Thousands of Jews lost their lives each day in these chambers and they were then thrown into pits to be burned.

> **Make the Link**
>
> You will learn about Judaism if you study RMPS.

„Die Judennase ist an ihrer Spitze gebogen. Sie sieht aus wie ein Sechser..."

Figure 22: *Example of anti-Jewish propaganda from a Nazi children's book in 1938; a German teacher demonstrating how all Jews had evil eyes and a large nose and scared innocent German children.*

In **Source H** the commander of Auschwitz Birkenau speaks out in 1949 about how he felt about murdering 1 000 000 Jews.

> I had to watch mothers take laughing children to the gas chamber. I had to watch the burning of the bodies, pulling the teeth, cutting the hair …
>
> I had to watch, because I was the one who gave the orders and I had to show that I was also ready to be there when it was happening. So I had to bury all the human feelings as deep as I could.

In **Source I** an SS officer answers a question about the gassing of Jews:

> **Q** 'Were you present at a gassing operation one day?'
>
> **A** 'They opened the door, threw the children in and closed the door. There was a terrible cry. A member of the SS climbed on the roof. The people went on crying for about ten minutes. Then the prisoners opened the doors. Everything was in disorder and contorted. Heat was given off. The bodies were loaded on a rough wagon and taken to a ditch. The next batch were already undressing in the huts. After that I didn't look at my wife for four weeks.'

GO! Activity 13

Answer the questions below using the information about the victimisation of Jews.
1. How did the SS men feel about the extermination of Jews? (Give a detailed explanation using the **Sources H** and **I**.)
2. Explain why the SS men committed these atrocities. (Think about why people were following the Nazis in the first place and how the SS maintained control.)

(Unit outcomes: National 4/5: Outcome 2.2)

Exam style question

Source J is from the diary of a German writer, Von Hassell, who was writing on 25 November 1938.

> I am writing under the crushing emotion evoked by the evil persecution of the Jews after the murder of Von Rath. Not since the Great War have we lost so much credit in the world. Goebbels has seldom been so disbelieved as when he said that an unplanned outburst of anger among the people had caused the outrages. As a matter of fact, there is no doubt that we are dealing with an officially organised anti-Jewish riot which broke out at the same hour of night all over Germany.

Source K is from a report by the American consul in Leipzig in November 1938.

> The attacks on Jewish property, which began in the early hours, were hailed subsequently in the Nazi press as a 'spontaneous wave of righteous indignation throughout Germany, as a result of the cowardly Jewish murder of Von Rath'. As far as many Germans are concerned, a state of popular indignation that would lead to such excesses can be considered as non-existent. On the contrary, all of the local crowd I observed were obviously stunned over what had happened and horrified over the unprecedented fury of the Nazi acts.

3. Compare the views shown in **Sources J** and **K** and say how they agree about attacks on the Jews? **SH 4**

    (Compare the views overall and/or in detail.)

Who else was victimised by the Nazis?

- Jehovah's Witnesses were targeted because of their religious views and refusal to follow the Nazi ideals, and several thousand were sent to their deaths in concentration camps.

- Homosexuals were made targets because they did not fit into the Nazis ideal. They were convicted, imprisoned, sent to concentration camps and sometimes even castrated.

- Romani gypsies were sent to ghettos, concentration camps and sometimes shot.

- Disabled people were seen as a massive burden on German society. They did not comply with the Nazi ideal of the master race. Disabled people were among the first to be victimised under the Nazi regime. An estimated 275 000 people with disabilities are suspected to have been killed under the Nazi regime.

Who opposed the Nazis and what happened to them?

It would be easy to think that Hitler and the Nazis managed to eliminate all opposition but in fact, if you looked at the election results of March 1933, you'll see that even with the huge propaganda machine and the mass intimidation from the SS, the Nazis still only managed to gain 44% of the vote. It would be impossible to calculate how much opposition remained in Germany after Hitler became Chancellor and this is something that has troubled historians for many years.

J. Noakes and G. Pridham wrote in their book *Nazism 1919–1945*: 'Trying to understand what Germans really felt during these years the historian is faced with serious problems. Not only were there no opinion polls but it was impossible for people to express their views in public with any freedom: the results of elections and plebiscites were rigged; the media were strictly controlled.'

It is important to point out that opposition did exist and while thousands emigrated to escape the Nazis regime, many opponents did speak out against the Nazis.

White Rose Group

This group were formed in Munich by a collection of university students. They distributed anti-Nazi leaflets, but Sophie and Hans Scholl were caught and executed in 1943.

Catholic Church

The Pope openly condemned the Nazis and one priest led a campaign to stop the mass execution of mentally disabled people.

Figure 23: *German students Hans and Sophie Scholl, 1940.*

Confessional Church

In reaction to the abolition of any religion other than Hitler's Nazi Church, a group of Protestants, under the leadership of Martin Niemöller, established the Confessional Church to oppose Hitler's church. Niemöller was later captured and sent to a concentration camp. He would write a poignant poem called *First they came* all about how he wished he had spoken out and acted sooner.

Reichsbanner

They were Social Democrats, who destroyed railway lines and often acted as spies.

Kreisau Circle

On 20 July 1944 the most famous of the opposition groups attempted to bomb Hitler in a secret bunker in Berlin. The group, led by Graf Helmut von Moltke, met at his house in Kreisau to discuss how to bring down Hitler. They were convinced the country was being led to military ruin. They were able to infiltrate the inner circle of Nazis as they had recruited members of the Nazi Party, like Colonel Klaus von Stauffenberg, who placed the bomb. The attempt failed and Stauffenberg was shot along with 5000 others.

Edelweiss Pirates

This was a group of young Germans who opposed the way the youth of Germany were being controlled. They were not seen as a major threat to the Nazi regime as, for most part, their activities seemed to be restricted to going on hiking trips and singing songs banned by the Nazis. This changed when they were accused of collecting anti-Nazi propaganda that had been dropped by a British bomber and posting them through people's letterboxes. In November 1944, on Himmler's orders, thirteen youths were hanged in Cologne, in public. It was believed that at least six of these youths were Edelweiss Pirates.

GO! Activity 14

1. Using the basic information given about the resistance groups that existed in Germany during the Nazi regime, create an anti-Nazi leaflet. You should use textbooks and the internet for your investigation. You should ensure that the leaflet clearly shows which group you are part of. The aims of the group should be clear in the leaflet, as well as information on how the group opposed and resisted the Nazis.

   (Unit outcomes: National 5: Outcome 2.3)

Exam style question

2. Explain the reasons why it was so difficult to oppose the Nazi government after 1933.　　　　　　　　　　　　　　　　　　　　　　　**KU 6**

   (Unit outcomes: National 4/5: Outcome 2.2)

4 Nazi social and economic policies

In this section you will learn about:

- Nazi economic policies.
- Nazi militarism.
- Youth movements and education during the Nazi regime.
- The important role women played.
- The Nuremberg Rallies and their purpose.

Nazi economic policies

1. Employment

To replace trade unions the Nazis created the German Labour Front, which controlled the majority of workers in Germany. Working hours went up from 60 to around 72 hours a week. By 1935, the Nazis had created a Labour Service, which was compulsory and meant that all Germans had to work for the German government for six months. This was a step introduced to target the huge unemployment problems that had plagued Germany during the Weimar years.

Hitler offered some very simple solutions to reducing the unemployment level. However, the strategy in large part involved Jews being fired from their civil service jobs which opened up job opportunities for the racially pure Germans. Jews were also not counted in the unemployment figures which helped the Nazis in their pledge to ensure all Germans were employed. When people were offered a job as part of the Labour Service they were given no choice in the matter and would be punished if they chose not to take it.

One of the biggest employment programmes created by the Nazis was the construction of a huge motorway network that would run throughout Germany. This employed thousands of Germans and removed them from state dependency. It also meant that the economy took an upturn as the taxes people paid would be fed back into the German government revenue.

Hitler was also responsible for suspending the reparation payments to France and Britain and also started to build up the German army, which allowed thousands of German men to become soldiers and thus help economic recovery.

Make the Link

You may look at how statistics can be used to show things that aren't really true in Maths.

2. Rearmament

Rearmament contributed greatly to economic improvement: army divisions grew from seven divisions (100 000 men) to fifty two divisions by 1939 and Luftwaffe planes went from zero to over 4000 in this same

Figure 24: *German soldiers in 1939.*

Figure 25: *You must save 5 marks a week if you want your own car.*

Make the Link

In Business Management you learn about how workers are motivated today.

time period. In 1935, even though the Nazis were clearly flaunting the Treaty of Versailles, Britain supported Germany's rearmament by signing the Anglo-German naval agreement. This allowed Germany to have an equal number of submarines and to build its naval forces up to 35% of Britain's. Rearmament would also mean the creation of weapons factories, which again led to more jobs.

3. Kraft durch Freude (KdF, Strength through Joy)

This scheme, under the leadership of Doctor Robert Ley, offered workers cheap holidays and a salary sacrifice scheme to award cars to ensure that their work and leisure time was bombarded by Nazi propaganda. The KdF would often arrange outings to the theatre to watch Nazi films. At Hitler's request the Volkswagen car was offered to Nazi workers on a hire purchase scheme where they could pay a small amount from their wages each week. However, this entire scheme was a con and not one German got a car.

Although these programmes and schemes made Germany appear economically stable the full employment figures were largely down to the removal of Jews and women from their jobs. In addition to this, Germany stopped paying the reparation bill and this obviously led to more revenue for the country. Finally, towards the end of the 1930s, Germany began to expand into other countries such as Austria and Czechoslovakia and take over their industries, which benefited the German economy.

GO! Activity 15

1. Write a summary (the main points) of the three areas above that helped create a stable economy in Germany under the Nazi regime. You should not copy the book as it will help your revision better if you put the three sections into your own words.

Exam style question

2. Describe the reasons why Germans were happy with the changes that the Nazis made to the economy. **KU 4**

   (Unit outcomes: National 4/5: Outcome 2.1)

How did militarism develop in Nazi Germany?

Hitler believed in the 'Führer Prinzip' – that the country should have one strong leader everyone obeyed. He felt that militarism and the organisation of the German armed forces were crucial in ensuring that Germany was strong and able to defend itself. He reorganised the Wehrmacht (German armed forces during the Third Reich) and reintroduced conscription. In 1938, the OKW (Oberkammando der Wehrmacht) or Supreme High Command was created. This was in addition to the OKH (Oberkammando des Heeres – the Army High Command) and the OKM (Oberkammando der Marine – the Navy High Command) and OKL (Oberkammando der Luftwaffe – the Air Force High Command).

Youth movements and education

Youth movements were introduced and education was changed dramatically under the Nazis. The table below shows you how girls were introduced to the 3Ks (Kinder (children), Küche (kitchen) and Kirche (church)) at an early age and how boys were encouraged at an even younger age to become Hitler's perfect soldiers.

Age	Boys	Girls
6–10	Pimpfen (Little Fellows)	
10–14	Jungfolk (Young Folk)	Jungmädel (Young Girls)
14–18	Hitlerjugend (Hitler Youth)	Bund Deutscher Mädel (German Girls League)

Schools were taken over by Nazi ideology. Hitler appointed Bernhard Rust as head of German education and he got rid of anti-Nazi teachers. All school books had to be approved by Nazi authorities. Nazi school textbooks encouraged pupils to hate and victimise the Jews as well as encouraging a militant way of life.

An extract from a Nazi textbook shows how Nazi ideals were taught to pupils in Maths: 'A squadron of forty five bombers drops incendiary bombs (to start fires) on an international centre of Jews. Each bomb weighs 1·5 kilos. What is the total weight of the bombs dropped?'

Anyone who spoke out about Nazis was sacked. All teachers had to attend Nazi re-education centres to ensure they understood the importance of teaching anti-Semitic ideas.

The boys would attend Hitler Youth summer camps where they would train using live ammunition and played war games. They would also be required to march for miles with heavy packs. Many were taken ill but still had to attend these camps.

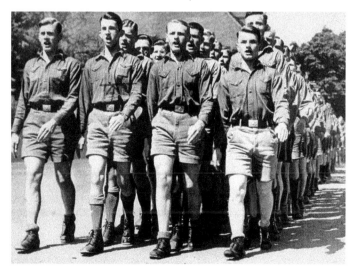

Figure 26: *A German youth camp in 1933.*

Key Word

- **Anti-Semitism**
Prejudice, hatred or discrimination against Jews for reasons connected to their Jewish religion.

Make the Link

When Germany occupied certain areas of Europe they took with them their ideas of anti-Semitism. Many of the concentration camps that held Jews and other political prisoners were based in Poland.

GO! Activity 16

1. Pretend you are part of a Hitler youth movement and write a few days of diary entries to detail how the organisation is ran and how you feel about the changes to your school work.

   (Unit outcomes: National 5: Outcome 2.3)

Exam style question

Source L was written by a member of the League of German Maidens.

> We had to be present for meetings with local leaders and businessmen. We had to attend events relating to health and well-being. Our week-ends were crammed full with camps and sporting activities. It was fun in a way. We certainly had a lot of exercise, but it had a bad effect on my school work. None of this was going to help me get a good career in the future.

Source M is by a modern historian.

> Many young Germans enjoyed the emphasis on activity and sport. However, those who had wanted to achieve success were frustrated and resentful at the amount of time spent on outdoor activities. Girls in particular felt that their education was being downgraded and their future prospects were being limited.

2. Compare the views in **Source L** and **Source M** on the effects of Nazi policies on young people.

   SH 4

   (Compare the views overall and/or in detail.)

Figure 27: *Mother pushing a pram decorated with Nazi flags.*

📖 Key Word

- **Lebensraum**

  A German word meaning living space. It was used to describe German expansion.

What role did women play in Nazi Germany?

German women were also indoctrinated in the Third Reich and forced to follow the three Ks. Women were forced to leave their jobs as doctors (3000), teachers (100 000) and civil servants. Instead they were to be occupied with looking after their husbands and family.

Kinder (children), Küche (kitchen), Kirche (church)

Using the powers of the Enabling Act, Hitler passed a law to try to ensure all women had at least four children. His hope was to increase the German birth rate so there would be more pure blood Germans to fulfil his desire for Lebensraum. Hitler also passed the Law for Enforcement of Marriage, which meant that each newly married couple would receive 1000 marks when they had four children. The money was paid in increments of 250 for each child born. Each year, on the birthday of Hitler's mother there would be an awards ceremony for the women who had produced more than eight children. It was also arranged that unmarried pure blooded women could go along to a location where they could be impregnated by an SS member.

As housewives German women had to follow the Nazi ideal. They were discouraged from slimming as it was believed that thin women were not good at bearing children. They also were not supposed to wear make-up or dye their hair. Women were encouraged to wear their hair in a bun and wearing trousers was not allowed.

The final K was the role the church would have to take in the women's lives. Hitler removed all religious members from the churches and each church was altered to follow the Nazi faith. The Bible was replaced with a copy of Mein Kampf and the crucifix was replaced by a sword to represent Hitler's strength.

⚙ Activity 17

1. Create a word-search that contains all the important words that are associated with the crucial role women played in making the Nazi regime a success. The words should be taken from these two pages and from your own notes on the subject in your jotter.

   (Unit outcomes: National 4/5: Outcome 2.1)

   Exam style question

   Source N outlines a new law that was planned in 1943 by the Nazi leaders. The new law never came into effect, but gives an idea of how women were viewed by the Nazis.

   > All single and married women up to the age of thirty-five who do not already have four children should be obliged to produce four children by racially pure … German men. Whether these men are married is without significance. Every family that already has four children must set the husband free for this action.

2. Evaluate the usefulness of **Source N** as evidence of how women were viewed and treated in Germany under the Nazi regime. **SH 5**

   (You may want to comment on who wrote it, when they wrote it, why they wrote it, what they say or what has been missed out.)

⚫ Make the Link

In Modern Studies and RMPS you look at the role of women in the UK and around the world.

📖 Key Word

- **Mein Kampf**

Hitler wrote this book, which outlined his ideas for a strong Germany, while in jail after the failed Munich Putsch. It outlined his ideas for Lebensraum and his idea of Germans being the 'master race'.

Figure 28: *One of Hitler's speeches during a Nuremberg Rally.*

Nuremberg Rallies

The Nuremberg Rallies were held every year in the Nuremberg Arena. Attended by thousands, Hitler demonstrated his strong military power with huge displays of fireworks, marches and mock battles. One of the main elements of the rallies was Hitler's speeches where he had the undivided attention of everyone in the crowd.

One rally was filmed by Leni Riefenstahl, which would become her famous film *Triumph of the Will*. The film expertly depicts the organisation and sheer military strength that Nazi Germany was able to demonstrate.

GO! Activity 18

1. Create a poster that advertises a Nuremberg Rally. You should include what will be shown at the rally and the importance of Hitler's speech. Think about the way you depict the importance of certain elements of the rallies; for example, what do you think should be the biggest thing on the poster? What would the Nazis want people to see first when looking at the poster?

   (Unit outcomes: National 5: Outcome 2.3)

Exam style question

2. To what extent was propaganda the crucial element that ensured the Nazis maintained control of Germany from 1933–1939?   **KU 9**

   Hint: Your essay should have an introduction, four paragraphs (one on propaganda, one on SS fear, one on youth organisations and one on the role of women) and a conclusion.
   (Unit outcomes: National 4: Outcome 1.2; National 5: Outcomes 1.2, 1.3 and 2.3)

Summary

In this topic you have learned:

- how the Weimar Republic was created and what caused its ultimate downfall
- what events and people helped the Nazis to rise to power between 1919 and 1933
- how the Nazis changed the way Germany was run, militarily, socially and economically
- how Adolf Hitler maintained power in Germany between 1933 and 1939.

You should have developed your skills and be able to:

- evaluate the usefulness of a source
- compare two sources by saying what they agree or disagree about
- put a source into context by saying how fully it describes an issue.

Learning Checklist

Now that you have finished **Hitler and Nazi Germany, 1919–1939**, complete a self-evaluation of your knowledge and skills to assess what you have understood. Use traffic lights to help you make up a revision plan to help you improve in the areas you identified as red or amber.

- Describe how Germany was affected by the Great War.

- Describe what peace settlements Germany had to agree to.

- Explain how the Treaty of Versailles affected Germany.

- Describe how the Weimar Republic was created.

- Describe the revolutions and putsches that affected the Weimar Republic between 1919 and 1923.

- Explain what economic problems weakened the Weimar Republic between 1919 and 1933.

- Describe the appeal of Hitler and the Nazis.

- Describe how the National Socialists (Nazis) took power in 1933.

- Describe the events that surrounded the Reichstag Fire.

- Explain how Adolf Hitler made Germany a dictatorship.

- Describe the changes Hitler made to the German government.

- Explain how fear and intimidation was used by the Nazis to maintain power in Germany.

- Describe the members of society that were victimised by the Nazis.

- Explain what happened to those who opposed the Nazis.

- Describe the Nazis' economic policies.

- Describe the military changes that were introduced under the Nazis.

- Explain how the youth of Germany were affected by the Nazi regime.

- Describe the propaganda that was used to maintain control of Germany.

Studying this topic will provide you with a good understanding of the fundamental changes that happened in the USA with regard to civil rights between 1918 and 1968. You will study how immigration patterns changed after the First World War, with the previous 'open door' policy giving way to a much more divisive system. You will also learn about the iniquities of black segregation and how racism and discrimination led to the growth of the civil rights movement, the ghetto riots and the emergence of black leaders such as the pacifist Martin Luther King and the radical Malcolm X.

You will develop your skills and be able to:

❖ evaluate the usefulness of a source

❖ compare two sources by saying what they agree or disagree about

❖ put a source into context by saying how fully it describes an issue.

This topic is split into four sections:

❖ The 'open door' policy and immigration, to 1928

❖ 'Separate but equal', to 1939

❖ Civil rights campaigns, 1945–1965

❖ The ghettos and Black American radicalism

Level 4 experiences and outcomes relevant to this topic:

I can evaluate conflicting sources of evidence to sustain a line of argument. **SOC 4-01a**

I have developed a sense of my heritage and identity as a British, European or global citizen and can present arguments about the importance of respecting the heritage and identity of others. **SOC 4-02a**

By studying groups in past societies who experienced inequality, I can explain the reasons for the inequality and evaluate how groups or individuals addressed it. **SOC 4-04a**

I can describe the main features of conflicting world belief systems in the past and can present informed views on the consequences of such conflict for societies then and since. **SOC 4-04b**

I can make reasoned judgements about how the exercise of power affects the rights and responsibilities of citizens by comparing a more democratic and a less democratic society. **SOC 4-04c**

I have investigated a meeting of cultures in the past and can analyse the impact on the societies involved. **SOC 4-05c**

Having critically analysed a significant historical event, I can assess the relative importance of factors contributing to the event. **SOC 4-06a**

I can assess the impact for those involved in a specific instance of the expansion of power and influence in the past. **SOC 4-06d**

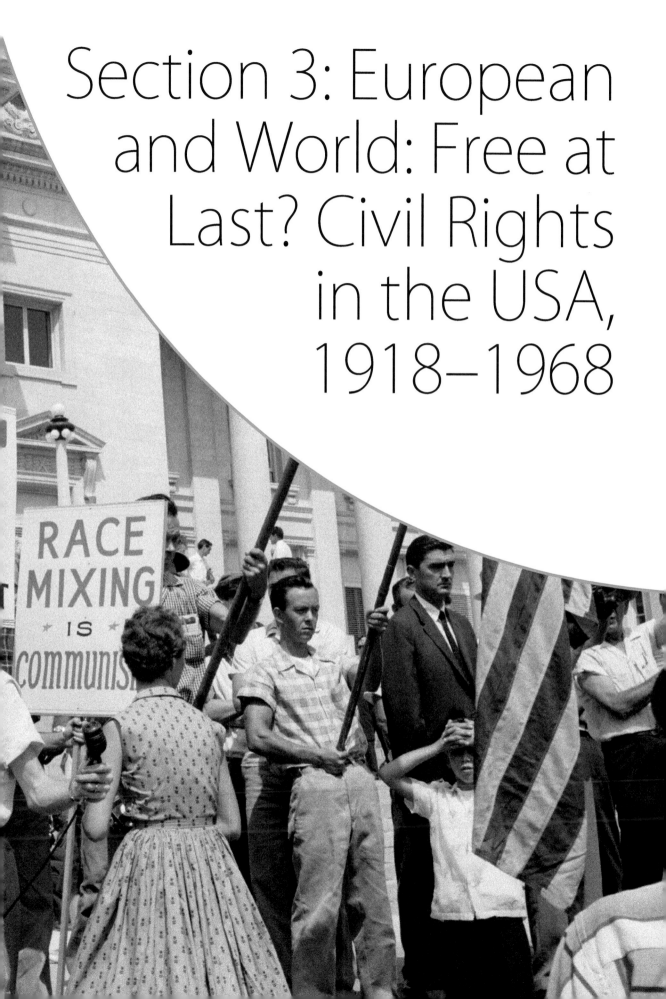

Section 3: European and World: Free at Last? Civil Rights in the USA, 1918–1968

Background

By the end of the Great War America had become a beacon of hope for many who had suffered during the war. Promises of health, wealth and land encouraged thousands to start afresh in the USA. Immigration into America was not a new idea and had really flourished at the tail-end of the 1800s. However, the immigration patterns had changed and more people were starting to move over from Southern and Eastern Europe. Unfortunately these immigrants would not feel as welcome as the previous waves of immigrants. Divisions would cause unrest, discrimination and a huge increase in crime.

Immigration in the USA went through huge changes after the war. Prior to 1863 nearly all black Americans were slaves. Slaves had been bought and sold all over America for hundreds of years, it was a 'peculiar institution' that had been allowed to survive even though the country was becoming more democratic. Although it was more commonly used by white plantation owners in the South, the North had also been guilty of owning slaves in the past. When the American Civil War ended in 1865, it marked a colossal turning point in the country's history. Abraham Lincoln was the President of the USA and he passed the Emancipation Proclamation on 1 January 1863. This gave all black Americans freedom, and meant they would become fully fledged American citizens. This law was further amended in 1868 when the American constitution was changed to state that black people would now be treated exactly the same way as white people. In 1870 another amendment gave black Americans the right to vote.

However, it was very clear even at these times that slavery in America would not be easy to forget and white people would find it extremely difficult to see people, who had previously been seen as property, as members of society with the same access to rights and laws as them. This might be a reason why some states, who could make their own laws, decided to introduce specific laws for black people that would restrict their rights.

As time passed it became clear that black Americans were not willing to continue being treated as unequal. The time period 1945–1964 was revolutionary for the civil rights movement. With every success, confidence increased, determination grew and more and more black and white people started to join the fight for equal civil rights for black Americans.

One of the crucial elements in this success was the use of media; technological improvements meant that images of peaceful protestors being attacked by white racists were being broadcast around the world. Many sympathised with the black Americans whose only wish was to have access to the basic human rights awarded to them by the Emancipation Proclamation in 1863.

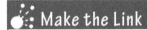

Make the Link

You may have studied the slave trade in Unit 2.

Key Words

- **Plantation**

An estate on which crops such as coffee, sugar, and tobacco are grown.

- **American Civil War**

The war between the Northern US states (usually known as the Union) and the Confederate States of America, 1861–1865.

- **Constitution**

The basic written set of principles the US government established in 1789.

Figure 1: *The Emancipation Proclamation, 1863.*

However, by 1964, despite everything the civil rights movement had achieved, including the passing of new laws to ensure discrimination was to stop, it was clear there were still huge issues to combat and it was at this point the civil rights campaigns became more militant and violent. Many felt this was out of frustration and anger at how slowly the American government was dealing with the racism that was still very apparent in many areas of the USA.

GO! Activity 1

Write down a list of questions you want to find the answers to after reading the background information. At the end of this topic, check your list and write the answers to your questions in as much detail as possible. An example of a question is given below to help you get started:

What devastation caused people to leave their home countries after the First World War?

1 The 'open door' policy and immigration, to 1928

In this section you will learn about:

- What America was like at the end of the First World War.
- Why immigrants came to America.
- The differences between 'old' and 'new' immigrants.
- How immigrants were treated in America.
- The 'Red Scare'.
- Sacco and Vanzetti.
- Why America changed its policy towards immigration in the 1920s.

America at the end of the First World War

Make the Link

You might learn about immigration to the USA in Modern Studies.

Make the Link

If you studied 'The Era of the Great War' in Section 1 you will have learned about post war economic problems.

At the end of the First World War America was seen as the land of opportunity. Immigrants arrived in search of the American Dream, the hope that if a person worked hard then even the poorest person could become richer and have a much better standard of living than if they had stayed in their old country.

After the devastation of the First World War in Europe, countries struggled to get back on their feet financially. Although countries like Britain promised to build 'homes for heroes' the government found they were financially unable to fulfil this promise. It was the same in several European countries and this led to hundreds of thousands of people looking for something better, away from unemployment and bad working and living conditions. America seemed the answer.

In 1800 the population of the USA was only 2 000 000. By 1920 it was 120 000 000! Many people believed that all of these different cultures and languages would eventually blend together in a 'melting pot'. One immigrant gave their opinion of Americans in 1925 as 'Americans? There ain't such a thing. Americans are a mix of every people in the world!' However, it became clear very quickly that the immigrants would gravitate towards their own and they created areas such as 'little Poland' and 'little Italy'.

Reasons people immigrated to America

Make the Link

If you studied Migration and Empire in Unit 1 you will have learned about Scots moving to America during this time in detail.

One of the main reasons immigration to America surged during the late 1800s and early 1900s was that America went through a period of huge prosperity and this pulled people to relocate to the USA. This, together with the devastating living and working conditions being suffered at home, pushed people to leave their own country. These push and pull reasons were to be the foundations of the American Dream, something that every immigrant strove to achieve.

Push reasons:

- Many lived in overcrowded squalor that led to disease in their own countries.
- Lack of working hour restrictions meant people were sometimes working up to 18 hours a day.
- Working conditions were often dangerous and even deadly.
- Lack of laws to protect people meant that men, women and children were exploited by their employers.
- Unemployment pressures.
- Specific crises, like the Irish potato famine and the Scottish Highland Clearances, led to mass immigration as these families were left with nothing to lose.

Pull reasons:

- The promise of land that could be farmed and provide for the whole family.
- The pull of bustling industries in the US.
- A guarantee of a job and financial stability.
- A better life away from the problems of their own country.
- People were promised wealth and prosperity if they moved to America.
- Hearing great things from friends and family who had already made the move.
- America offered political freedom and democracy.
- Propaganda posters in their own countries promised health, wealth and prosperity.

The United States held a promise of freedom, symbolised by the Statue of Liberty, her torch a beacon of hope and light for all immigrants. The statue, which stands in New York harbour, was unveiled in 1886 and for many it was the first thing they saw when they arrived in the country.

Figure 2: *The plaque at the foot of the Statue of Liberty reads: 'Give me your tired, your poor, Your huddled masses yearning to breathe free, The wretched refuse of your teeming shore. Send these the homeless, tempest tossed to me I lift up my lamp beside the golden door!'*

GO! Activity 2

Push and pull factors:

- families lived in poverty and faced starvation
- voyages overseas were often free or subsidised by landowners
- low wages and long, monotonous work
- job losses due to new technology
- lack of healthcare, no education, few prospects
- chance to start a new life/find better opportunities overseas
- landlords charged very high rents
- posters encouraged people to emigrate
- poor diets: oatmeal, barley, potatoes – little fresh meat
- promise of cheap land and job opportunities in America
- miserable living conditions, overcrowding
- poor soil and harsh climate led to low crop yield
- friends and family had already emigrated.

Using the information gathered during your reading, decide which of these factors above are PUSH factors (the residents are pushed out due to the issues in their home country) and which are PULL factors (they are pulled to a country with better opportunities).

Use a coloured pencil to make your notes stand out and ensure you use a key.

PUSH factors =

PULL factors =

(Unit outcomes: National 5: Outcome 2.3)

Who were the 'old' and 'new' immigrants?

'Old immigrants' were people whose families had lived in the USA for many generations, sometimes descended from some of the first immigrants to the country. They were commonly known as WASPs (White Anglo Saxon Protestants). This name came about because these 'old' immigrants were white, they originated from the Anglo Saxon race in Northern Europe (the UK, Germany and Scandinavia) and followed the Protestant religion. Over the years, many of these families had made money and they were well-off. As the years had passed the 'old' immigrants had given up the language of their home country and instead spoke English. As a result, the USA had become an English speaking country.

By 1900, 'new' immigrants had started arriving. Many were poor and had left their country in desperation. The majority came from Southern Europe, countries like Italy or Greece. However, some of the 'new' immigrants came from Eastern Europe: Poland and Russia. Few could speak English and most were Roman Catholics, Jews and Orthodox Christians. Tensions between the WASPs and the 'new' immigrants became quickly evident.

Make the Link

You might learn about the tensions between different religious communities if you study RMPS.

Figure 3: *European immigrants arriving at Ellis Island, 1920.*

WASPs feared that the continued influx of immigrants could lead to threats to employment and a possible attack on the WASP control of business and government. This often led to discrimination and prejudice towards the newer immigrants who were looking for work and advancement.

Figure 4: *Typical WASP family in the 1920s.*

GO! Activity 3

1. Take a sheet of paper and split it down the middle. On one side draw a picture of a WASP. On the other side draw an image of a 'new' immigrant. Now label typical characteristics for each immigrant using the preceding information.

Exam style question

Source A was written by a Senator from Alabama in 1921. He is explaining why he wanted immigration controls.

> As soon as the immigrants step off the decks of their ships our problem has begun – Bolshevism, red anarchy, crooks and kidnappers. Thousands come here who never take the oath to support our Constitution and to become citizens of the United States. They do not respect what our flag represents. They pay allegiance to some other country and flag while they live upon the benefits of our own. They are of no service whatever to our people. They constitute a menace and a danger to us everyday.

Source B is a description by Robert Coughlan of the growth of support for the Ku Klux Klan in the 1920s.

> It may be asked why, then, did the town take so enthusiastically to the Klan? Many old stock Americans believed they were in danger of being overrun. The 'foreigners were running our country'; and so anything 'foreign' was 'un-American' and a menace. Cars were draped with the American flag and some carried homemade signs with Klan slogans such as 'America for the Americans'.

2. Compare the views of **Sources A** and **B** about American attitudes to immigrants in the 1920s. (Compare the views overall and/or in detail.) **SH 4**

How were immigrants treated when they arrived in America?

After travelling for weeks in terrible conditions on overcrowded ships many immigrants found that their American Dream would become an American Nightmare. The immigrants found themselves living in poverty in slum conditions and frequently suffered harsh discrimination when trying to gain employment. Cultural and language differences increased racial tension and there was much resentment of the new arrivals.

Immigrants tended to be ignorant about the American political system and this often meant many immigrants became the followers of corrupt politicians who bribed them by offering them help in return for votes.

🔍 Hint

In New York City, an organisation called Tammany Hall attracted a lot of support from Irish immigrants by helping them find jobs. It did great work by assisting the poor but also was famous for political corruption.

Figure 5: *Lodgers in a crowded and squalid tenement, which rented for five cents a spot, Bayard Street, New York City.*

GO! Activity 4

1. Create a poster that compares the **American Dream** with **American Reality**. This should show what people were being promised on one side, using images and buzz words and, on the other side what many immigrants found when they arrived in America, which was poverty and deprivation. Below are some words that will help you with each side of your poster, which should be colourful, easy to read and informative.

American Dream	American Reality
Health	Disease
Wealth	Unemployment
Land	Discrimination
Jobs	Slum housing

(Unit outcomes: National 5: Outcome 2.3)

Exam style question

Source C is from an interview with an immigrant.

> Apartments had no heating. Running water was only available in the filthy hall. The smell was terrible and in winter we froze. But we froze back in Russia so what's the difference? At least now we had a dream to aim for.

2. Evaluate the usefulness of **Source C** as evidence for the reasons why people were willing to suffer in an attempt to achieve the American Dream. (You may want to comment on who wrote it, when they wrote it, why they wrote it, what they say or what has been missed out.)

SH 5

How did the 'Red Scare' affect immigrants in America?

The 'Red Scare' was a period of anti-communism in the USA following the Bolshevik led Russian Revolution in 1917. A nationwide fear of communists, socialists and anarchists caused people to be suspicious and fearful of newcomers. Economic difficulties and worker unrest increased as many people returned from the First World War to no jobs. Strikes broke out in several regions. The strikers were branded as 'Reds' (referring to them being communists) and accused of being unpatriotic. There was a real fear that strikes would lead to a communist revolution spreading throughout the USA.

The Palmer Raids

In 1919 President Woodrow Wilson made A. Mitchell Palmer his attorney general. At this time Americans were becoming increasingly worried that, in the wake of the 1917 Russian Revolution, communist agents were going to overthrow the US government. When thirty eight bombs were sent to various American politicians and an Italian anarchist, Carlo Valdinoci, blew himself up outside Palmer's home, the government acted. Over 10 000 suspected communists and anarchists were arrested in 1919, and 248 were deported to Russia. 6000 were arrested and held without trial in 1920.

This period of serious unrest led to more discrimination of 'new' immigrants. They were often blamed for crimes and imprisoned without a fair trial.

Figure 6: *Woodrow Wilson*

Figure 7: *A. Mitchell Palmer*

Make the Link

You will also look at the reasons for and effects of strikes in Modern Studies and Business Management.

Make the Link

In Modern Studies you may learn about how and why people are held without trial today.

📖 Key Words

- **Communism**

When the workers control the country and economy, and wealth is equally shared among everyone.

- **Bolshevik**

A member of the Russian Social Democratic Party, which seized power in the October Revolution of 1917.

- **Russian Revolution**

The revolution in the Russian empire that happened in 1917, in which the Tsar (Emperor) was overthrown and replaced by Bolsheviks.

- **Anarchist**

A person who believes in or tries to bring about anarchy, chaos and disorder.

🔵 Activity 5

1. Create an American propaganda poster for the government warning about the threat of a communist takeover and the 'Red Scare'. Use the information from the section above to help you. Your poster should contain a clear slogan and images that demonstrate what the Americans are afraid of.

   (Unit outcomes: National 5: Outcome 2.3)

Exam style question

2. Explain the ways in which America was affected by the 'Red Scare' following the First World War.

   (Unit outcomes: National 4/5: Outcome 2.2)

   KU 6

The case of Sacco and Vanzetti

The case of Italian immigrants Nicola Sacco and Bartolome Vanzetti was typical of many at this time when 'new' immigrants were being targeted and often not given a fair trial. Sacco and Vanzetti were anarchists who were arrested in the wake of a robbery of the payroll of a shoe factory in 1920 when several bystanders claimed that the robbers looked Italian. Despite the men having alibis they were both found guilty and were executed in 1927. Many believed that the two men had been targeted because of their radical beliefs and that the testimony of the defence witnesses was rejected because they were also Italian immigrants.

Figure 8: *Sacco and Vanzetti.*

Issues with the case:

- Neither man had committed a crime before this.
- Both men had alibis that were supported by immigrants.
- None of the eye witnesses saw the robbers properly.
- The USA was becoming more and more segregated and lived in fear of a communist take-over.
- The two men's 'radical' beliefs were held against them at the trial.

⏵ Activity 6

1. Write a newspaper front page for this case. It will need to contain the following:
- headline
- outline of the incident, trial and verdict
- picture.

Exam style question

2. Describe the problems facing European immigrants to the USA in the 1920s.　　**KU 4**
   (**Unit outcomes: National 4/5: Outcome 2.1**)

Why did America start to close its 'open door' policy in the 1920s

The USA had practised an 'open door' policy, which meant that anyone could enter the country provided they weren't 'feeble minded', extremely poor or had a serious disease. However, restrictions were put in place by the American government to try to halt immigration from certain countries. The Dillingham Commission (1907–1911) was set up to clarify the 'issue' with immigration. Their findings were that most immigrants in the early twentieth century were coming from South and Eastern Europe and with this in mind the commission recommended literacy tests to stop 'inferior' immigrants.

Below is a list of regulations that were introduced in America to stop immigration:

- 1921 – Congress encouraged immigration from Western Europe: Germany, UK, Ireland and Scandinavia; discouraged immigration from Eastern and Southern Europe.
- 'Quota system' introduced – only a certain number of immigrants from each country allowed.
- 1924 – a cut off for immigrants was set at 150 000 for each year.

These laws were seen by the American government as necessary to stop the immigration of people seeking the 'American Dream'. Fear, war, deprivation, crime and poverty had led the country to breaking point and it was this that caused the immigration laws to be changed drastically.

 Activity 7

Exam style question

Using information from this whole section write an essay answering the question:
To what extent did attitudes towards immigration change in the 1920s? **KU 9**
Hint: Your essay should have an introduction, four paragraphs (one on crime, one on discrimination, one on immigration laws and one on language and culture) and a conclusion.
(Unit outcomes: National 4: Outcome 1.2; National 5: Outcomes 1.2, 1.3 and 2.3)

2 'Separate but equal', to 1939

In this section you will learn about:

- The 'Jim Crow' laws.
- How 'separate but equal' affected Americans.
- The Ku Klux Klan.
- The importance of Emmett Till.
- How voting rights were restricted in America for black civilians.
- The migration of black Americans to the North.

How were black Americans affected by the Jim Crow laws?

The Jim Crow laws were Southern state laws, which aimed to keep black and white people separate and ultimately denied black people access to their civil rights.

Who was Jim Crow?

The 'Jim Crow' figure was a fixture of the minstrel shows that toured the South. Jim Crow was typically played by a white man made up as a black man who sang and mimicked the stereotypical behavior of black people. The character was dressed in ragged clothes and would come across as clumsy, incompetent and unintelligent, all in the name of comedy.

The Jim Crow laws

The Jim Crow laws were created after 1870. They imposed legal punishments and formed a segregated society.

> 📖 **Key Word**
>
> - **Segregate**
>
> Set someone or a group of people apart from each other.

Figure 9: *A segregated drinking fountain.*

Some of the more common examples of Jim Crow laws:

- Florida: All marriages between a white person and a black person were prohibited forever.
- Alabama: Every employer of white or black males had to provide separate toilet facilities.
- Louisiana: Separate schools would have to be provided for black and white children.
- Maryland: Every railroad company would have to provide separate coaches/cars for black and white people.

Some other facilities that were designated as separate were: bus station waiting rooms, restaurants, lunch counters, public parks, public toilets, drinking fountains, cinemas, even graveyards.

The states insisted that the introduction of these laws was simply to keep black and white people separate under the *separate but equal* idea. However, it was quickly clear the facilities may have been separate, but they were in no way equal.

The facilities in black schools were also worse than in white schools. Teachers in black schools would teach in overcrowded classrooms without adequate resources.

Figure 10: *Separate waiting room for white people at a bus terminal.*

Activity 8

Supreme Court:

> Laws, which keep the races apart, do not mean that one race is better or worse than the other.

President Wilson 1916:

> Segregation is not humiliating and is a benefit for you Black gentleman.

A black businessman gives his view of Jim Crow laws:

> Wherever Black people lived or travelled in the south they were faced with the humiliation of seeing doors that were open to White people and legally closed to them.

A businessman from North America:

> I saw a modern rest station with gleaming counters and picture windows labelled 'White'. A small wooden shack beside it was tagged 'coloured'. The coloured waiting room was filthy, in need of repair and overcrowded.

1. Above are a series of statements taken from the time of Jim Crow laws in the Southern states of America. Write each statement down and say whether it is 'for' or 'against' Jim Crow laws. Then answer the following questions:

- How do Jim Crow laws make white people feel?
- How do Jim Crow laws make black people feel?

(Unit outcomes: National 5: Outcome 2.3)

Exam style question

Source D was written by an old black farmer in 1920.

> I remember my granddaddy telling me how he felt he was 'free at last' after the civil war. 'Free at last boy', he said, 'thanks to these northern laws.' He died a few years ago. He knew he had been fooled. Jim Crow broke his spirit.

Source E is from a diary kept by a white woman in 1920.

> My grandmother told me that freeing the slaves was the ruination of the South. Our plantations lost money and worst of all nigra folks (black people) walked the streets as if they were the equals of White folks. Something had to be done – I thank the lord for good old Jim Crow.

2. Compare the views in **Sources D** and **E** about the treatment of black Americans after the Civil War. **SH 4**
(Compare the views overall and/or in detail.)

How did 'separate but equal' affect black Americans?

On 7 June 1892, a thirty year old man named Homer Plessy complained after being asked to move from a seat that was allocated for a white person on a train carriage. He was arrested and after losing at the State court of Louisiana, he chose to push the case further up to the Supreme Court. Plessy's lawyer argued that the Separate Car (train carriage) Act was against the 13th and 14th amendments that clearly said that black people were equal citizens in America. When the Judge ruled that *'separate but equal'* would be upheld as part of Federal (national) law it had huge implications for black Americans.

This meant that although the American Constitution had agreed that black people would be seen as equal they wouldn't necessarily be allowed to co-exist with whites. The Plessy decision outlined that 'separate' facilities for blacks and whites were constitutional as long as they were 'equal'.

Black people felt betrayed by the decision of the Supreme Court. They knew that white Southern states were unlikely to provide equal services. As a result of the 1896 Plessey decision more Jim Crow laws spread across the South than ever before and segregation became the normal way of life in the South up until the 1950s.

Figure 11: *Homer Plessy*

Activity 9

Write a summary of the Homer Plessy court case. Give detailed information about the event and how it was taken to the Supreme Court by Homer's lawyer. You should also outline the implications for black people once 'separate but equal' had been confirmed at Federal level. You should include witness statements from both black and white people to show how they would have felt about the court's decision.

(Unit outcomes: National 5: Outcome 2.3)

The Ku Klux Klan

The Ku Klux Klan is a white separatist terrorist organisation that was established in the Southern states of America after the American Civil War. The Klan was an elitist group that had a specific set of rules for those who wanted to join.

Klan Rules:

- Each Klan was led by a man who had the title, Grand Wizard.
- Klan organisations were called Klaverns.
- All members had to be native-born Americans, white and Protestant male. Members could join from the age of sixteen.
- No black Americans, Roman Catholics or Jews were allowed.
- Klan members typically wore robes or sheets and masks topped with pointed hoods.

Klan members terrorised black people, Jews, Catholics and divorced women. They would target these people by using extreme forms of violence like lynching, mutilating, whipping or even murder. They would strike fear into the hearts of their targets by erecting huge crosses near their homes. The Klansmen were very proud of their group and often participated in large patriotic rallies and marches, which were legal.

Figure 12: *A Ku Klux Klan member.*

Figure 13: *A Ku Klux Klan march/rally.*

> ### 📖 Key Word
> - **Lynching**
> When a group of people kill a person, commonly by hanging.

Although the Klan membership dwindled towards the end of 1915, this dramatically changed in 1920 for many reasons, such as increasing unemployment and the arrival of 'new' immigrants. The Klan also attracted judges, police officers and politicians. This made a conviction in any case against the Klan almost impossible to achieve. Even high profile cases with evidence proving the involvement of the Klan were often thrown out of court.

> **Hint**
>
> The KKK still exist as a terrorist group today, but are more secretive about their actions and activities.

The Ku Klux Klan would continue to terrorise and inflict violence on the black population of America all through the civil rights movement in the 1950s and 1960s. As acts were passed to secure the equal position of black Americans, Klan membership actually increased.

Activity 10

1. Write a recruitment advert for the Ku Klux Klan to show you understand who was encouraged to join and who was excluded. You should include some of the events that members can attend and demonstrate the patriotism that was displayed at many of their rallies and marches.

Exam style question

Source F was part of a booklet published in 1966 by a friend of Martin Luther King. It refers to events in the 1950s.

> Ever since the Civil Rights Movement began the leaders have received death threats over the phone and through the mail. Police joined in the harassment. Phones were tapped. One man, the Rev. Charles Billups, was arrested. Later he was tied to a tree and beaten by the Ku Klux Klan.

2. Evaluate the usefulness of **Source F** as evidence that fear and terror were used against the civil rights movement and black Americans. **SH 5**

   (You may want to comment on who wrote it, when they wrote it, why they wrote it, what they say or what has been missed out.)

The murder of Emmett Till

Emmett Till was visiting relatives in the Southern state of Mississippi in August 1955. Coming from Chicago he was well aware of the laws of segregation and attended an all-black school. However, he was not aware of the strict laws in Mississippi and thought nothing of showing off a picture of his white girlfriend back in Chicago. His new friends took advantage of Emmett's ignorance and encouraged him to go up to a white girl in the shop nearby and talk to her. Emmett didn't see what the big deal was and entered the shop, bought some gum and said 'bye baby' on his way out.

Days later Emmett was kidnapped by two men; his body was recovered three days later in the local river. His body was horribly mutilated and his corpse was almost unrecognisable by his own mother. The two kidnappers were quickly identified and arrested. At first it seemed both white and black Americans were horrified and this was demonstrated by the lack of any white lawyers willing to represent the two accused. The case attracted widespread publicity and media attention increased when Emmett's mother insisted on his coffin being open so everyone in America could see what had happened to her fourteen-year-old son.

Figure 14: *Emmett Till.*

Although the country seemed to cry out for justice, when the trial was heard in the segregated, all-white Mississippi court, no white person was willing to speak up against the two men and all the black witnesses, including Emmett's uncle, were ignored. It only took the jury an hour to return a not guilty verdict.

Although many saw the case of Emmett Till as a failure, it did clearly show the rest of the country the extent of black intimidation in the South and sparked the beginning of the civil rights movement.

 Activity 11

Write a summary of this case using the following questions to help you cover all the information:

- What did Emmett Till do to upset the white people of Mississippi?
- How did the white people of Mississippi deal with Emmett?
- What happened to the two men accused of Emmett's death?
- Why did Emmett's mother insist on an open casket?
- What role did the media play in Emmett's death?

(Unit outcomes: National 4: Outcome 1.2; National 5: Outcomes 1.2, 1.3 and 2.3)

How were Black Americans prevented from voting?

Although black Americans technically gained the vote in 1867, the Southern states, using the Jim Crow laws, made it increasingly hard for black Americans to vote in elections. In order for anyone to vote in the USA, you first have to register. It was at this point a black American would come up against a literacy test, to be sat before elections, which contained questions like 'How many bubbles in a bar of soap?' The Southern states knew that if black people were able to vote they would elect people who pledged to put a stop to the Jim Crow laws. To avoid this, they used different means to simply exclude black Americans from the voting process, for example introducing a tax black people had to pay, preventing them from voting because they simply could not afford it. As a last resort white separatists would simply beat the black people up as they made their way to the polling station.

An Alabama politician said in 1900: 'We take away the Nigra's votes to help them. They don't understand politics. It makes their life easier. We know what is best for them.'

 Key Word

- **White separatist**
Someone who believes that whites should live separately from other races.

 Activity 12

Below are the **answers** to a series of questions. Your task is to write what the question would be.

- 'How many bubbles in a bar of soap?'
- 1867
- Literacy tests and a poll tax
- Black people would vote for politicians who would help them.

(Unit outcomes: National 5: Outcome 2.3)

Why did so many black Americans migrate to the North of America?

In the late nineteenth and early twentieth centuries there was an influx of black people moving to the North with the promise of a better life away from the segregation laws and fear of the Ku Klux Klan, as well as the growing industries that needed cheap labour. This was known as the 'Great Migration'.

There were positive and negative aspects to this mass movement. The table below gives you some examples of both.

Positive	Negative
Harlem Renaissance encouraged black culture.	Competition for jobs and housing, which led to discrimination and segregation.
Black-influenced music – jazz.	Black ghettos emerged as poor black Americans from the South could only afford to live in the poorest areas of the North.
Increased number of black artists.	Riots in East St Louis in 1917.
	Riots in Chicago in 1919.
	Riots in Detroit during the Second World War.

Although it seems that the negative aspects outweigh the positive, the 'Great Migration' did have some dramatic long-term effects. It helped the Federal government see the massive inequalities black Americans suffered and forced them to make changes to improve the situation.

GO! Activity 13

1. Create a propaganda poster that shows what the North offered the black Americans if they moved. Your poster should have a clear slogan and images to support your slogan. You can use any of the positive aspects to encourage black Americans to move. However, you could also create an ironic version of the poster and show all the negative aspects that would be waiting for them when they arrive in the North.

Exam style question

Source G is a table that shows where black people lived in the 1890s and 1960s.

	1890s	1960s
% of black Americans living in the South	90·3%	10%
% of black Americans living in the North	9·7%	90%

2. Describe the effects of the 'Great Migration'. **KU 4**
   (Use the information in **Source G** and the above section to help you answer the question.)

   (Unit outcomes: National 4/5: Outcome 2.1)

3 Civil rights campaigns, 1945–1965

In this section you will learn about:

- Early civil rights campaigns.
- The effect of the Second World War on civil rights.
- Brown vs. Topeka court case.
- Improvements to civil rights in education.
- Montgomery bus boycott.
- Student campaigns: 'sit ins' and the 'freedom rides'.
- Martin Luther King's protest in Birmingham.
- The importance of Martin Luther King's 'I have a dream' speech.
- The Civil Rights Act of 1964 and the civil rights protest in Selma.

How effective were the early civil rights campaigns?

One of the fundamental problems with the early civil rights organisations was their disjointed aims. They all looked for very different things and this meant that they came across as weak.

NAACP (National Association for the Advancement of Coloured People)

Leader: W.E.B. DuBois

Founded: 1909

Aim: To campaign for equal civil rights for black Americans legally.

Booker T. Washington

Active: Early 1900s

Aim: To stop black Americans demanding civil rights and instead show they deserved them by working hard, gaining a better education and more employment training. He taught at the Tuskagee Institute that specialised in training in agriculture and industry.

UNIA (Universal Negro Improvement Association)

Leader: Marcus Garvey

Founded: 1914

Aim: Black separatist organisation that believed all black Americans should return to Africa. Garvey encouraged black Americans to be proud of their heritage and return to govern Africa. He even set up a steamship company called the Black Star Line, which promised to take black Americans back to their 'homeland'. However, Garvey was arrested and deported in 1925 after it became apparent that he was fraudulently taking money from the company.

Figure 15: *W.E.B DuBois (top), Booker T. Washington (middle) and Marcus Garvey (bottom).*

Hint

Marcus Garvey's aims were adopted, in part, by Stokely Carmichael when he founded the militant Student Non-violent Coordinating Committee in the 1960s.

Activity 14

1. After reading the different aims and methods of the early civil rights organisations answer the following questions to help you understand why they were unsuccessful.
   * In your own words, outline the three different aims of each civil rights organisation.
   * Why did the early civil rights groups fail?

   (Unit outcomes: National 5: Outcome 2.3)

Exam style question

Source H is a speech written by Booker T. Washington in the 1890s.

> You should stop demanding equal rights. Education is the answer. Show White people that you can work hard and save for the future and then they will see that the Black man is a respectable person. Then we will be granted our rights.

2. Evaluate the usefulness of **Source H** as evidence of the aims of the early civil rights organisations. **SH 5**
   (You may want to comment on who wrote it, when they wrote it, why they wrote it, what they say or what has been missed out.)

How did the Second World War affect the civil rights movement?

When America entered the Second World War in 1941 black Americans were quickly recruited into the army. However, the awareness that they were fighting against a country (Germany) which was actively discriminating against a minority group (the Jews), when black Americans were suffering from discrimination in America, led to the 'Double V' campaign. This stood for Victory in the war and Victory for civil rights at home.

One man who saw a great opportunity was A. Philip Randolph, the president of a black trade union.

In 1941, Randolph met with US President Franklin D. Roosevelt and threatened that unless he passed an executive order that would halt all discrimination in the defence industry Randolph would organise a fifty thousand-strong black protest in Washington that would highlight the similarities between Germany's racist laws and US laws that allowed segregation and discrimination. Randolph put forward three demands:

* Government assistance to stop all discrimination and segregation in employment in America.
* A stop to all discrimination and segregation in Federal government positions of work.
* An immediate stop to discrimination and segregation in the armed forces.

Figure 16: *A. Philip Randolph.*

Key Words

* **Trade union**

An organisation that represents workers' rights.

* **Executive Order**

An order having the force of law issued by the President.

Although Roosevelt was nervous about making such radical changes, he passed Executive Order 8802 and introduced the Fair Employment Practices Committee. He knew he needed the black soldiers to fight and couldn't face the embarrassment of the protest.

Hint

The Congress of Racial Equality (CORE) was established in 1942 and would go on to play a huge part in the civil rights movement in the 1950s and 1960s.

GO! Activity 15

Exam style question

To what extent was the growth of the civil rights movement due to the experience of black Americans in the Second World War? **KU 9**

Hint: For this 8 mark essay you will need to collect information on the three other factors, which are:

- hardship and humiliation caused by Jim Crow laws
- segregation of schools, transport, etc.
- inequality faced by black Americans in employment and housing.

(Unit outcomes: National 4: Outcome 1.2; National 5: Outcomes 1.2, 1.3 and 2.3)

Brown v. Board of Education of Topeka

The case of *Brown* v. *Board of Education of Topeka* in 1954 was a turning point in the campaign for civil rights. The case involved a black child, Linda Brown, who had to walk a mile through a dangerous railroad yard to get to school, even though there was a 'white' school much closer to her house. Linda's father tried to enrol her in the 'white' school, but was refused and decided to enlist the help of the NAACP, which saw this as the perfect opportunity to fight against the Federal 'separate but equal' law. When the case was rejected by the district court in Kansas they decided to take it further and have it heard in the Supreme Court. On 17 May 1954, the Supreme Court finally threw out the 'separate but equal' law and desegregated all schools.

Figure 17: *Linda Brown walking beside railway tracks to school.*

📖 Key Word

- **Desegregate**

To eliminate racial segregation/separation.

GO! Activity 16

Source I is from the Supreme Court in 1954 on how they felt 'separate but equal' affected the children who were segregated in schools.

> … causes a feeling of inferiority as to their status in the community that may affect their hearts and minds in a way unlikely ever to be undone …

Source J is from a judge who worked in a district court in the South and how he felt about desegregating schools.

> Black Monday is the name used to describe Monday, May 17, 1954. Black for darkness and terror. Black meaning the absence of light and wisdom.

Using the sources above, write a detailed answer to the following question: Explain how the district and Supreme courts differ on their decision in the *Brown* v *Topeka* case.

(Unit outcomes: National 4/5: Outcome 2.2)

Improvements to civil rights in education after Brown v Topeka

In September 1957 nine black students (later called the Little Rock Nine) were granted the right to attend Little Rock Central High School in the State of Arkansas. On their first day the Governor of Arkansas, Orval Faubus, ordered the National Guard to surround the school. He was against the integration of the school. He claimed the soldiers were there to protect the black students from an angry mob, but they in fact prevented them from entering.

📖 Key Word

• **Integrate**

Bring together and incorporate as a whole; in this case it is the bringing together of black and white people.

Figure 18: *Elizabeth Eckford failed to receive a message to say the students had been warned not to attend school due to the crowds of state soldiers and white racists surrounding the school. She attempted to go to Little Rock on her own and remained calm and peaceful even though people were verbally abusive to her, these images were spread through the media and caused more supporters for the Civil Rights movement.*

Figure 19: *Students being blocked from entering Little Rock Central High School.*

Faubus was instructed by the Federal government to remove his soldiers but when the nine students tried to return to school they found an angry crowd of racists stopped them entering again.

Sending a strong message in support of desegregation, US President Eisenhower sent 1000 Federal soldiers to protect the black students. These soldiers were with the students every day for a year to ensure they were able to attend the school without harm.

The media played a crucial role in the civil rights movement, particularly with this case, as it attracted worldwide attention, portraying the Little Rock Nine as peaceful students attempting to gain an education and the racist white mob as violent and aggressive.

🔍 Hint

During the 1950s Britain invited labour and transport workers from Jamaica to fill jobs in this country to help rebuild after the Second World War. As the number of immigrants increased so too did the level of racial abuse the Jamaican people suffered.

🟢 Activity 17

Answer the following questions to show you understand how education changed for black Americans after the *Brown v Topeka* case.

• Explain why the Little Rock Nine attracted so much media attention.

  (Unit outcomes: National 4/5: Outcome 2.2)

• Describe how the Federal government used the situation to ensure States followed Federal law.

  (Unit outcomes: National 4/5: Outcome 2.1)

How the Montgomery bus boycott helped the civil rights movement

In December 1955, in Montgomery, Alabama, Rosa Parks, a member of the NAACP, refused to move from a seat on a bus although she was legally obliged to give up her seat to a white person. Her arrest would signify another turning point in the fight for civil rights.

Figure 20: *Rosa Parks.*

The law that allowed segregation on buses had already been identified as a target for an NAACP campaign and the leaders of the campaign, who included a young black preacher called Martin Luther King, immediately organised a bus boycott. From then on the black people of Montgomery refused to use the buses.

> 📖 **Key Word**
>
> - **Boycott**
>
> Refuse to have an involvement with a person, organisation or refuse to buy a product.

Figure 21: *Black people boycotted the buses in Montgomery.*

> **Hint**
>
> Martin Luther King and Reverend Ralph Abernathy created the SCLC (Southern Christian Leadership Conference) in 1957. Inspired by Ghandi, King was a great supporter of non-violent protests, and felt this was the way to achieve civil rights for the black people of America.

The boycott went on for over a year and saw black people sharing their cars to avoid the bus. The police in Montgomery even attempted to outlaw car sharing and Rosa Parks was arrested a second time for car sharing. It wasn't long before the bus companies realised they had to desegregate the buses or go out of business. This was an example of how powerful the black population were economically (75% of passengers were black). The bus companies relied on their fares and they could no longer afford to discriminate against them.

In December 1956, the courts decided that segregation on buses was against the American Constitution. Although the desegregation was limited to the buses, and many other areas of Montgomery were still segregated, this was a powerful win for the NAACP and the civil rights movement, as it demonstrated the power of organised protest.

> **GO! Activity 18**
>
> 1. Write a three day diary entry for Rosa Parks, detailing the day she refused to move from her seat, the day she is arrested for car sharing and finally the day the buses were desegregated. How did she feel at each stage of this campaign? How did she feel about the support the campaign gained?
>
>   **(Unit outcomes: National 5: Outcome 2.3)**
>
> **Exam style question**
>
> 2. Describe the main events of the Montgomery bus boycott.   KU 4
>
>   **(Unit outcomes: National 4/5: Outcome 2.1)**

'Sit ins' and the 'freedom rides' campaigns

The success of *Brown* v *Topeka*, Little Rock and the Montgomery bus boycott led to President Eisenhower passing the Civil Rights Act in 1957:

- The Federal Justice Department would now support black Americans if they went to court to ensure they could vote freely.
- A Civil Rights Commission was started nationally.

Spurred on by the successes of past campaigns, four black students, on 1 February 1960, walked into a café in Greensboro, North Carolina. They sat at a whites-only lunch counter and were asked to leave. Their response was to return peacefully the next day with eighty protestors, both black and white. The students had heard about Martin Luther King's campaign of non-violence and had chosen this as their form of protest. The eighty protestors were subjected to physical and verbal attacks but refused to react. When these images were shown in the national media, the peaceful protestors gained much sympathy and support. By the end of 1960 approximately 70 000 protestors had participated in a 'sit in'.

Figure 22: *A 'Sit In'.*

The next major campaign came in 1961. The multiracial Congress of Racial Equality (CORE) had been set up in 1942 by a group of students from Chicago. Their campaign was to test a Supreme Court ruling in 1960 that said blacks could freely travel from one state to another. This campaign was called the 'freedom rides'. The media attention ensured the route of the travellers was well known, which meant the racist Southern whites found it easy to target them with physical violence and verbal abuse. Even in the face of this aggression and violence, the protestors remained peaceful.

Figure 23: *Guards surround a 'Freedom Riders' bus.*

Many tried to get the students to stop. The FBI (Federal Bureau of Investigation) were sent in to try to protect but ultimately stop the 'freedom riders', but they refused. Even Martin Luther King pleaded with them to stop. By this time the CORE group had been joined by the SNCC (Student Non-violent Coordinating Committee) and they both refused to stop until the Federal government forced all bus companies to desegregate their buses.

GO! Activity 19

1. Create a cartoon strip using either six or nine boxes that shows, visually, the 'sit in' or 'freedom ride' campaigns. Above each box should be a space for a caption that details what is happening in the box.

2. Explain the growth of the civil rights movement in the Southern states of America during the 1950s and 1960s.

   Hint: You should write an essay that contains an introduction, four paragraphs (one about *Brown* v *Topeka*, one about Little Rock, one about the 'sit ins' and one about the 'freedom rides') and a conclusion.

   (Unit outcomes: National 4: Outcome 1.2; National 5: Outcomes 1.2, 1.3 and 2.3)

Figure 24: *Martin Luther King holds a news conference in Birmingham, Alabama, 1963.*

Figure 25: *Police Chief 'Bull' Connor: President Kennedy said 'Bull Connor has done more for civil rights than anyone else.'*

Why was Martin Luther King's Birmingham protest so important?

In May 1963, Martin Luther King and the SCLC led a campaign in Birmingham, Alabama, aimed at ending discrimination in employment and desegregating public areas and shops. Using the influence of the media, King made the decision to allow teenagers and even some younger children to take part in a protest, convinced images of children being racially abused would draw huge media attention.

One of the main reasons the Birmingham protest was so effective was because the police chief at the time was very racist. 'Bull' Connor ordered fire hoses and police dogs to be set on protestors. These images shown in newspapers and on television would shock the whole country and lead to a huge rise in civil rights support.

Figure 26: *A police dog attacking a black protestor in Birmingham.*

Figure 27: *Fire hoses knocking black protestors off their feet.*

This campaign would convince President Kennedy and the Federal government to take action and pass a civil rights bill.

As a result of Birmingham, shops were desegregated and discrimination in employment was stopped. However, the changes were not immediate and discrimination in employment would be hard to monitor.

📖 Key Word

- **Bill**

A proposal for a new law.

Activity 20

Campaigns	Albany, Georgia	Birmingham, Alabama
Date	1961–1962	1963
Governor	Earnest Vandiver	George Wallace
Police Chief	Lawrie Pritchett	'Bull' Connor
Reaction to protest	No racist mob attacked them. Police were gentle when arresting protestors. Lawrie Pritchett encouraged the police to be peaceful and non-violent when dealing with protestors.	'Bull' Connor set dogs and water hoses on the protestors, who included children. Protestors arrested and jailed.
Media coverage	None	Images of police turning water hoses on the protestors shocked America.
Group that started campaign	SNCC	SCLC
Outcome	King leaves Albany defeated. Instead of being desegregated, parks were closed. Chairs were removed from the desegregated library.	Civil rights movement received even more support. Persuaded the President and the Federal government to take action: civil rights bill.

Above is an outline of two Martin Luther King protests. One was extremely successful while the other failed.

Answer the questions below using the information from the table.

1. What were the differences between the Albany and Birmingham civil rights campaigns?

   (Hint: think about what was different about the towns, what caused the different reactions.)

2. Write a developed answer using all the information you have gathered over the last two lessons.

   (Unit outcomes: National 5: Outcome 2.3)

Exam style question

Source K is from a statement made by President Kennedy in May 1963.

> I think that the situation in Birmingham will be peacefully settled in the next 24 hours. Quite obviously the situation was damaging the reputation of Birmingham and the United States. It seems to me that the best way to prevent that kind of serious damage it to take steps to provide equal treatment for all of our citizens. That is the best remedy in this case and other cases.

3. Evaluate the usefulness of **Source K** as evidence of the effects of the civil rights protest in Birmingham.   **SH 5**

   (You may wish to comment on who wrote it, when they wrote it, why they wrote it, what they say or what has been missed out.)

'I have a dream'

The March on Washington 'for jobs and freedom' took place in Washington, D.C., on 28 August 1963. It was attended by upwards of 250 000 people, the largest demonstration ever seen in the nation's capital, and one of the first to have extensive television coverage. President Kennedy had even agreed to the march happening, as he did not expect over a quarter of a million people to turn out to hear King speak.

Figure 28: *Crowds at the demonstration, Lincoln Memorial in Washington D.C.*

Protestors marched to the Lincoln Memorial where King delivered his 'I have a dream' speech beside a statue of Abraham Lincoln. The march was attended by both black and white supporters and this demonstrated a desegregated show of unity.

Civil Rights Act 1964

In response to the civil rights campaigns the 1964 Civil Rights Act was passed.

- Segregated restaurants, stores and other public places were banned.
- The legal system could now file law suits to speed up desegregation, improve desegregated education and voting rights.
- The Fair Employment Practices Commission was set up on a permanent legal basis. No racial, sexual or religious discrimination would be allowed.
- No discrimination on any federally aided programmes was allowed.
- A Community Relations Service was set up to deal with any remaining disputes.

Civil rights protest in Selma

On 7 March 1965, Martin Luther King set out to repeat the success of Birmingham by having a march in Selma, Alabama, to protest about the lack of voting rights black Americans had in that state. In Selma there were 15 000 black people, but only 325 were registered to vote. King deliberately got arrested about a month before the protest to gain publicity for the march. King was confident that the well-known racist sheriff of Selma, Jim Clark, would react in a similar way to 'Bull' Connor. Many historians argue that King was only too aware of the potential for violence, and that was what he wanted, in order to gain even more publicity for the cause.

There were two attempts at the march that was planned to start in Selma and end in Montgomery. The first, on Sunday 7 March, was extremely violent and was even given the name 'Bloody Sunday'. The marchers were attacked with tear gas, beaten, whipped and trampled by horses. The death of James Reeb, a white minister, shocked America.

Figure 29: *Martin Luther King in Birmingham jail for demonstrating without a permit.*

Figure 30: *Civil rights demonstrators pass by federal guards in March 1965.*

The demonstrators were not deterred and on 21 March the march began for a second time. However, this time the protestors were heavily protected by US troops sent by the Federal government. At the end of the march, King delivered a moving speech to 25 000 supporters. This demonstration was seen as a great success, especially when the Federal government and the President, Lyndon B. Johnson, passed the Voting Rights Act in August.

President Johnson said:

'What happened in Selma was an American tragedy. The blows that were received, the blood that was shed, the life of the good man that was lost must strengthen the determination of each of us to bring full and equal and exact justice to all of our people … There is no Negro problem. There is no Southern problem. There is no Northern problem. There is only an American problem.'

Provisions of the Voting Rights Act:

- Literacy tests were removed.
- No more poll tax payments in order to vote.
- Any kinds of restrictions on the black population were removed.

This Act was a huge victory for the civil rights movement and within the space of three years the majority of the black population were registered to vote.

% of black population registered to vote		
State	1964	1968
Alabama	14	56
Florida	26	62
Georgia	22	56
Mississippi	4	59
South Carolina	11	56

 Make the Link

You will learn more about representing statistics in Maths.

 Activity 22

1. Using the statistics above, create two pie charts to show the increase in voting rights for black Americans following the Voting Rights Act 1965.

Exam style question

2. Explain the reasons why black Americans felt that progress towards civil rights had been made between 1945 and 1964. **KU 6**

(Unit outcomes: National 4/5: Outcome 2.2)

4 The ghettos and Black American radicalism

In this section you will learn about:

- Problems faced by blacks in the Northern Ghettos and the importance of the ghetto riots.
- The role Malcolm X played in the radicalisation of the civil rights movement.
- How Stokely Carmichael made the SNCC more militant.
- The importance of the Black Panthers.
- 'Free at Last?' The impact of the campaigns on US society.

Problems faced by blacks in the Northern Ghettos and the importance of the ghetto riots

By the 1960s the civil rights movement had become more militant, shifting its focus to the North. Black Americans had been led to believe that life would be better there but the industrial cities of the North were just as segregated as the South and often were divided into communities that became known as ghettos.

> **Key Word**
>
> - **Ghetto**
>
> A slum or run down area of a town or city, usually where people of the same ethnic group live.

- In August 1965, in the **Watts** area of Los Angeles, a riot started after a young black man was stopped by the police and accused of drunk driving. The population in Watts was 98% black, with an all-white police force. The accusation led to a fight that erupted into a six day riot, which left thirty four people dead, 900 injured and 4000 arrested.

- In the summer of 1966, on a hot summer's day in **Chicago**, the police shut off one of the fire hydrants that had been illegally opened by black teenagers desperately trying to cool down. The incident led to a fight that involved ten people being hurt and some shop windows being damaged. Martin Luther King was concerned it was the start of a riot. The next evening he was proved right when petrol bombs and stones were thrown at city fireman and even some cases of sniper fire were reported.

Figure 31: *The Watts riots.*

The race riots continued throughout the 1960s and over the course of 1966 there were forty three more riots. The riots were caused by a series of frustrations: unemployment, bad housing, poor education and health facilities, and drugs gangs.

Activity 23

1. Create a newspaper front page that describes the riots detailed in this section. Ensure you include what witnesses could have said after seeing the riots happen. Include a 'made-up' point of view/eye witness statement from a rioter and also from a member of the public who witnessed it but was not involved.

(Unit outcomes: National 4/5: Outcome 2.1)

Exam style question

Source L is from an eye witness to the Watts riots.

> Last night a police officer stopped us and said, 'OK, everybody get off the street!' I said 'Hey man, it's summer. It's really hot. We don't have air conditioned rooms like you rich White folks. We like to hang out till late in the cool night air. We got no job to get up to in the morning.

2. How fully does **Source L** describe the reasons for the riots that happened in America during the 1960s?

   SH 6

   Hint: To answer a 'how fully' question you need to ensure that you first point out what the content of the source contains to answer the question and then, very importantly, you must say what information is missing from the source. In order to gain full marks you must include both.

   (Unit outcomes: National 4/5: Outcome 1.1)

How did Malcolm X influence the civil rights movement?

Figure 32: *Malcolm X.*

Make the Link

You may study the slave trade in detail in Unit 2.

- Born Malcolm Little in Omaha, Nebraska, 1925.
- Son of a West Indian mother and black Baptist preacher.
- His father was a local organiser for Marcus Garvey's United Negro Improvement Association (UNIA) that promoted black separatism. His father was beaten and murdered by white racists who threw him under a tram car. His mother was admitted to a mental hospital when he was only thirteen years old. After this Malcolm lived in several different foster homes.
- At the age of twenty, he went to jail for burglary and while there became a member of the Nation of Islam.

The Nation of Islam was founded by black Muslims in Detroit in 1929. They only accepted black Americans as members as they saw white people as 'devils'. Elijah Muhammed became the leader of the Nation of Islam in 1934 and encouraged members to follow three main ideas:

1. Black Americans needed to be established as a separate nation in America.

2. All black Muslims should be proud of their identity.

3. Businesses, shops and services should be established and run by the Nation of Islam.

After joining the group Malcolm Little changed his name to Malcolm X and claimed that the 'X' represented his lost African name that had been stolen by slave owners who bought and sold his descendants. He encouraged black Americans to reject the European names which connected them to the world of slavery.

Malcolm X felt very strongly that the non-violent campaigns had not tackled the problems faced by the blacks in the northern cities of America. He saw Martin Luther King's non-violent methods as 'defenceless', having gained little for most black people. He accused sympathetic whites of being 'wolves in sheep's clothing' and helped establish temples where black Muslims could come and hear his preaching. The FBI were extremely concerned by his actions and felt he was encouraging black people to become more militant in their demands for civil rights. The government were already worried after the riots in Los Angeles and Detroit and felt Malcolm X's methods could lead to further violence.

Although Malcolm X's messages attracted many who were tired of the slow progress of the civil rights movement, serious arguments with the Nation of Islam's leader, Elijah Muhammed, led Malcolm X to leave the group. He travelled to Africa and the Middle East, where he visited Mecca and changed his beliefs completely after finding that so many of his fellow Muslims were white.

Malcolm X was assassinated on 21 February 1965 by three members of the Nation of Islam.

GO! Activity 24

1. Create a story board using either six or eight boxes to describe Malcolm X's life. It might be easier for you to write the numbers 1–6 or 1–8 and then write a brief description of what you are going to draw in the box. This written description can also be placed above the image in the caption box to describe what is going on in the box below.

Caption	Caption	Caption
Image	Image	Image
Caption	Caption	Caption
Image	Image	Image

(Unit outcomes: National 4/5: Outcome 2.1)

Exam style question

Source M is about the opposition of Malcolm X to non-violent protest.

> Malcolm X was mistreated in his youth and this gave him a different set of attitudes to Martin Luther King. Later, while in jail, he was influenced by the ideas of Elijah Muhammed who preached hatred of the white race. In his speeches he criticised non-violence. He believed that the support of non-violence was a sign that black people were still living in mental slavery. However, Malcolm X never undertook violent action himself and sometimes prevented it. Instead he often used violent language and threats to frighten the government into action.

2. How fully does **Source M** explain the views of Malcolm X on non-violent protest? **SH 6**
   (Use **Source M** and recall.)

Figure 33: *Stokely Carmichael.*

Figure 34: *H. Rapp Brown.*

Stokely Carmichael and 'Black Power'

After Stokely Carmichael was elected Chairman of the SNCC (Student Non-violent Coordinating Committee) in June 1966, there was a huge change in the way the group functioned. What kicked off this change was a non-violent protest march against fear and racism from Memphis to Jackson led by James Meredith. Soon after the march began Meredith was shot by a sniper and killed. The three leaders of the SNCC (Stokely Carmichael), CORE (Floyd McKissick) and SCLC (Martin Luther King) decided to finish the march in Meredith's name.

When the march was completed, Carmichael made his, now famous, 'Black Power' speech:

'The only way we gonna stop them white man from whippin' us is to take over. We been sayin' freedom for six years and we ain't got nothin'. What we gonna start saying now is Black Power.'

It was at this point that Carmichael changed the aims of the SNCC, later to be known as 'Snick' to the following:

- Black Americans should be prepared to defend themselves, fight back and use violence if needed against white racist attackers.
- Black Americans should no longer rely on the 'white' people to give them their civil rights. Instead black people should take back the power by building their own schools, hospitals, communities and businesses.
- Black Americans should be proud of their heritage and create a separate identity to that of the 'whites'.

Many believed that Stokely Carmichael was too simplistic with his 'Black Power' slogan and that all it did was create more anger and frustration. He claimed he just wanted to take the power away from the white people and instead give black Americans the chance to decide their own destiny.

Stokely Carmichael eventually left the SNCC in 1968 to follow an even more extremist group called the Black Panthers. H. Rapp Brown replaced him and he too supported the new militant ideas saying:

'The white man won't get off our backs so we intend to knock him off.'

242

Activity 25

The following is from a speech delivered by Stokely Carmichael in 1966:

> I maintain that every civil rights bill in this country was passed for white people, not for black people. For example, I am black. I know that. I also know that while I am black I am a human being. Therefore I have the right to go into any public place. White people don't know that. Every time I tried to go into a public place they stopped me. So some boys had to write a bill to tell that white man, 'He's a human being; don't stop him.' That bill was for the white man, not for me. I knew I could vote all the time and that it wasn't a privilege but my right. Every time I tried I was shot, killed or jailed, beaten or economically deprived. So somebody had to write a bill to tell white people, 'When a black man comes to vote, don't bother him.' … I know I can live anyplace I want to live. It is white people across this country that is incapable of allowing me to live where I want.

Using the passage to help you, answer the following questions:

1. Martin Luther King said in one of his speeches, 'The Negro needs the white man to take away his fear.' Carmichael did not share this view. Extract a quote from the passage above to show this is not true and explain how you have come to this conclusion, comparing the two quotes.

2. Which part of the passage above clearly outlines Stokely Carmichael's position on the issue of the civil rights movement; you must explain why you have chosen this quote.

   (Unit outcomes: National 4/5: Outcome 2.2)

Exam style question

3. Describe the major changes Stokely Carmichael effected on the civil rights movement in the 1960s.   **KU 4**

   (Unit outcomes: National 4/5: Outcome 2.1)

Who were the Black Panthers and why were they important?

Remember who they were using the five 'W's:

- What? The Black Panther Party.
- Who? A group of young black men, aged 16–19.
- When? November 1966 until 1982.
- Where? Oakland, California until 1968, then around the country and the world.
- Why? To address the needs of the black community and other poor communities.

Figure 35: *Black Panthers march to a news conference in New York to protest at the trial of one of their members, Huey P Newton.*

Figure 36: *Police and Black Panther members often clashed.*

The Black Panthers created a 'Ten Point Plan' to achieve equal civil rights for black Americans:

1. Freedom and the power to determine the destiny of the black community.

2. Full employment for all black people.

3. An end to 'robbery' of black people.

4. Housing that is fit for the shelter of human beings.

5. Access to decent education.

6. Black exemption from military service.

7. An end of acts of brutality and murder by the police.

8. Freedom for all black people who are held in jail.

9. Fair juries in courts of law, black juries for black people.

10. Land entitlement as well as bread, clothing, housing, education, justice and peace.

The Black Panthers chose to focus on police brutality and the murder of black Americans. Members would carry guns to protect the streets that housed their fellow 'brothers'.

The Black Panthers were openly pledged to using violence and force and images shown in the media often focused on this. The media failed to mention the group's community programmes in the ghettos:

• Free breakfasts for children.

• Free clothes for the poor.

• Free health clinics.

• Campaigns to target and stop drugs and crime in some of the poorest areas.

It wasn't long before the government instructed the police to spy on the Black Panthers. In August 1967, the FBI initiated a programme which aimed to disrupt and 'neutralise' organisations they called 'Black Nationalist Hate Groups'; this included the Black Panthers. The FBI director J. Edgar Hoover even said the Black Panthers were: 'The greatest threat to the internal security of the country'.

The government made attempts to stop the free breakfast programme and disrupt the local education classes that the Black Panthers were running. Many people now believe that the Black Panthers were not as violent as the media portrayed and that images were used to try to destroy the group in order to prevent them gaining any success. It is even thought police specifically targeted the group in order to create violent images for the media to use.

The Black Panthers broke up after internal arguments between the leaders led to the group losing its focus and strength.

'Free at Last?'

On 20 January 2009, African American Barack Obama was sworn in as the 44th President of the United States of America. Is this a sign that the black people of America are now 'Free at Last'? There are certainly many successful black people in US society today.

However, in 2007, the Nobel Prize winner James Watson created huge controversy when he suggested that blacks were less intelligent than whites. Unemployment statistics also show interesting facts. In June 2009, black unemployment was 15·3% compared to an 8·8% unemployment rate for whites.

In 1980, three Ku Klux Klan members shot four elderly black women (Viola Ellison, Lela Evans, Opal Jackson and Katherine Johnson) in Chattanooga, Tennessee, after a Ku Klux Klan initiation rally. As recently as 2008, there was believed to be 6000 members still remaining of the Ku Klux Klan.

In June 1998, an African American called James Byrd was brutally murdered in Texas by three white supremacists. Lawrence Russell Brewer, Shawn Berry and John King dragged James behind their truck for miles, his body was ripped to shreds and the remaining parts of his body were later dumped in front of an African American graveyard.

So is it true to say black Americans are 'Free at Last'?

Figure 37: *Barack Obama making his first speech as President in 2009.*

Black Lives Matter

More recently, the spotlight has focused on the Black Lives Matter movement – an international movement which was started in America. It began following the high profile case of the fatal shooting of Treyvon Martin, a 17 year old black man who was shot by George Zimmerman, a neighbourhood watch volunteer. Zimmerman claimed that he shot Martin in self-defence and the police did not charge him. In 2014, Michael Brown was shot dead by a police officer and Eric Garner was killed after the police officer put him in a chokehold even when Garner could audibly be heard to tell the police officer he couldn't breathe. Several other deaths of black people have prompted mass protests, the use of #blacklivesmatter and even a BLM Freedom Ride after the killing of Michael Brown. Black Lives Matter has since organised thousands of protests and demonstrations. Furthering the protest, Colin Kaepernick an NFL player refused to stand during the National Anthem before a football game in 2016. After the game he stated: "I am not going to stand up to show pride in a flag for a country that oppresses black people and people of colour. To me, this is bigger than football and it would be selfish on my part to look the other way. There are bodies in the street and people getting paid leave and getting away with murder." Many athletes and their supporters have joined the protests directed at the Trump presidency to highlight the inequalities that continue for black people in America today.

Summary

In this topic you have learned:

- what the 'open door' policy was in America and how it affected immigration between 1918 and 1928
- how black Americans were separated from white society and how unequal their lives were
- how black Americans were victimised in society
- how the civil rights campaigns started and progressed between 1945 and 1964
- in what ways the civil rights movement changed and became more militant.

You should have developed your skills and be able to:

- evaluate the usefulness of a source
- compare two sources by saying what they agree or disagree about
- put a source into context by saying how fully it describes an issue.

Learning Checklist

Now that you have finished **'Free at Last?' Civil Rights in the USA, 1918–1968,** complete a self-evaluation of your knowledge and skills to assess what you have understood. Use traffic lights to help you make up a revision plan to help you improve in the areas you identified as red or amber.

- Describe what America was like at the end of the First World War. ○ ○ ◯
- Explain why immigrants came to America. ○ ○ ◯
- Describe the differences between 'old' and 'new' immigrants. ○ ○ ◯
- Describe how immigrants were treated when they got to America. ○ ○ ◯
- Explain what the 'Red Scare' was and how it affected America. ○ ○ ◯
- Describe the events of the Sacco and Vanzetti case. ○ ○ ◯
- Explain why America changed its policy on immigration in the 1920s. ○ ○ ◯
- Describe the Jim Crow laws. ○ ○ ◯
- Explain how the Jim Crow laws affected black Americans. ○ ○ ◯
- Describe how the Ku Klux Klan intimidated black Americans. ○ ○ ◯

- Describe what happened to Emmett Till.

- Describe the early civil rights campaigns.

- Explain how the Second World War affected civil rights.

- Describe how the civil rights movement improved the education of black students.

- Describe the Montgomery bus boycott.

- Describe the 'sit-ins' and 'freedom rides'.

- Explain how Martin Luther King improved civil rights in America.

- Explain how the civil rights movement became more violent in the 1960s.

- Explain how the Black Panthers tried to achieve civil rights for black people in America.

Activities indexed by Outcome

Section 1: Migration and Empire, 1830–1939

National 4

Outcome	Activity
1.1	Activity 2 (page 10) Activity 7 (page 19) Activity 10 (page 27) Activity 14 (page 32)
1.2	Activity 11 (page 28)
1.3	Activity 3 (page 12) Activity 10 (page 27)
2.1	Activity 5 (page 14) Activity 6 (page 17) Activity 8 (page 22) Activity 9 (page 22) Activity 12 (page 30) Activity 16 (page 34)
2.2	Activity 2 (page 10) Activity 4 (page 13) Activity 11 (page 28) Activity 14 (page 32) Activity 15 (page 33) Activity 17 (page 35)

National 5

Outcome	Activity
1.1	Activity 2 (page 10) Activity 7 (page 19) Activity 10 (page 27) Activity 14 (page 32)
1.2	Activity 11 (page 28)
1.3	Activity 3 (page 12) Activity 10 (page 27)
2.1	Activity 2 (page 10) Activity 5 (page 14) Activity 6 (page 17) Activity 7 (page 19) Activity 8 (page 22) Activity 9 (page 22) Activity 10 (page 27) Activity 12 (page 30) Activity 14 (page 32) Activity 16 (page 34)

2.2	Activity 2 (page 10) Activity 4 (page 13) Activity 11 (page 28) Activity 14 (page 32) Activity 15 (page 33) Activity 17 (page 35)
2.3	Activity 9 (page 22) Activity 17 (page 35)

Section 1: The Era of the Great War, 1900–1928

National 4

Outcome	Activity
1.1	Activity 2 (page 44) Activity 5 (page 50) Activity 6 (page 53) Activity 8 (page 55) Activity 12 (page 61) Activity 15 (page 65) Activity 20 (page 68)
1.2	Activity 6 (page 53) Activity 8 (page 55)
1.3	Activity 9 (page 56) Activity 13 (page 63)
2.1	Activity 4 (page 48) Activity 5 (page 50) Activity 6 (page 53) Activity 7 (page 54) Activity 8 (page 55) Activity 11 (page 60) Activity 13 (page 63) Activity 14 (page 64)
2.2	Activity 2 (page 44) Activity 3 (page 46) Activity 4 (page 48) Activity 6 (page 53) Activity 10 (page 57) Activity 12 (page 61) Activity 15 (page 65) Activity 16 (page 66) Activity 17 (page 67) Activity 18 (page 67) Activity 19 (page 68) Activity 20 (page 68) Activity 21 (page 69)

National 5

Outcome	Activity
1.1	Activity 2 (page 44) Activity 5 (page 50) Activity 6 (page 53) Activity 8 (page 55) Activity 12 (page 61) Activity 15 (page 65) Activity 20 (page 68)
1.2	Activity 6 (page 53) Activity 8 (page 55)
1.3	Activity 9 (page 56) Activity 13 (page 63)
2.1	Activity 2 (page 44) Activity 4 (page 48) Activity 5 (page 50) Activity 6 (page 53) Activity 8 (page 55) Activity 11 (page 60) Activity 12 (page 61) Activity 13 (page 63) Activity 14 (page 64) Activity 15 (page 65) Activity 20 (page 68)
2.2	Activity 2 (page 44) Activity 3 (page 46) Activity 4 (page 48) Activity 6 (page 53) Activity 8 (page 55) Activity 10 (page 57) Activity 12 (page 61) Activity 15 (page 65) Activity 16 (page 66) Activity 17 (page 67) Activity 19 (page 68) Activity 20 (page 68) Activity 21 (page 69)
2.3	Activity 8 (page 55) Activity 11 (page 60) Activity 16 (page 66) Activity 22 (page 70)

Section 2: The Atlantic Slave Trade, 1770–1807

National 4

Outcome	Activity
1.1	Activity 2 (page 76) Activity 4 (page 81) Activity 10 (page 94)
1.2	Activity 5 (page 83) Activity 12 (page 100)
2.1	Activity 5 (page 83)
2.2	Activity 3 (page 78) Activity 10 (page 94)

National 5

Outcome	Activity
1.1	Activity 2 (page 76) Activity 4 (page 81) Activity 10 (page 94)
1.2	Activity 5 (page 83) Activity 11 (page 97) Activity 12 (page 100)
2.1	Activity 5 (page 83)
2.2	Activity 3 (page 78) Activity 10 (page 94)
2.3	Activity 7 (page 87) Activity 9 (page 93) Activity 14 (page 102)

Section 2: Changing Britain, 1760–1914

National 4

Outcome	Activity
1.1	Activity 5 (page 113) Activity 15 (page 128) Activity 18 (page 132)
1.2	Activity 4 (page 111) Activity 7 (page 116) Activity 9 (page 118) Activity 11 (page 120)
2.1	Activity 11 (page 120)
2.2	Activity 6 (page 113) Activity 11 (page 120)

National 5

Outcome	Activity
1.1	Activity 5 (page 113) Activity 15 (page 128) Activity 18 (page 132)
1.2	Activity 4 (page 111) Activity 7 (page 116) Activity 9 (page 118) Activity 11 (page 120)
2.1	Activity 2 (page 109) Activity 11 (page 120)
2.2	Activity 6 (page 113) Activity 11 (page 120)
2.3	Activity 15 (page 128) Activity 19 (page 133) Activity 20 (page 136)

Section 3: Lenin and the Russian Revolution, 1894–1921

National 4

Outcome	Activity
1.1	Activity 2 (page 142) Activity 21 (page 170)
1.2	Activity 7 (page 146) Activity 10 (page 151) Activity 18 (page 160) Activity 19 (page 165) Activity 20 (page 168)
2.1	Activity 4 (page 143) Activity 7 (page 146) Activity 10 (page 151) Activity 13 (page 154) Activity 15 (page 157) Activity 17 (page 160) Activity 18 (page 160) Activity 21 (page 170)
2.2	Activity 3 (page 143) Activity 5 (page 144) Activity 6 (page 145) Activity 7 (page 146) Activity 8 (page 148) Activity 9 (page 149) Activity 11 (page 152) Activity 12 (page 153) Activity 13 (page 154) Activity 14 (page 157) Activity 15 (page 157) Activity 16 (page 158) Activity 19 (page 165) Activity 21 (page 170)

National 5

Outcome	Activity
1.1	Activity 2 (page 142) Activity 21 (page 170)
1.2	Activity 7 (page 146) Activity 10 (page 151) Activity 18 (page 160) Activity 19 (page 165) Activity 20 (page 168)
1.3	Activity 7 (page 146) Activity 10 (page 151) Activity 18 (page 160) Activity 19 (page 165) Activity 20 (page 168)
2.1	Activity 4 (page 143) Activity 7 (page 146) Activity 10 (page 151) Activity 13 (page 154) Activity 15 (page 157) Activity 17 (page 160) Activity 18 (page 160) Activity 21 (page 170)

2.2	Activity 3 (page 143) Activity 5 (page 144) Activity 6 (page 145) Activity 7 (page 146) Activity 8 (page 148) Activity 9 (page 149) Activity 11 (page 152) Activity 12 (page 153) Activity 13 (page 154) Activity 14 (page 157) Activity 15 (page 157) Activity 16 (page 158) Activity 19 (page 165) Activity 21 (page 170)
2.3	Activity 7 (page 146) Activity 10 (page 151) Activity 18 (page 160) Activity 19 (page 165) Activity 20 (page 168)

Section 3: Hitler and Nazi Germany, 1919–1939

National 4

Outcome	Activity
1.1	Activity 2 (page 176) Activity 6 (page 182) Activity 9 (page 190)
1.2	Activity 9 (page 190) Activity 18 (page 204)
2.1	Activity 1 (page 174) Activity 3 (page 178) Activity 5 (page 181) Activity 6 (page 182) Activity 7 (page 186) Activity 9 (page 189) Activity 15 (page 200) Activity 17 (page 203)
2.2	Activity 2 (page 176) Activity 6 (page 182) Activity 8 (page 188) Activity 11 (page 193) Activity 12 (page 194) Activity 13 (page 196) Activity 14 (page 198)

National 5

Outcome	Activity
1.1	Activity 2 (page 176) Activity 6 (page 182) Activity 9 (page 190)
1.2	Activity 9 (page 190) Activity 18 (page 204)
1.3	Activity 9 (page 190) Activity 18 (page 204)
2.1	Activity 1 (page 174) Activity 3 (page 178) Activity 5 (page 181) Activity 6 (page 182) Activity 7 (page 186) Activity 9 (page 189) Activity 15 (page 200) Activity 17 (page 203)
2.2	Activity 2 (page 176) Activity 6 (page 182) Activity 8 (page 188) Activity 11 (page 193) Activity 12 (page 194) Activity 13 (page 196) Activity 14 (page 198)
2.3	Activity 7 (page 186) Activity 9 (page 189–190) Activity 10 (page 192) Activity 11 (page 193) Activity 14 (page 198) Activity 16 (page 202) Activity 18 (page 204)

Section 3: 'Free at Last?' Civil Rights in the USA, 1918–1968

National 4

Outcome	Activity
1.1	Activity 23 (page 240)
1.2	Activity 7 (page 218) Activity 11 (page 225) Activity 15 (page 229) Activity 19 (page 233)